A Year in the Shrub Garden

The author's garden in May.

A
Year in the
Shrub Garden

by
Sybil Emberton

Faber and Faber
London

First published 1972
by Faber and Faber Limited
3 Queen Square
London W C 1

ISBN 0 571 09382 5

Acknowledgements

When first I tried my hand, two books ago, at writing for publication I certainly did not anticipate much encouragement, whether from official or other sources, since when I have found friendly help and stimulus from all quarters to increase with each new venture of the kind.

In expressing my gratitude to those to whom I am chiefly indebted on this occasion my warmest thanks go to my publishers for exceptional kindness, patience and understanding in unusually trying circumstances.

I am also grateful for much practical help from Miss Ann Bonar, B.Sc. (Hort.), who not only compiled the list of Recommended Reading in Appendix One but also provided expert criticism and advice on the complicated subject of gardening chemicals in particular.

I count myself fortunate to have as a near neighbour so distinguished a plantsman as the Earl of Morton, M.A., F.L.S., V.M.H., whose good nature I constantly abuse with horticultural queries of which he never seems to tire, no matter how trivial or recondite.

My thanks are also due to the well-known plant photographer, Miss Elsa M. Megson, for her professional skill in producing the coloured illustration of a part of my shrub garden which appears as a frontispiece and on the jacket. Though primarily decorative in purpose, it also serves to illustrate much of the message I have tried to convey in print.

Contents

❧❧❧❧❧❧❧

Working-Calendar

Line Drawings

Line Drawings: continued

Line Drawings: continued 𝕏𝕏𝕏𝕏𝕏𝕏𝕏𝕏𝕏𝕏𝕏𝕏

Part One

Introductory — Aims

Someone, I think, had to write this book, but so far as I can discover none of the experts has yet come up with a detailed working calendar for the *shrub* gardener. Even without any thought of publication, sooner or later I suppose I should have been compelled to work out something of the sort merely to keep myself up-to-date throughout a year of seasonal tasks of this kind, and it is a fact that my trees and shrubs have received far more appropriately timed attentions since my rough draft for the six working-periods took shape. So I hope that in getting this rather stodgy subject on to paper it may at the same time be of some service to others as well as to me.

Discussions over recent years with flower arrangers and other readers of my two previous books suggest that my own horticultural tastes are widely shared. But a number of converts now appear to need some help with the initial planning, if they are to make the most of their shrub material for garden decoration rather than hide it away in their cutting beds; they also seem to be unnecessarily apprehensive about the subsequent care and maintenance of newly acquired trees and shrubs.

This, then, is an attempt to take things a step further for those to whom I feel I owe some kind of after-sales service. My aims are fourfold, with the emphasis on number 4:

1. To clear shrub gardening of any false mystique, in order to persuade the diffident that it really is as easy and undemanding as its reputation claims
2. To give what elementary help I can as regards the initial planning and planting
3. To explain the more important operations in the greatest possible detail for the benefit of the out-and-out novice
4. To provide a ready-reference guide to seasonal jobs in the shrub garden.

As regards the third of these, in order to avoid cluttering up the calendar unnecessarily and wearying the experienced with superfluous detail, the general instructions on such recurrent items as planting, control of pests and diseases, pruning technique and so on are given a section to themselves (Part Three), which may be ignored by those who know it all.

Nothing Up My Sleeve

For the would-be shrub gardener some intrinsic feeling for colour, texture and design is obviously an advantage, though, even when initially lacking, these artistic instincts quite often develop along with increasing experience of planning and plant habits. What is even more essential from the start is, I think, a modicum of common sense and a determination to succeed. This is often all too glibly referred to as 'green fingers', but one of my professed aims is to debunk the superstition that shrub gardening is an occult science and 'green fingers' the supernatural gift of some good fairy. Though totally inexperienced at the start and wholly dependent for guidance on a couple of intoxicating books on the subject, I reckon that my own shrub garden took shape without the intrusion of any such fairy godmother, unless I had her to thank for a congenital capacity for taking pains, both mental and physical – no doubt a more serviceable endowment for the job on hand, be that hand a workaday, grubby pink, or green as jealousy. Given a sufficiently absorbing interest and tenacity, first-hand experience will do the rest (the next chapter, on the making of a shrub garden, contains a rather more practical approach to both the creative and technical aspects of the problem).

While many of us are busy acquiring this experience we may take comfort in the fact that, provided they are kept regularly and adequately mulched with suitable material (as described under Mulching in Part Three), ornamental trees and shrubs are on the whole so well able to take care of themselves when once established that they are almost more likely to be killed by kindness than to die of neglect. I have known some novices to be as fidgety as an over-zealous young mother with an initially healthy first-born infant; indeed, I can think of one shrub gardener of some experience so much addicted to over-cosseting, over-feeding, over-doctoring and general foreboding that I doubt whether she herself derives much pleasure from her well-chosen plantings, among which disease is thought to lurk in every bush and any vestige of leaf-scorch or distortion is tantamount to a death warrant. To combine enjoyment with reasonable watchfulness should be our aim from the outset, and if at first we make mistakes—as we surely must—there will be salutary lessons to be learnt from them, while at the same time the end product as a whole will be increasing in beauty and in stature year by year.

Admittedly the first years of semi-nakedness in the shrub borders are a little tricky, especially in cold or windy districts, but before long the plants will begin to afford one another mutual shelter, if not too sparsely spaced, and from then on will in most cases suffer very little permanent setback from a year's neglect, or more—though one should expect to have to make up for lost time once in a while. But just think what a mess a herbaceous border would become if left untended for only half as long!

Not from idleness, but from sheer pressure of circumstance, I was recently obliged to leave my shrub borders to look after themselves over a period of almost five years. Only at infrequent intervals, and then only for a brief hour or so, could I make time for any gardening at all, so that even jobs normally regarded as essential had to be scamped or left undone. Fortunately the grass is my husband's responsibility, for lawns cannot be neglected, even briefly, during the growing season without creating an immediate air of dilapidation; he also saw to it that the indispensable leaf-mulch was annually topped up. When once again it became possible to get down to some serious gardening I half expected to uncover a trail of death, disease and general disaster, but although there were plenty of jobs crying out to be done, few signs of long neglect would have been evident to any but the most critical observer. I am not suggesting that one may let things rip indefinitely, but I hope that the experience of my readers will endorse my contention that the shrub garden is a fairly accommodating task-master.

That is not to say that no hard labour is involved. Though much of the seasonal work is far from strenuous the planting period in particular, which is mostly concentrated in the winter months of dormancy, demands considerable physical effort in the first instance. However, those unwilling or unable to make this effort might safely employ unskilled labour, under constant supervision (to ensure that topsoil is kept separate from subsoil and so on), for preparing planting holes or expanses of ground to receive new trees and shrubs, and also to help in the removal of bulky established specimens within the garden.

But perhaps I am taking too much for granted. In talking of 'hard labour' I have assumed that you are either about to make a shrub garden, in which case the initial exertion involved will surprise no one, or that you already have one—and if so you may well wonder why so much hard work in winter, once the original planting has been completed. Admittedly the bulk of winter work is non-recurrent, provided one is satisfied with the garden as it is. But so few real gardeners ever are and I, for one, cannot leave the plants alone just as long as it is still possible to improve their siting or alter a part of the layout without serious damage either to the plants or to the operator. Those who have not yet caught the fever should not let this attitude discourage them, because there is of course not the slightest necessity to switch things around year after year in the un-relenting search after better colour combinations, more telling contrasts of shape and texture, more favourable situations for individual needs, or a fairer allocation of flower power between the succeeding seasonal displays, discarding subjects which have fallen short of expectations after fair trial, or stealing a few extra yards of *lebensraum*, perhaps, from part of a lawn, to accommodate new possessions. And so on, and on.

Those of us who persist in making work for ourselves, as our experience and our love for our hobby grow, do so purely because we derive from it a deep satisfaction and an absorbing creative interest which will almost certainly last us all our active lives. But, I repeat, this kind of frenetic activity is compulsive rather than compulsory. For the unambitious 'caretaker' the really inescapable winter jobs in the shrub garden are comparatively few. Even though the summary of the more important operations for winter (mid- or late December to early or mid-March) in the Working-calendar may appear to be longer than most, it should be remembered that much of it may not apply to your particular garden: for example, you may grow only a few of the shrubs requiring regular pruning at this time, or you may be lucky enough to be free from the pests and diseases needing winter control, or from the savage kinds of winter weather which make protective measures necessary only in certain districts.

The first title which suggested itself for the kind of book I had in mind was *Time Permitting*, which was altogether too uninformative even to hint at the nature of the subject matter. But it does suggest the kind of attitude to shrub gardening which I believe to be the right one: the garden should not be allowed to become a tyranny, but can largely be fitted in—or periodically ignored—to suit one's convenience, without disastrous results. When the needs of a garden of any kind are allowed to nag at one's conscience, arousing a feeling of guilt or, worse still, resentment, it is time to look for an upstairs flat or to take to window-box gardening with plastic daffodils, marigolds and asters. Or what could be more everlasting than plastic Immortelles?

The compilation of the Working-calendar in particular has made it clear to me just how irregularly I practise what I preach. But the garden does not often give me away, except perhaps to the more hawk-eyed of horticulturists. I hope I shall not be thought guilty of sales-talk if I say that for me, at least, this has been a very salutary exercise, sending me scurrying out of doors to attend at the right moment to a number of highly desirable, if not essential tasks, for which the appropriate season had come and gone unheeded all too often hitherto.

Territory which a State believes is needed for its natural developement. (G = living space)

Part Two

Making a Shrub Garden

Having had no training in garden design I have always refused to give advice on the subject, except to rescue floundering personal friends in doubt and difficulty. But I have so often been asked by readers for help in the initial layout of a shrub garden that a few basic hints derived from personal experience may perhaps be welcome here. Though entirely non-professional, the advice which follows is, I hope, mostly too elementary to be debatable for a garden of its kind.

Often in the past I have stressed that my garden is a small one by any standards, and I must say so yet again. It covers less than half an acre. Much as I should like to find room for many more plants I have no desire to add to its size, which is just as much as I can comfortably manage, nor would I advise others to cultivate an area greater than they can conveniently look after (either single-handed, or between them in the case of husband and wife) without the 'aid' of a jobbing gardener. I have no experience in the management of broad acres requiring a full-time professional staff and am concerned only with the self-taught, or untaught, owner-gardener on a modest scale, who will find it increasingly difficult to get even unskilled help for a couple of days a week, or less.

For my own part, so long as I am sufficiently able-bodied to look after my own shrub plantings nothing would induce me to let one of these casual hands loose among them. The bus driver, bricklayer or postman who may still occasionally be willing to oblige with an hour or two of his time on summer evenings may usefully keep the grass cut or weed the vegetables, but will almost certainly be so ignorant about the care of trees and shrubs that, if allowed any responsibility for these, as like as not he will chop them to the bone without discrimination and without prior consultation. So for me 'all my own work' is the motto for success, and in this chapter I shall have in mind the small shrub garden in which outside help will not be required except perhaps for the mowing.

First I shall propose some preliminary homework for those with neither theoretical knowledge nor practical experience in garden-making. As I myself had neither when I started, this was my own approach to the problem.

1. Join the Royal Horticultural Society, which offers many in-
estimable benefits in return for a modest annual subscription.
These include admission to the Society's Garden at Wisley, to
frequent shows in London and to other meetings such as the
Chelsea Flower Show, the Royal National Rose Society's Shows,
and so on, and to various lectures and practical demonstrations;
a copy of the monthly Journal; advice on horticultural problems,
and the use of the Society's extensive library.

2. Visit the shows and the Wisley Garden as often as possible, and of
course any of the many fine shrub gardens in the British Isles
which are opened to the public annually. The best way to decide
what to grow is to have a look at growing specimens in suitable
surroundings, rather than to judge a plant from a small sample
in a showman's vase or, even worse, from a catalogue description.

3. Make a collection of the more detailed shrub nursery catalogues
and do not begrudge payment of the small charge which may be
made for them, because some are a 'mine of information' (as one
justifiably claims on its cover). The meat is what counts, so look
for this rather than for fancy garnish in the shape of coloured
illustrations. Some I find over-optimistic about hardiness, some
not sufficiently discriminating about lime-haters; but many
supplement the regulation plant descriptions with facts about
flowering periods, estimated ultimate heights (not enough include
the ultimate spread, which is no less important), individual
cultural needs, hints on planting, pruning and general aftercare
and, in many cases, a selection of 'horses for courses' which may
help a beginner with problems of wet soil, dry soil, chalk, shade,
salt- and sand-laden coastal gales and so on. I must, however,
make it clear that the object of the list which follows is not to
make an invidious selection of the best shrub nurseries, but
rather to recommend some of the more instructive shrub catalogues. Most costly, yet remarkably cheap at £1·75p. (£1·25p.
in paperback), the new *Hilliers' Manual of Trees and Shrubs* is both
a catalogue of some 8000 woody plants and a unique reference
work of 576 pages, providing a fund of information of incalcul-
able value. Among the more helpful of the ordinary catalogues
are those of Jackman, Notcutt, Pennell, L. R. Russell, J. Scott,
Slieve Donard, Sunningdale, Toynbee and Wyevale. Specialist
information on clematis comes from Fisk, Great Dixter Nurseries

and Treasure (also from the general catalogues of Jackman and Pennell); from Bayles on eucalyptus (with a free leaflet of planting instructions); from Slocock in their special rhododendron catalogue; from Trehane on camellias and evergreen azaleas and from Mrs Desmond Underwood on silver-leaved plants. Sunningdale is especially helpful on ground-cover, as well as trees and shrubs. Finally, the brief double sheet issued by M. Haworth-Booth deserves a separate word or two of commendation, providing— for a very few pence—a valuable and remarkably comprehensive lesson in selecting plants for a shrub garden. Stocking only such trees, shrubs and carpeters as satisfy his exacting definition of 'effective', he divides these into four flowering periods, so that we have only to choose an equal proportion from each seasonal section in order to achieve an 'unbroken succession of flowering effects' from April until late autumn, with evergreen foliage effects for winter.

A general list of nurserymen, with addresses, is included in Appendix Two. *245*

4. The next best thing to practical experience is the right kind of reading. Apart from their instructive articles, the Royal Horticultural Society's Journal and other good horticultural periodicals will contain book reviews to guide your choice and public libraries will obtain almost any book they are asked for if they do not have it in stock. To my mind omnibus tomes entitled *The Complete* . . . this or that tend to say too little about too much and least of all on the subject of shrub gardening. If your dilemma is intractable clay, solid chalk, salt sea winds and sprays or whatever, a book devoted to that one subject is far more likely to tie up all the loose ends and will probably have been wrung from the author by stern experience. A number of excellent cheap paperbacks, such as Christopher Lloyd's *Gardening on Chalk and Lime*, J. R. B. Evison's *Gardening by the Sea* and Kenneth Midgley's *Garden Design*, deal with problems of this kind. The Royal Horticultural Society also publish useful pamphlets on a variety of specialized subjects. (See Appendix One for the list of Recommended Reading.) *244*.

5. Keep a large loose-leaf garden notebook in which to record anything useful you may read concerning the needs of the trees and

shrubs you grow or hope to grow. In time your personal study
of plant behaviour in your particular soil and climate will make a
valuable contribution to your own home-made 'mine of information'.

A record of orders for plants is not only useful for reference as
planting time approaches but also for later determining the age,
source and price of one's trees and shrubs.

Layout   These are, so to speak, the pre-preliminaries and we are
now ready to start work. So first let us consider a few points
connected with the layout. It was as a golfer that I first discovered
how much might be learnt from a good, hard look at how not to do
it. To study a 'rabbit' on the practice ground was almost as good
as an hour with the professional. The hideous absurdity of that
almighty slice or of that jerky snatch at the ball must in future be
avoided at all costs. The principle seems to me no less true of
garden design, in which there are salutary lessons to be learnt from
the bad example as well as from the good. So I propose first to deal
with a few 'don'ts'.

Positioning of Borders   Why, I wonder, is the amateur planner
so often hypnotized by the visionary dream of a colourful, ever-
changing panorama spread broadside on before the drawing-room
window or the terrace, when in practice the build-up of colour in
depth is so much intensified when looking *along* a border rather
than *at* it? Then again, even in a very small garden it is usually
possible to lead the eye into the distance, perhaps towards a view
beyond the garden boundary or towards some centre of interest
such as a specimen tree or other ornamental feature—and by this
I do not mean a plastic gnome dipping a plastic fishing rod into a
plastic pool! But away goes one's vista if one deliberately cuts
across the middle distance with a shrub border for the sake of a
head-on confrontation.

Contours   I have nothing whatever against straight lines and
formal shapes when these fit their setting; indeed many fine examples
of formal design are to be seen in large and famous gardens. But on
the whole I think ornamental trees and shrubs look more at home
in borders of less angular outline. And a series of bold sweeps and
graceful curves will accommodate a larger variety of the verge
plants which give such a decorative finish to the plantings. 'Bold

sweeps' and 'graceful curves' have however become such mis-
applied clichés of horticultural jargon that I hesitate to use them
lest they be interpreted as those mean, identical waves and wiggles
too often masquerading as gracefully curved contours. 'Bold' really
must *be* bold. Where space is restricted, far better one generous
sweep than all that mini-scalloping. And where there is room for
more, let your ample bays and bulges vary noticeably in their
proportions.

A long length of thoroughly pliable hosepipe is the best aid I know
for planning the contours of borders, lawns and paths because it is
so clearly visible when the effect is surveyed from a distance, as it
should be during the planning, and it is so easily manipulated to
vary the curves until one hits on the ideal outline; it is as well, however, to put in some more permanent markers once the lines have been
decided. Mapping out on the spot and judging the effect from a
number of viewpoints from house and garden will almost certainly
provide more pleasing perspectives than the plotting of mathema-
tically precise contours on the unnatural flatness of squared
paper.

Lawns and Paths   Do not be tempted to skimp either lawns or
paths in your enthusiasm for trees, shrubs and ground-cover, for the
beauty of these will be immeasurably diminished in effect without
an ample setting of green grass, or perhaps of paved areas, not only
as a foil to their colours but to create an atmosphere of restfulness
in contrast to the busy pattern of branch, flower, fruit and leaf. On
the other hand, the idea that the grassing down of large areas is
labour-saving is not founded on fact. Rough grass may be so, but
well-kept lawns demand considerable care and expertise.

It is even more difficult to force oneself to allow for paths of a
generous width when space is limited. Aesthetically a broad walk is
much more pleasing, but it is also desirable for more practical
considerations, such as the passage of a loaded wheelbarrow without
impediment. And when planting alongside paths we should make
ample allowance for the future spread of low-growing shrubs and
verge plants which will otherwise one day become a menace,
catching in the mower, barring our way and drenching our feet
after rain. I speak from sorrowful experience; and yet I am none
too sure that paths *must* be wide enough to accommodate two
people walking abreast if we are really short of space, as is so
frequently laid down by horticultural writers. On sloping sites paths

may include steps for ease of human access from one level to another, but if so a ramp or ramps must be provided where necessary to enable wheelbarrows, mowers etc. to circulate to all parts of the garden.

Grass paths are usually so much more visually pleasing in the shrub garden that I prefer to ignore the advantage of walking dry-shod on gravel, paving or other materials which require no mowing. Despite the cheaper cost of clinker or straightforward concrete I find these too unsightly to be considered except as a last resort in kitchen garden and utility areas. Like stone paving, concrete is also inclined to be slippery when wet.

One last point about paths. These are primarily functional and should therefore lead somewhere. By all means let them curve round a bend to lead away out of sight, but if they bend or wander let there be some visible reason why. A path that wriggles for the sake of wriggling looks both unpractical and ridiculous, but if it can rationally be made to disappear beyond or behind a clump of trees or shrubs it not only looks invitingly mysterious but it also makes sense. I know of a garden of about one acre which has been most lovingly planned and tended, and yet I used never to pass it without wondering why I found it so boring. I ceased to wonder when at length it occurred to me that even from the road the entire layout was simultaneously visible at a glance. So let us resist the temptation to display all the goods at once in the shop window, and keep a surprise or two up our sleeve.

Before leaving the subject of grassed areas let me put in a word for the chap in charge of the mower. Our broad sweeps and graceful curves bordering the lawn can comfortably be taken in his stride, but my husband reminds me that in this garden two snags in particular make his task more laborious than need be. One is that my carpeters and other front row subjects, having been planted too close to the edge of the beds in the first instance, have now grown out over the grass in many places to impede the mower; the other is the brick edging to the beds at the foot of the house walls which prevents the machine from cutting close up against the bricks.

Windbreaks and Screens On sites exposed to fierce gales or salt sea spray one of the first essentials will be an outer shelter-belt of cheap and hardy trees and shrubs, well furnished to the ground and including a high proportion of evergreens, in order to filter the force of the wind before it reaches the choicer ornamental plantings within its shelter. Subjects for this purpose are chosen not for their looks but for their toughness, and include poplar, ash, laurel, privet, holm-oak, *Rhododendron ponticum* (soil acidity permitting), gorse, hardy conifers and, for seaside in particular, sea buckthorn, the hardier olearias and tamarisk. This rather specialized problem is dealt with in some detail in J. R. B. Evison's *Gardening by the Sea* (Pan Piper Small Garden Series).

In less extreme exposure a well-furnished hedge, strongly made wattle hurdling, or only semi-solid wooden fencing makes an adequate wind filter, providing protection for a distance of about ten times its height. Any of these are to be preferred to a solid wall, which creates a great turbulence on its leeward side because the wind cannot penetrate it and so is forced up and over, to descend with vicious force on to the plants it is intended to protect.

For screening purposes or to provide privacy I think the comparatively cheap and expendable wattle hurdling, with a foreground planting of ornamental trees and shrubs, is not only more practical but better-looking than the more conspicuous fencings, or than hedges which demand regular trimming, take up more space and use up much of the moisture required by the more valuable plants. Hurdles vary in quality of material and workmanship and even the best have a shorter life than other types of screen, but if a group of shrubs or a border containing a generous proportion of evergreens is planted against them the plants should have grown to form a living, decorative screen by the time the wattles are beginning to fall apart.

The Furnishings–Two Basic Facts of Life (Soil and Climate)

Soil Before beginning to think about what you propose to grow you will need to know whether your soil is acid, neutral or limy (indeed you may find it varies in this respect in different parts even of a small garden), because certain subjects known as calcifuge will not tolerate lime in the soil. So one of the first needs is to equip yourself with a soil-testing kit, so as to be able to test samples from any part of the garden where you may wish to grow these lime-haters. The very cheapest kind of kit is quite good enough and extremely simple to use, because the pH value of the soil is all one needs to know (that is, its degree of acidity or alkalinity). The more elaborate outfits provide a thorough-going soil analysis, which is quite unnecessary for our purposes. Though it is possible to have one's soil

tested by application to one's local Horticultural Officer, or by the
Royal Horticultural Society on payment of a fee, I am strongly in
favour of the 'do-it-yourself' process, if only for the reason that one's
tests can be much more numerous when one does not have to count
the cost of each sample tested.

The subject of soil pH values has been dealt with in detail on
pp. 37–44 and all that is left to do here is to stress the advisability
of gardening *with* one's soil, rather than trying to fight it. If there
is any choice in the matter one should certainly settle for a soil on
the acid side, but for those whose lot has fallen on limy ground it
would be wiser to forget all the fastidious beauties which insist on
acid, or at least neutral, soil conditions, and to content themselves
with a wide range of other fine trees, shrubs and foliage plants
which will not object to, and in a few cases actually prefer, an
alkaline soil. Those who are unwilling to follow this advice will
find some hints on the cultivation of calcifuge plants in limy
gardens in the Soil section of Part Three referred to at the beginning
of this paragraph.

Climate   As already mentioned, it may be possible to provide a
good measure of wind protection on exposed sites, but there is not a
great deal one can do about the rigours of winter and an insufficiency
of summer sun in a naturally cold garden such as my own, for
instance, which lies on a north-east slope in an uncompromisingly
cold district. Assorted gadgetry in the form of frost protection is
described on pp. 142–51, but here I have found that there is little
satisfaction in attempting subjects of doubtful hardiness, except as
a calculated risk now and again. My own maxim is: 'if at first you
don't succeed, don't try again—or not more than once'; though
it may be found that what turned up its toes in one part of the
garden may flourish in another. The half-hardy plants, for instance,
may be quite happy against a warm wall; and here I have often
found that in the open garden certain failures of earlier years will
today come through severe winters without much harm, thanks to
the shelter now derived from matured neighbouring evergreens or
from a canopy of bare branches. Hydrangeas, which at first were
killed to the ground each winter except in beds at the foot of the
house walls, are a case in point.

Some parts of a garden may be more naturally frost-prone than
others, as for instance the lower end of a sloping site. It is not
always possible to do as one is told about providing an escape route

at the bottom for the cold air which flows downhill, in which case
it will remain trapped in a frost pocket down below in which only
the hardiest plants will survive, whereas shrubs higher up the hillside will find the winter temperature much less trying to their
constitution.

Choice of Plants and Their Arrangement In deciding how
to furnish the shrub borders it is important to be meticulously fair
in catering for each of the flowering seasons, leaving subtly contrasted evergreen foliage to take care of winter interest, unless, that
is, one is particularly addicted to winter-flowering trees and shrubs.
If so, it should be borne in mind that they really need a prominent
site within view of the house, to be enjoyed in comfort in winter,
and that most will be mere passengers for the best months of the
year, unless they have other virtues such as the fine, sculptural
foliage of *Mahonia japonica*, or may serve as a host to a spring- or
summer-flowering climber. If any one seasonal display is stepped
up at the expense of another there will be some pretty dreary gaps
in what should be a non-stop show from early spring until late
autumn.

As regards the grouping of trees and shrubs, guiding principles
are the same as for herbaceous borders, with a gradual stepping
down from tall to medium, dwarf and carpeting plants. Gradation
of heights should not be too rigid, but where it is ignored the shrub
border takes on the forbidding appearance of the typical Victorian
'shrubbery', coming to a steep and abrupt halt at the edge of the
plantation to reveal a lot of gaunt legginess and knobbly knees. So
when deciding what to grow, keep some idea of the ultimate overall
effect in view.

A certain number of flowering trees will carry colour into the
upper levels, but do not overdo them, as I did here, or you will land
yourself with overshady borders later on. In cold districts it is of
course especially important to invite all the sunshine available into
your garden. And be careful not to underestimate the ultimate
spread of the young sapling cherry, robinia or eucalyptus which
occupies so little space for the first years of its life. On the other
hand, do not be in too much of a hurry to scrap existing trees on
the site, even though they may not contribute large crops of
flowers. In my garden I must have removed seven or eight pine
trees (mostly too close to the house) without subsequent regret;
but I congratulate myself that I had the *nous* to keep a clump of

graceful silver birches and a singleton elsewhere, which were in
fact the only growing things worth retaining, and instantly lent
some air of maturity to the garden-in-the-making, despite the fact
that they steal an unfair share of moisture from the shrubs planted
among their roots.

Spacing has been discussed in Part Three (pp. 48–50), giving the
pros and cons of 'close boscage' versus more orthodox planting
distances, and garden planners may find a close study of established
plantings in shrub gardens open to the public a help in deciding
which method they favour. When in doubt about planting distances
between certain trees, for instance, I have brazenly paced it out in
famous gardens in my time, to my temporary embarrassment and
permanent advantage.

My own planning methods are somewhat unorthodox. Having
bought what I estimate to be roughly appropriate as regards
quantities and graded heights, I map out the basic groupings with
the live plants on the site rather than on the drawing-board. For
me the design only begins to come alive when I see it on the ground,
first getting the key plants properly spaced and then juggling around
with the rest of them until I am satisfied with the result. Labelled
bamboo canes make useful planning markers, using different
lengths to indicate approximate heights. Subjects such as magnolias,
cornus, ceanothus and so on, which dislike being moved, should be
carefully positioned once and for all, whereas more portable items
such as rhododendrons and azaleas, or more expendable ones such
as tree lupins, cistus and brooms, may be packed close for rapid
results and later transferred in the one instance, or removed, in
the case of the more short-lived subjects, when they reach the
scrawny stage. Almost 'instant' gardening may be achieved if two
or three evergreen azaleas, the smaller potentillas, or other dwarf
shrubs are grouped closely enough to give the effect of a single
specimen. By the time that one alone will fill the space portable
spares from the group may perhaps serve to replace a casualty
elsewhere, or to contribute to a new planting as one's appetite grows.
Trees and shrubs which may well outlive their owner by many
years, if conditions are to their liking, deserve the best possible
start, not only in respect of individual fads about sun or shade, acid
or limy soil, sharp drainage or moist root-run, shelter or full
exposure and so on, but also by suitably preparing the site to receive
them and by providing adequate protection in cold areas for all
but the hardiest plants during their first critical winter or two.

These and other aspects of planting and aftercare are dealt with in detail in Part Three.

Plant Orders and the Nurseryman   One is usually at the mercy of the supplier as regards delivery unless one has made special arrangements, but the earlier the order is placed the better one's prospects of priority treatment from a trade which tries to deal with orders in strict rotation, and the less the likelihood of scarcer items being sold out or the best specimens gone before one's turn comes. If you are asked to sign for a package on delivery without having inspected the contents, make a note to this effect on the document; and if you are dissatisfied with the quality of a plant on arrival, do your complaining at once – not months later when you find it dying or dead, by which time the fault is as likely to be yours as that of the supplier. Difficult though it may be to persuade oneself that 'best' is not necessarily 'biggest', it is a fact that, despite the greater cost of the larger sizes, a young specimen will almost always grow away more rapidly than an older one when transplanted. Nor is the cheapest by any means always the most economical and the nurseryman's 'Bargain Collection – our choice' is another temptation to be resisted. If you do not know what you want to grow, you would do better to wait until you do, lest the nurseryman's choice later fails to coincide with yours. Being unwilling to accept the nurseryman's 'nearest', which may otherwise turn up in place of an item he is unable to supply, I find it advisable to mark my orders: 'No substitutes without reference to me'.

In this connection may I urge the beginner (and others) to make the initial effort required to master botanical Latin names in full, that is, the first name or genus, the second name or species, and a third in some cases, representing a particular variety of the species. The use of correct botanical nomenclature ought to be so commonplace that it would cease to create a pompous air of name-dropping and so put an end to the misunderstandings between gardeners and growers, for it is the only certain means of avoiding confusion when ordering. Close study of the best catalogues soon makes such names familiar and the subject has also been explained in great detail in my book, *Garden Foliage for Flower Arrangement*.

It will be seen that I have, as usual, used botanical nomenclature throughout this book, adding synonyms vernacular names or nicknames in brackets alongside. Where single quotation marks are given they have a recognized botanical significance and apply to a garden variety (cultivar), that is, a variety originally found in cultivation, rather than in the wild.

Whether you wish to plant the general run of trees and shrubs while there is still some warmth in the soil, or whether you prefer spring delivery in order to avoid the hazards of the first critical winter for plants of border-line hardiness, the nurseryman will usually co-operate if he knows your wishes in good time. If on the other hand you propose to fetch your plants, give him some warning and a suggested date for collection, so that they may be lifted and made ready on time (for the grower's convenience as well as for yours).

Whereas it is often unpopular to drop in at a nursery without warning during the busy lifting season, expecting to drive away with a boot-load of plants not previously ordered and disrupting the routine work of the establishment in the process, it is of course now possible to pick up as many potted plants as required at your convenience, without prior arrangement and at any season, by calling at a Garden Centre, where you will always be a welcome visitor. And convenience it is, so long as you are not an 'impulse buyer' and can find exactly what you came for. Fortunately the rarer items of special interest to the serious plantsman may now quite possibly be found at certain Garden Centres catering for the connoisseur. Even where the stock is limited to more commonplace best-sellers there will be a number of these worthy of a place in an initial planting, so long as they have been well and truly pot-grown (see p. 44).

Taking the Plunge   This has been rather a long chapter. I hope it is long enough. If it and the detailed general advice in Part Three between them serve their purpose as intended, the rest is now up to you. With all the prescribed homework behind you, you should now be ready to take the plunge without misgiving, remembering that there is little inevitability about most of one's initial blunders in garden-making. Happily for the amateur shrub gardener the canvas may be re-worked at least as freely as that of an oil painting— indeed after 20 years or so I am still cheerfully daubing away at mine.

Part Three

Some Technical Aspects of Shrub Gardening

Though the more experienced shrub gardener will no doubt find much of Part Three superfluous, beginners are bound to need advice on certain essential techniques of what is to them an unfamiliar undertaking, requiring some understanding of the basic principles of planting, pruning, feeding, control of pests and diseases, winter protection and so on. By including all such general instructions in this separate section I aim to keep the Working-calendar uncluttered by repetitive explanations for the sake of easier immediate reference to the tasks due for attention at various seasons. For the same reason all the explanatory line drawings are concentrated in Part Three.

Before we become too deeply involved at a later stage in references to proprietary horticultural products such as fertilizers, pesticides and fungicides, I should like to make it clear that the mention of certain manufacturers and their wares and the omission of others should not be taken to mean that the latters' products are necessarily inadequate. If too few are thought to get a mention it is for the reason that I am above all concerned to make things as simple as possible for the novice, for whom too wide a choice of chemical dusts, sprays and granules is likely to be more bewildering than helpful.

A list of some of the leading manufacturers of gardening chemicals, with addresses, will be found in Appendix Three, p. 249.

Acid, Neutral and Limy Soils

Even the non-gardener is usually aware that soils differ widely in structure, from heavy clay to hungry sand, with plenty of variations in between, and the newcomer to gardening tends to think of soil in terms of this sort, if at all, often unaware that it also varies in its chemical reaction from acid to neutral or limy, although this is the aspect of chief importance to the shrub gardener. Fortunately there are ways of improving awkward soil structures; but whereas even the sands of the desert can now be made to blossom like the rose science has not yet devised any entirely practical, large-scale method of altering a limy soil to suit those calcifuge (lime-hating) plants which provide some of the finest ornaments of a shrub garden, soil permitting.

The improvement of difficult textures such as that of heavy clay or solid chalk (the latter will, however, remain limy despite the increased fertility resulting from such 'improvement') has been well covered by specialist writers, and when faced with a problem of this kind our wisest course is to read up the subject in detail or to seek the advice of the local county horticultural officer before embarking on anything as permanent as the making of a shrub garden, which we may delight in, or deplore, for the rest of a lifetime (see Recommended Reading in Appendix One). However, although a few ornamental trees and shrubs show some preference for a limy diet they will nevertheless grow perfectly well on acid or neutral soils, whereas the lime-haters will pine and die in alkaline conditions.

So the pH value of the soil is what matters most to us—that is to say, whether it is acid (pH 6.5 and less), neutral (pH 7.0) or alkaline (i.e. limy, pH 7.5 upwards). Until this has been determined there is little point in planning what to grow. To give one example, owing to the common misconception that camellias insist on a peaty soil they are often written off as impossible to grow on clay. The calcifuge camellia will however flourish exceedingly on a clay foundation so long as it is on the acid side, as it very well may be, despite the widespread misconception that clay is invariably alkaline. Indeed, I have known one expert to claim that camellias grow best on acid clay.

I hope you have not taken fright at the mention of the pH scale used to gauge soil acidity or alkalinity. This is not at all the same as a thoroughgoing soil analysis which, fortunately, is not necessary for our purpose. An elementary soil-testing kit costing under thirty new pence is very uncomplicated and will tell us as much as we need to know about samples taken from different parts of the garden where shrub planting is intended—and it will also offer one piece of advice which I must warn you to ignore: the instructions regarding the addition of lime 'to correct acidity' are intended for vegetable and kitchen gardens and must on no account be applied in the shrub garden, where acidity is to be cherished rather than 'corrected', unless it is extreme.

Every aspiring shrub gardener should be equipped to make such simple tests, and here are some of the reasons why.

When about to make a garden in a new district disregard the often repeated advice to look around the neighbourhood, observing what grows in the wild as well as what prospers in local gardens. This is to by-pass certainty for guesswork, and just is not good enough. For instance, though you may observe formal bedding displays or massed plantings of dahlias on the other side of the fence this is no help at all because, no matter what the nature of his soil, your neighbour may simply prefer his French marigolds, begonias and dahlias to the choice, lime-hating trees and shrubs that you hope to be able to grow.

Fig. 1. A cheap, simple soil-testing kit

A. Drip-nosed bottle of testing fluid.
B. Double-ended spoon, B1 being partially filled with soil sample to be
   saturated with testing fluid, which is
   later drained off into B2. Result is
   judged by colour of the drained fluid.
C. Spatula for handling soil samples.
(A leaflet of directions for use is also included in the outfit.)

On the other hand, if he has been sufficiently determined to cultivate such lime-haters himself he may have been obliged to import suitable acid soil to accommodate the group of azaleas which catches your eye next door.

Or perhaps you may find pine woods or wild heathland at your gates and rhododendron thickets within your property, but these are no guarantee that some parts of your garden have not been heavily limed by your predecessor or that he has not replaced the naturally acid soil of his rose beds or kitchen garden with imported limy loam. Some say that the effect of artificially liming an acid soil is leached out within three years or so, but I side with those experts who hold the results to be a lot more permanent.

Then again, dumps of builders' lime and mortar rubble may come to light when preparing shrub borders on a naturally acid soil. As might be expected, beds at the foot of house and other walls are particularly suspect. Anyone building a house around which it is proposed to lay out a shrub garden would be wise to persuade the builders to mix their mortar and to contain other noxious offal within a prescribed area (preferably on a future driveway or paved precinct of some kind), so that it does not interfere with the siting of shrub borders later on. While its harmful effect may, I suppose, be less significant on a naturally limy soil, this kind of rubbish is a poor growing medium for almost anything except, I believe, *Iris unguicularis*!

It is in fact also possible for virgin soil to vary, without man's intervention, from acid to neutral or alkaline, just as soil textures too may vary, even within the comparatively small compass of half an acre, or less. So, all things considered, it is safer to take nothing for granted in this respect.

This is not to suggest that all the lime-hating tribe must be utterly forsworn by those with limy gardens, but rather to dissuade the latter from attempting to grow them in any quantity without being aware of the difficulties. There are various ways of overcoming this soil obstacle, but only on a limited scale and with certain provisos.

1. Plants in tubs and garden vases

It is common practice among gardeners on lime to grow individual specimen rhododendrons, camellias, pieris, kalmias and other calcifuge plants in tubs or garden vases containing acid soil, which must be topped up or renewed from time to time and should never be allowed to dry out—and this means constant watchfulness. If the mains water supply is alkaline, rain-water should be collected to supply the necessary moisture. The risk of frost damage both to plants and to earthenware containers has been dealt with in the chapter on winter protective measures, pp. 145–46, and should not be overlooked when contemplating patio-style gardening of this kind and in this climate.

2. Polythene-lined holes

Dig a hole of suitable size to allow adequately for root growth and line it with fairly strong polythene sheeting so that this extends a little way beyond the top of the hole. Pierce a few small holes in the lower parts of the lining for drainage purposes and fill up with a suitably acid soil mixture.

3. Raised beds

If you are rich and can also command the necessary labour,

you may consider the construction of a raised bed of suitable soil for a collection of rhododendrons and other shallow-rooted lime-haters, where natural circumstances are against them. The bed should be on the flat, since lime only seeps downwards and sideways and will not harm calcifuge plants if it is well below the root ball and if this is safe from contamination by limy water draining down from above. A layer of acid, peaty soil deep enough to accommodate the roots is thus built up above the level of the naturally alkaline soil, sandwiching a drainage layer of pebbles or some such between the two if possible, which may, however, be impracticable over a large surface. A generous

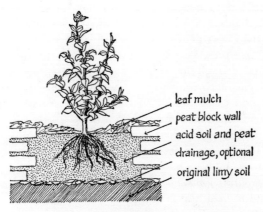

leaf mulch
peat block wall
acid soil and peat
drainage, optional
original limy soil

Fig. 2. Raised bed for calcifuge plants on limy soil
(cross-section)

18 in. of acid soil and peat should be adequate for most plants, since deep-rooted subjects are not suitable for this kind of cultivation. This acid top layer is retained within walls made, preferably, from horticultural peat blocks (which your garden sundriesman should be able to obtain for you), though brick or stone walls are sometimes substituted. For a rather lesser depth, lengths of natural log as favoured by the late King George VI in the Savill Garden have found some popularity in recent years, though the risk of the dreaded honey fungus developing on what must sooner or later become rotting wood and thence spreading to attack live trees and shrubs would rule out this alternative for me. Assuming therefore that we settle for the peat blocks, these must first be thoroughly soaked and then

bonded in layers as in bricklaying, using some of the acid, peaty soil of which the bed is to be made in place of mortar at the joints. This, too, should be well moistened. Speaking without personal experience of this form of cultivation it occurs to me that one would need a lot of vigilance and rain-water to prevent such a raised bed from drying out—and rhododendrons, together with many other ericaceous subjects, are especially allergic to drought, even when growing in the most favourable natural circumstances.

4. Iron Sequestrene

When sequestrated iron was first introduced some years ago one was tempted to hope that the problem of the calcifuge plant had been finally overcome. But on more sober reflection this strikes me as yet another rich man's panacea, if it is to be used in any quantity. A pack costing 34p at the time of writing would be enough to treat 1½–3 rhododendrons or perhaps 3 hydrangeas, according to size, degree of soil alkalinity and so on. In most cases the solution needs to be applied yearly at the correct season. For most of us I would say that wholesale use would be unpracticable, but at least it affords yet another means of growing a few of the pernickety but most desirable lime-haters in alkaline conditions, and may also provide a welcome fillip for such plants growing in neutral soils, as an extra aid to healthful living.

Neutral Soils A neutral soil comes half-way between acid and alkaline—that is to say, it has a pH value of 7.0. I was about to describe it as the exact centre of the see-saw, but in practice there is a definite bias in the shrub gardener's favour, since the lime-haters are fortunately able to tolerate a neutral soil, provided a generous amount of acid peat is mixed into the planting hole and that they are kept well mulched thereafter, preferably with fallen leaves from an acid district. Crushed bracken rhizomes are also splendid mulching material for individual specimens, if available. Sequestrene should help to put things right if calcifuge plants show any signs of sickliness such as abnormally slow growth, or some yellowing of the leaves, often particularly noticeable between the veins.

I make no apology for giving what may seem to be a disproportionate amount of space to the matter of soil pH values because, although a great deal has been written to help gardeners with

difficult soils, this particular aspect of the problem seems to me to
have been much less fully and frequently aired in print. And yet
it is as fundamentally important to start right in this respect in the
shrub garden as it is to condition cut flowers and foliage according
to their needs before arranging them indoors, if we wish them long
life.

Some Calcifuge Trees, Shrubs and Climbers

Berberidopsis
Calluna
Camellia
Cassiope
Clethra
Conifers (some)
Cornus kousa (most other cornuses are lime-tolerant)
Crinodendron hookeranum
Cytisus scoparius varieties and similar types
Daboecia
Desfontainia
Disanthus
Embothrium
Enkianthus
Erica, almost all except *carnea, mediterranea* and *terminalis*
Eucryphia, except x *nymansensis*
Exochorda racemosa
Fothergilla
Gaultheria
x Gaulthettya
Halesia
Hamamelis (tolerates a very small degree of alkalinity)
Kalmia
Lapageria
Ledum
Leiophyllum
Leptospermum
Leucothoe
Liquidambar
Lithospermum diffusum varieties
Magnolia (some)
Menziesia

Nyssa sylvatica
Oxydendrum
Pernettya
Pieris
Rhododendron (including azalea)
Stewartia
Styrax
Vaccinium
Zenobia

This list includes some of the most widely grown members of the family *Ericaceae*, which almost all need acid soil conditions, with the exception of certain ericas noted in it, and also of some of the Strawberry Trees, of which *Arbutus unedo* is generally considered the most lime-tolerant of the genus.

Planting – General

Planting Seasons In this age of Garden Centres planting seasons no longer appear to make sense, when an 'instant' garden may be knocked up with container-grown goods at any time of the year. But even today the planting of a shrub garden or border is not quite such an all-season affair as may at first appear.

To begin with, if a tree or shrub is to have the stamina required to survive summer planting conditions it must have been well and truly pot- or container-grown, not merely popped into a pot for a quick cash-and-carry sale. The customer should therefore check that it has been growing in its container long enough to have filled it fairly solidly with roots, often showing some reluctance to be knocked or eased out of it. On the other hand, it should be remembered that a shrub rarely gets a proper grip when planted out if it has outgrown its container to the point where the main root has been forced to curl round and round the pot in a despairing spiral, for lack of room to extend.

Also, whereas it may theoretically be feasible to plant suitably grown 'containerized' trees and shrubs in high summer, I for one would not elect to do this in a big way, because each will need constant and copious watering throughout the growing season, except in the very wettest ones.

Then again, not all of us live within reach of a good Garden

Centre. And so, it seems, we are still quite largely dependent on open-ground nursery stock and traditional planting seasons.

As mentioned in the Working-calendar, evergreens should, ideally, be planted either in autumn or, in the case of the more tender ones, in spring. But in these days of soaring carriage charges the shrub gardener usually tries to make do with a single mixed consignment if the plant order includes both evergreen and deciduous subjects *of reasonably tough constitution*, taking delivery of them any time during the latter's dormant period, i.e. roughly between early November and late March (though it varies a good deal in different areas). In this exceptionally cold garden I cannot recall more than one or two casualties resulting from the practice over many years.

Fig. 3. Pot-bound plant

This is all very well for the entirely hardy kinds. But, additional carriage charges notwithstanding, winter planting is not worth risking for the more delicate subjects, whether deciduous or evergreen. For evergreens some gardeners favour autumn planting, while the soil still retains some of its summer warmth, to encourage the root action which helps to withstand the drying winds and drought so often characteristic of spring or early summer. In an average garden climate, or worse, this I consider safe only for bone-hardy subjects and for those of only very slightly suspect constitution. For anything less tough the rigours of the first winter following autumn planting are bound to constitute a risk in all but the mildest districts. Elsewhere it is advisable to leave the grower to bear the brunt of bringing the more fragile nurselings, whether deciduous or evergreen, through the winter, for despatch or collection when the weather begins to warm up, especially if the plants are to share the comparative nakedness of a new border. Spring planting does however necessitate meticulous attention to watering, or spraying to check transpiration when circumstances require it— not just for a week or two, but throughout the growing season.

Since garden climates vary so widely in the British Isles from the coldest and bleakest to the mildest and most sheltered (the latter being mostly confined to the south-west and southern counties), to attempt to distinguish between subjects suitable for spring planting in preference to autumn would be more misleading than helpful. Even in a garden as small as mine the micro-climate from about half-way down the steep north-east slope is a great deal colder than that higher up, where I can grow certain slightly tender subjects, with care, which would have no hope of survival lower down, though the distance between the two positions is probably no more than 30 yards.

In acknowledging an order for plants the nurseryman usually indicates any for which spring despatch is the general rule and will advise, if asked to do so, on suitable planting times for the customer's special climate and other relevant circumstances. If the shrub gardener is to decide upon the best planting season as applied to local conditions (and incidentally to avoid acquiring plants doomed to failure for climatic reasons in certain areas) awareness of the degree of hardiness in each case will be necessary. Such details are contained in the Royal Horticultural Society's *Dictionary of Gardening* and in Messrs Hillier's first-class shrub catalogue, amongst others, differentiating between subjects only suitable for growing in the open in the most favoured localities, those needing wall protection or other shelter in the average climate, those liable to be damaged by hard frost, those more nearly bone-hardy and others entirely so.

As far as really hardy trees and shrubs are concerned, I am treating planting and transplanting operations as continuous from late autumn to early spring, whenever the ground is neither water-logged, frost-bound nor blanketed in snow ('frost-bound' should be taken to mean too hard to cut into with a spade; a thin layer of icing may be skimmed off and set aside). Evidently, therefore, these operations must overlap several of the Working-periods. Pot-grown goods, as distinct from those known in the trade as 'open-ground' plants, may be transferred from container to planting hole with a minimum of root disturbance at any season in suitable weather.

Given frequent and generous watering—that is, not less than 2 gallons per mature plant at any one time—even a well established shrub may sometimes survive a move in high summer, though the risk is only justifiable in exceptional circumstances. Knowing she had nothing to lose I once helped a friend to transfer quantities of valuable adult shrubs from her old garden to a new one many miles away in early July in a heat wave: but I hardly expected much success. Having between us put them into a well watered temporary plot (in scorching sunshine) and commended them to the mercy of the incumbent, my friend did not move in for several months. I think there was not a single casualty, but I feel bound to mention that the seller behind the hosepipe happened to be a close friend of the buyer of the property!

Storing and Heeling In Plants which can be collected, by arrangement, from a nearby nursery present few problems, though unless these are to be immediately planted in their permanent positions they, too, need heeling in. But goods despatched from a distance (with or without notice) turn up, as often as not, when one is beside oneself with preparations for Christmas, laid up with influenza, or snowed up, frozen up, or awash. If circumstances prevent one heeling them in on arrival the plants are unlikely to come to any harm if the package is stowed away unopened for some days in a frostproof but unheated outbuilding—which few of us possess! If brought indoors they should not be kept in a heated room. One of the most satisfactory methods of undercover storage is to unpack the plants, soak the roots if dry, and put them in a dustbin, covering the roots with moist peat. Since the goods may have spent days or even weeks out of the ground and in transit the sooner their roots regain contact with the soil the better.

Even if the weather is totally unsuitable for the planting proper it need rarely prohibit the temporary operation known as 'heeling in' out of doors. A patch of ground may be prepared in advance of likely frost by piling straw or other kind of litter, or sacking, on to it, and by the same token it is often possible to push aside the thick leaf-mulch in the shrub borders during hard weather to find unfrozen soil beneath, in which new arrivals may be temporarily accommodated. Where frost penetration is only superficial the frozen layer of soil may be set aside, but be careful to avoid burying frozen lumps when heeling plants in or, or course, when planting. As a last resort a patch of ground may be thawed in advance by lighting a bonfire on it. In no circumstances should snow or ice be buried, because they are very slow to thaw underground, thus lowering still further the winter soil temperature when dug in.

In waterlogged conditions a supply of dry soil, compost or lightly moistened peat will blot up the surplus water if liberally sprinkled among the roots when heeling in. Dust-dry peat is so extraordinarily slow to absorb moisture that it should always be moistened before use.

A trench is practical for the purpose where space permits. Here, where it does not, new arrivals are temporarily winkled in anywhere in the shrub borders. Those with bare roots should be heeled in at an angle against one side of the trench rather than in an upright position, spreading the roots out carefully before covering them up. Those with root balls packed in hessian and pot-grown subjects are happier in an upright position, leaving the hessian wrapping undisturbed and burying pots right to the rim in the soil.

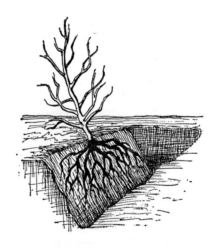

Fig. 4. Heeling in

Trench about to be filled in with soil, after spreading roots out against slope of one side.

Spacing Opinions differ markedly about spacing in the shrub borders. Personally I believe in the close boscage principles picked up when working for the plantsman and garden designer, Mr Michael Haworth-Booth, whose own spectacular shrub garden made a convert of me for all time. Not only does a new garden or planting become an effective spectacle far sooner than can be achieved by sparser methods, but at least in the colder gardens the mutual protection against winter weather to be derived from huddling plants together would in itself be sufficient recommendation.

The kind old friend who first aroused my interest in shrub gardening used to shake her head over my jam-packed spacing. 'My dear', she would say, 'what a problem you will have on your hands in ten years' time!' I am quite sure that many people today consider my garden overcrowded, but even if, after 15 years or so, some of the least precious trees and shrubs had to be scrapped to relieve congestion I felt that I had had my moneysworth from them from the earliest possible stage and, having always accepted some thinning out as inevitable, I can still part with one or two dry-eyed when I must. On the other hand, I have tried, according to my lights, to place more highly prized specimens, and those which most resent transplantation, where they have room to develop undisturbed.

So, on close boscage terms, the larger shrubs are spaced about 4 ft. apart (this applies to anything more than about 3 ft. in ultimate height), the dwarfer plants (ultimately 2–3 ft. high) about 2½ ft. apart and the carpeting plants along the verges 1–1½ ft. apart, on average. The seemingly illogical reference to height rather than to spread, in this context, is because of the greater unpredictability of the latter in individual specimens. But in practice, spacing will be found to work out well enough on the above basis.

Gardeners of a different persuasion insist that each shrub must have room to display its characteristic form unhampered and would therefore add at least 1 ft. to each of these distances, allowing quite 6 ft. between most of the tallest subjects. One is commonly advised that half the combined spread to be expected at maturity gives the correct spacing between two shrubs, but 'spreads' are difficult to predict and are only forecast in a few of the more detailed shrub catalogues, so it seems simpler to adopt one or other of the scales just mentioned.

In either case it is usual to fill gaps with some of the cheaper and more short-lived subjects such as most cytisus and genista, cistus, tree lupin and so on, which will be more or less ready for the scrap-heap by the time their neighbours need more room to spread themselves.

Close boscage or no, it is unwise to plant trees too close together, or too close to the house. The average minimum space necessary between two trees is about 15 or 16 ft., except of course for fastigiate (narrowly columnar) forms.

Climbers on walls, trellises and fences normally need a width of about 6 ft. apiece, but this does not rule out the planting of two climbers or wall plants to grow together and intermingle. Any fairly thin-habited climber such as clematis, rose or *Tropaeolum speciosum* may grow happily, for instance, against a backcloth of *Euonymus fortunei* 'Variegatus' or pyracantha, with their roots sharing one large, well prepared hole not less than 1 ft. away from the base of the wall.

Soil Preparation and Planting Instructions　Planting holes are supposed to be prepared in advance and allowed to settle, but I have found that on a fast-draining soil some short-circuiting is possible. If preparation is postponed until planting time I get away with it on my Surrey greensand by giving the lower layers of the filling some extra firming with the foot and then loosening the surface lightly with the tips of a fork. Such tactics would, however, probably result in a de-aerated mud-puddle on sticky clay, which should in any case be trodden much more gently than a light, sandy soil during planting.

Slack though I may be in the matter of advance preparation, I do not believe in skimping the job itself. Ideally, the whole planting area should be dug over to about two spits depth, carefully keeping the topsoil and subsoil apart, and replacing them in their relative positions; and some of my first plantings were prepared for in this way, which obviates the shock to the roots on reaching the bounds of the prepared hole to fetch up against a possibly unyielding and unfamiliar kind of earth. But this involves a lot of labour, and good results may be achieved with much less effort by excavating generously proportioned individual planting holes within the prospective shrub borders.

It is important that the holes should be really roomy, allowing for expansion as a child's shoe should allow for growing toes. Fortunately the simile ends there, because once the young tree or shrub has taken a good grip on its new surroundings its roots should have sufficient vigour to push through the undug soil beyond the hole's perimeter. Thus one well made pair of shoes will last a plant's lifetime, whereas shoddy initial workmanship may result in permanent crippling and retarded growth later on.

On my own exceptionally thin, hungry sand, which had not then been enriched by years of leaf-mulching, almost all my original plantings were given a good send-off with a generous forkful of farmyard manure not far beneath, but not in contact with, their roots, with a further layer on the surface of the soil, and the resulting growth was remarkably encouraging. Generally speaking, however, an over-rich diet only suits notoriously greedy subjects, since the majority of flowering trees and shrubs tend to put their energy into foliar rather than floral output when too well fed, and the resultant lush growth is likely to suffer in a hard winter.

Nevertheless, there are few soils so rich and fertile that a newly planted or transplanted tree or shrub in a state of dormancy—that is, from late October to the end of March in an average season—will not appreciate the addition to the soil of some slow-acting organic food such as bonemeal, to provide the phosphorus which helps in the development of root action during winter, when growth above ground is at a standstill. Recommended proportions are 1½ oz. of bonemeal to 1 bushel of soil. Fortunately it is not necessary to be meticulously precise in measuring dosage of such slow-acting organics, so we need not repeatedly trample mud into the house and mess up the kitchen scales if we are content to translate these weights and measures (I confess I have never known how to arrive at a bushel of soil and nor can any of my gardening acquaintances!) into the rather more approximate, if more workaday, gardener's terms of 1 large (male) handful of bonemeal to 4 average-sized bucketfuls or 1 medium-sized barrow-load of soil. But let the more slapdash mathematicians take note that there must be no guesswork and nothing approximate in the mixing or measuring of *inorganic* chemical products, for which the makers' instructions must be most faithfully observed.

The majority of soil textures are improved by the incorporation of some form of humus, my own preference being for peat. Though there is no food value in most kinds of commercial peat, natural bracken peat (which does possess some nutritional properties and is sometimes available from local sources) is ideally suited to the shrub garden, improving the texture of heavy, sticky soils where it acts as blotting paper and, conversely, helping to conserve moisture in porous chalk and in light, fast-draining sand. Among commercial brands Irish Moss Peat and Alexpeat are of particularly good texture and some of the best for our purpose.

The step-by-step instructions which follow apply to the general run of trees and shrubs. Much of it may look like elementary common sense, but the unfamiliar process seemed less so to me, as I remember, when planting a tree for the first time.

1. Try to do the job when soil conditions are favourable, avoiding planting in frozen or saturated soil. If dry it should be moistened, but not drenched.

2. Keep the topsoil separate from the subsoil when making the hole—and, of course, when filling it in.

3. Make the hole deep enough and wide enough to take the full spread of the roots with room to spare.

4. Break up the bottom and sides of the hole or loosen with a fork before starting to fill in.

5. If the subsoil is poor, porous or sticky, mix it well and evenly with moist peat, compost, hop manure or some other form of humus. This must be a thorough job, leaving no recognizable lumps of one or the other to shock exploring young roots.

6. At no stage should any fallen leaves be buried in the soil to rob the plant of the nitrogen which the dead leaves use up in the slow process of decomposition underground. Burying of snow or frozen soil should also be avoided, for the reasons mentioned on p. 48. Discard large stones, dead wood and other debris in the soil before replacing it.

7. Well rotted manure may be added if called for either by the hungry nature of the soil or by the plant's inordinate appetite. If not thoroughly rotted, place it so that the roots will not reach it until it has decayed (i.e. after several months), but not so deeply buried that they will obtain little or no benefit from it.

8. If the root system is dry immerse it for half an hour or so in water—rain-water if possible—before planting. In the case of a solid root ball the soil will be completely moist throughout when it stops emitting bubbles underwater. Bare roots should never be left exposed to cold, drying winds; even for a short spell they should be covered with a wet sack, bracken or something of the sort.

9. Any damaged pieces of root should be cleanly cut away, at an angle to bring the cut surface face downwards when in contact with the soil.

10. The straggling kind of root pattern common to many trees and shrubs makes it convenient to mound up the soil slightly within the hole at the level at which these will go in, so that the roots may be directed at a downward angle rather than spread out in an unnaturally horizontal plane. The level of previous planting usually leaves a soil mark at the base of the stem, and the same planting depth should as a rule be reproduced. This can, if necessary, be checked against a cane laid across the hole alongside the stem. Certain grafted plants, of which hybrid tree peonies are an example, may however be induced to form

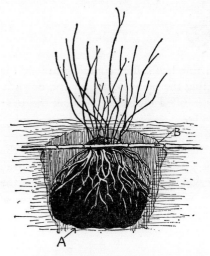

Fig. 5. Planting

A. Mounded earth over which roots may be spread in a natural position during planting.

B. Cane laid across planting hole as a guide to correct planting depth.

roots of their own if planted rather deeper. In the case of hessian-wrapped root balls, if the wrapping is very openwork it should be gently opened out in its planting position and left in place to rot beneath the roots; heavier-weave wrappings should be carefully slid out from under the roots once the plant is in position, with as little disturbance as possible to the soil around them. Paper pots are sometimes left on to rot in the ground, but these may possibly be confused with the slightly similar black polythene container now in favour and totally indestructible. It is just as necessary to remove the latter as to take the plant out of an earthenware or plastic pot before it is put into its permanent position.

11. If a permanent stake is necessary, put it in before the roots are covered up, to avoid damage; or use a temporary one at this stage if one pair of hands is not enough to keep the plant upright while filling in. When in difficulty I make do by propping the stem in the angle formed by a couple of long-handled tools laid crosswise over the hole.

Fig. 6. Makeshift method of propping plant in position while starting to fill in planting hole

12. Next scatter *moist* peat (or fine leaf soil or compost) among the roots, simultaneously joggling the plant gently up and down to ensure that every cranny is filled and also to allow the finer roots to settle more naturally.

13. Tread down gently but firmly round the *outer* part of the planting, so that the root tips will be directed on their way downwards. The reverse will happen if one starts from the centre, working outwards. Never tread a bare root for fear of

Fig. 7. Treading in the soil as planting proceeds, start at A on perimeter, following arrows to finish at B, centre.

abrasion, and keep even small stones away from the immediate root area for the same reason. The foot, or a part of it, is a better tool than the hands for firming the soil around any but the very smallest of shrubs; but although woody subjects need to be rammed home more firmly than herbaceous plants the soil should be fairly gently trodden down over the roots with heel or toe, making sure that all are in close contact with the earth, rather than heavily trampled with the whole foot or feet.

14. If the root system is of the loosely branching type, before starting to firm the soil covering the roots see if you can tease out a few rootlets from higher up the rootstock and spread these on the soil at their own level before covering with more earth. Then tread in with heel or toe, working in circles, as always, from the circumference inwards.

15. Fill up with a mixture of peat and topsoil, with or without bonemeal, depending on the natural degree of fertility of the soil. The rate is roughly one large handful to four average-sized bucketfuls of soil ($=1\frac{1}{2}$ oz. per bushel). The planting mixture should always be moist, but not soggy. Tread this in lightly, as before, and when the planted area reaches just above the level of the surrounding soil (to allow for subsidence) loosen the surface very lightly with a fork.

16. Water well if necessary, before topping with a moist surface mulch covering the root spread, but not packed closely against woody stems (see Mulching, p. 80).

17. Tie the plant to its permanent stake, if any, and attach a permanent label before the name on the paper one becomes obliterated (see Stakes, Ties and Labels, pp. 74–9).

18. When planting in hot, dry or windy weather excessive transpiration (i.e. loss of moisture through the leaves) may be prevented by spraying the foliage with S-600 (a modified polyvinyl resin, marketed by Synchemicals Ltd). This will coat it with a thin plastic film (also said to prevent Christmas trees from shedding their needles indoors), so long as it is not stored in the freezing temperature of garden sheds or outbuildings in

winter, in which case it will become too much coagulated to
be sprayable. Alternatively the plant may be sprayed with
water and all parts above ground enclosed in a plastic bag
allowing of only very little ventilation; this should, however, be
removed directly the plant can be seen to be perking up once
more. A miniature tent-like arbour formed by pushing evergreen branches of some sort into the ground round a really
small new plant so as to meet above it (see Fig. 41) may
provide brief but adequate protection for long enough to get
it established. I need hardly say that these anti-transpiration
measures do not apply to deciduous subjects planted during
the normal dormant period, when they have no leaves to give
off moisture.

Transplanting Within the Garden If a newly arrived plant
from a reputable shrub nursery appears to us to be disappointingly
small there is usually a good reason for it, quite apart from that of
keeping down carriage costs. For when stock has to be lifted, packed
and despatched by road or rail—often, in the latter case, meeting
with long delays and pretty rough handling en route—to be re-
planted at length in alien soil, climate and environment, the smaller
and younger the plant, within reason, the better it is likely to settle
down after the ordeal.

The shock of transplanting is however very much reduced when
a tree or shrub is to be moved within the confines of one's own
garden, and it is therefore often possible to transplant quite old,
established specimens without their suffering much of a check,
provided certain precautions are observed. Shrubs with compact,
densely fibrous root balls, such as rhododendrons, are among the
best movers (as proved by the huge flowering specimens on show
each year at Chelsea) and tap-rooted subjects such as eucalypts,
brooms, cistus, and ceanothus are some of the worst. These are
invariably pot-grown in order that they may be slid into position
in the first instance with the soil still intact around their roots. The
slender, tapering main root provides the chief anchorage for the
top-hamper and if it is torn up and probably damaged in the
process it is most unlikely to regain a firm hold in a new position
unless the plant is a very young one. I would only attempt to move
these in their earliest years, if at all; but I know of some flourishing
Genista cinerea and *G. tenera* (*virgata*) which were transplanted as tall
bushes of about eight or nine years old, for which I prophesied doom

at the time. I still think the odds against success in a case of this kind too high to be worth the risk unless the alternative were to scrap them altogether.

Now for a few safety precautions.

1. Make a really roomy hole to receive the transplantee *before* digging it up; but if it proves inadequate when you get the plant to the spot it is better to let it wait, with the roots well covered to prevent drying (see 3), while you enlarge the hole, rather than to cramp the roots.

2. Dig the plant up with as much of its existing root system as can be transported. If a solid root ball such as that of a large rhododendron is too heavy to move intact it will stand some careful chopping off round the perimeter, but will almost certainly die if allowed to split apart across the middle, as frequently happens if a plant with a heavy mass of roots is lifted by the stem, rather than eased up from beneath while keeping the weight supported all the time from below. If possible slide hessian, rabbit-wire, or something capable of taking the weight beneath a heavy root ball before moving it on the improvised carrier. Plants with a more loosely branched root system are said to re-establish themselves more quickly if they go naked into their new quarters, but if risking a move with a tap-rooted subject I would try to keep it encased in its soil in the hope that it might not notice the disturbance it so strongly resents. A square hessian carrier with a loop handle at each corner is useful for hauling any large or heavy plant from one part of the garden to another, since it can be handled by as many as four people, or more, if necessary.

3. If the plant has to be left lying about for more than a few seconds, wrap some damp sacking, bracken or straw round the roots. If they should happen to dry out soak them well before re-planting, as recommended for newly arrived plants which have dried out in transit.

4. Get the plant into its new position so fast that it has no time to realize what has happened until it is all over. It is unwise to start on the job unless you have a reasonable prospect of seeing it through without interruption.

5. For the actual planting proceed as detailed on pp. 52–6, not forgetting watering, which should be generous for a large trans-plantee, and continued as necessary throughout the growing season. Anti-transpiration measures should be taken if required, and firm staking is particularly important for top-heavy ever-greens until they are re-established.

6. If a long-established tree has to be moved it will probably be necessary to begin preparations some months in advance by taking out a circle of soil round the plant with a radius covering as much of the root-spread as it is proposed to move. Cut any thick roots at the perimeter and fill in the circular trench with moist peat or fine leaf soil or compost. Then forget it, apart from watering in dry weather, until the time comes for the move, during dormancy. This should encourage the formation of plenty of the finer rootlets through which the tree feeds, so that when faced with the shock of transplantation the patient should be better equipped to make a more rapid recovery.

Working Gear Having spent so many years in search of the most practical female gear for winter gardening, I venture to pass on a few of my conclusions for those in doubt.

No matter what one wears underneath, a thornproof outer covering such as an old macintosh is much more suitable than the more welcome thickness of a cast-off tweed or woollen overcoat for planting and other winter work among densely furnished borders. What counts is not so much the waterproofing as the smoothness of texture, which saves one from entanglement among snags and prickles, from which the plants as well as the gardener may suffer damage.

One's footwear will determine whether one works in comfort or in a state of constant irritation. Although rubber clogs are made specifically for the gardener, they seem to me precisely designed to collect all kinds of minor instruments of torture, in the shape of twigs and stones and other debris. Rubber *boots* of any kind are fine beneath trousers, but those who garden in skirts can scarcely avoid a certain amount of soil infiltrating even into knee-length boots, when heaving large-rooted shrubs about for transplantation, for instance. Oddly enough, the shorter boot is no worse than the longer one in this respect, and much easier to slip on and off. Entry for debris may be blocked by thick socks reaching to the top of the boots or rolled inside to fill spare leg-room.

Waterproof over-trousers made for golfers are especially useful in showery weather and when one is obliged to garden in the rain. I have never, in more than twenty years, found the ideal form of headgear versus wind and rain. Any form of vigorous exertion generates so much steam, after an hour or two, inside any kind of impermeable headcovering that one might just as well have worked bare-headed in the rain. The kind of waterproof kepi with retractable side-curtains once popular with women golfers is, I think, the most practical, for any who have hoarded such a relic from their past.

Specialized Planting Hints

Plants of less than reliable hardiness are most likely to succeed when grown in wall positions in the average to cold garden. Any wall aspect will afford greater protection than an open-ground site, but south and west facing walls (provided these are not situated in wind funnels, as in a narrow strip between two buildings) are of course the most hospitable for the more fragile subjects.

Abutilon vitifolium The hardiest of a not very hardy genus, this abutilon shares the ability of certain other Chilean shrubs to endure the very best that the British climate has to offer and may possibly do well, at least for a time, in sheltered gardens with a mild climate. Even so, it is likely to prefer a warm west wall. No matter how well situated, it has a way of declining, without warning, from a fast-growing, healthy specimen into an inexplicably dead or dying one. It is none too easy to place, since draughts or too much sunshine cause it to shed its flower buds unopened, but it is charming enough to be worth a try in reasonably suitable conditions. I think the soft blue-lavender form prettier than the white.

Acer japonicum, A. palmatum (Japanese Maples) Though pretty hardy both species are particularly susceptible to drying winds and drought and therefore do best in sheltered positions in moist but well-drained soil.

Arbutus (Strawberry Tree) This genus is calcifuge, in common with the other members of the *Ericaceae*, but there is one species that will grow in limy conditions, and that is *Arbutus unedo*.

Bamboos   Moisture-loving, but not to the extent of waterlogging, many species manage well enough in dry conditions, but prefer positions sheltered from cold winds. Most tend to be invasive and, once established, are very difficult to uproot, so should be appropriately sited in the first instance.

Berberis (Barberry)   Though the majority thrive in sun or shade, the purple-leaved varieties of *B. thunbergii*, including the pink-leaved, variegated 'Rose Glow', will only achieve a good colour in a sunny position. I find the same to be true of the delightful new yellow-leaved form of this species, *B. thunbergii* 'Aurea'.

Calluna vulgaris (Heather)   Full sunlight is also necessary for cultivars of heaths and heathers grown for their foliage colour. This heather and its cultivars are calcifuge, but not quite so intolerant of limy conditions as some.

Camellia japonica (and other hardy species and varieties)   These do best in semi-shade, in moist, rich, acid soil. They are particularly suitable for north or west walls, but perfectly hardy in the open in positions where plants in bloom have time to thaw after a night frost before the sun reaches them.

Cistus (Rock Rose)   Like other denizens of the Mediterranean *maquis*, these revel in sun-baked sites and light sandy soil. Only a few species are hardy enough for cold conditions. Pegging down outer shoots on the dwarfer sorts makes for extra density and increases vigour, once the layers have put down roots of their own (see Fig. 10, p. 74).

Clematis   Though shady situations suit quite a number of clematis, most prefer to grow with their heads in the sun and roots in the shade. The latter requirement is the more important for the majority, and may be provided either by covering the roots with a large flat stone or by planting a dwarf shrub on the sunny side of the main stem. They are greedy feeders, so that in all but the richest soils it will be necessary to incorporate old manure or compost with some bonemeal in the soil at planting time. Alternatively, clematis compost may be obtained from some of the specialist growers, but the cost of carriage is disproportionately heavy. Opinions differ about the addition of lime to acid soils (4 oz. per sq. yd.), but one of the specialists believes this reduces the incidence of clematis wilt. Good drainage is important. The crown should be planted 1–2 in. below the soil surface. Plants on their own roots are preferable, but grafted plants may be induced to form their own roots if the shoots springing from just above the graft are layered for a few inches, before being trained upwards. Plant 1 ft. away from walls or allow to trail through trees and shrubs, and protect the fragile main stem from kinking by tying in several places to a support near the base and enclosing in a barrier of wire netting.

Cornus grown for coloured bark (Dogwood)   *Cornus alba* 'Sibirica' and *C. Stolonifera* 'Flaviramea' and other coloured-barked forms are specially effective for waterside planting in coppiced clumps, where their naked wands of red and yellow are brilliantly contrasted in spring. Moist, rather than waterlogged sites, are most enjoyed. (See Fig. 17, p. 86.)

Cotinus (syn. Rhus) (Smoke Bush)   In the case of the purple-leaved forms the sunnier the position the more vivid the colour will be.

Danae racemosa (Alexandrian Laurel)   Does well in quite heavy shade.

Elaeagnus macrophylla   The long, sinuous sprays of silver-backed, evergreen foliage which are so valuable for cutting are only produced in fairly shady positions. In full sun this species becomes much more compact, if not actually stodgy of contour.

Embothrium coccineum lanceolatum 'Norquinco Valley' (Chilean Fire Bush)   This is the most effective in flower and is reputedly hardier than other forms. It needs a moist, acid soil and shelter from early autumn and late spring frosts. It seems to prefer a position similar to clematis, with its head in the sun and its feet in the shade.

Erica (Heath)   Most species are calcifuge and those grown for foliage colour need full exposure; *E. carnea* and the summer-flowering *E. terminalis* (Corsican Heath) will grow in limy soil.

Eucalyptus (hardy species)   Both roots and soil must be thoroughly moist at planting time. It is not advisable to add fertilizers when

planting, except in specially poor or dry, sandy soil (otherwise the
speed of the top growth outstrips the root system). Bonemeal may
however be added to poor soils and moist peat to dry, sandy ones.
Deep planting is important. The ball of soil must be kept intact
and its top buried 1½–2 in. below the natural soil level, in a depression about 1 ft. wide so that the necessary water during the plant's
first summer is collected where it is wanted. Fill in the depression
in late autumn to ensure that the basal bump just above the roots
(the lignotuber) is adequately protected during the winter. Stake
firmly. (For this abridged information I am indebted to Mr A. J. T.
Bayles, who succeeded Mr R. C. Barnard at his well-known
eucalyptus nursery in S. Devon, and who supplies a helpful leaflet
of detailed planting instructions free of charge, together with a list
of eucalypts for planting in the British Isles which also contains
much valuable information.)

Eucryphia   At least in the case of *E. glutinosa* (the only species of
which I have cultural experience) I have found it necessary, in this
cold garden, to plant in full sun for generous flowering, despite the
fact that part-shade is usually recommended. It needs a moist,
acid soil. I believe *E.* x *nymansensis* to be the only eucryphia to
tolerate limy conditions.

Euonymus fortunei 'Variegatus' (syn. *E. f.* 'Gracilis')
This makes a compact, rounded shrub of no more than 2 ft. or so in
an open-ground position but, surprisingly, climbs a wall to the
height of at least one storey, with the help of a little support. The
cultivar 'Silver Queen' is a finer foliage plant, but rather less
hardy.

Fuchsia (outdoor varieties)   Many not commonly guaranteed as
hardy will survive the winter, even in a garden as cold as mine, if
planted with the top of the root ball about 2 in. below the soil
surface and given some form of winter protection. The roots are
said to find decaying bracken so delectable that if this is deeply
buried in the planting hole it will attract the roots downwards,
away from frozen winter topsoil. For the same reason bracken is
unsuitable for surface mulching of fuchsias.

Ginkgo biloba (Maidenhair Tree)   This historically fascinating
tree, which may also be had in a fastigiate form, is quite hardy,

given a little shelter, but it is most unhappy on a bleak site. It also requires good drainage.

x Halimiocistus and **Halimium**   These are closely related to the *Cistus* genus and require the same conditions.

Hebe armstrongii and **H. hectorii** (Shrubby Veronica)   These should be planted in full sun for good foliage colour and compactness of growth.

Helianthemum (Sun Rose)   Though also belonging to the *Cistus* family, helianthemums are hardier than most of their relations, but these dwarf carpeters also need full sun and light soil.

Hoheria glabrata and **H. lyallii**   Both are reputed to be slightly tender, but all that they seem to need here is a winter protection of low evergreens at their feet.

Hydrangea   The hydrangea's chief requirement is plenty of moisture. On light, fast-draining soils in particular, more rain-water will reach the roots if the crown is planted a little below the level of the surrounding soil, leaving a slightly concave surface over the root area when filling in at planting time. Mature specimens transplant best as soon as they have lost their leaves, but spring planting is wiser in cold districts for new plants in new gardens lacking the shelter of mature shrubs.

For treatment of the soil at planting time to alter flower colour, see under Miscellaneous in Period I of the Working-calendar.

Kalmia latifolia (Calico Bush)   As for eucryphia.

Kolkwitzia amabilis (American Beauty Bush)   This has the merits of flowering during the 'June gap' in the shrub garden and of tolerating limy soils. Since it sometimes produces particularly shy-flowering forms, it is as well to reserve a floriferous plant when in bloom in the nursery, if possible. It will only flower freely in a sunny position.

Lonicera nitida 'Baggessen's Gold' and the climbing **L. japonica 'Aureoreticulata'**   Both need sunny positions to do full justice to the yellow leaf colour. Many climbing types of honeysuckle (to which genus these two plants belong) do well in shade, and are useful for growing over tree stumps or large shrubs. 'Baggessen's Gold' is a bush type, of dense, yet spraying habit.

Magnolia (both evergreen and deciduous) All are bad movers (and for this reason ought always to be pot-grown by the nurseryman), so planting should be once and for all, treating the delicate, fleshy roots with care and not treading in too heavily. Plants should be firmly staked to prevent root breakage. Good catalogues usually indicate which species need acid soil conditions. All enjoy a rich soil.

Mahonia These range from the bone-hardy to the more than somewhat tender. Among the former, which will put up with any soil and situation, are the familiar *M. aquifolium* (Oregon Grape) and its purple-leaved form, and *M.* 'Rotundifolia' which so far appears to be equally unfussy. These are all dwarf to medium-sized types. *Mahonia* 'Charity', one of a number of recently raised clones from a cross between *M. lomariifolia* and *M. japonica*, fortunately inherits the hardier constitution of the latter parent and will grow in sun or shade, making quite a tall plant of 8 ft. or so.

Mahonia japonica is the one with the drooping, fragrant, pale yellow flower sprays, unlike *bealei* (with which it is often confused) in that *M. bealei* has less strongly scented flowers carried in erect sprays. *M. japonica*, with its great whorls of pinnate evergreen foliage, has a handsomely sculptured appearance which makes of it a suitable ornament for courtyards, patios and positions alongside buildings, where its scent may also be enjoyed at close range in wintertime. Nevertheless it is equally fine in the open garden, where it is best suited by fairly moist, semi-shady and preferably lime-free soil conditions. It grows to about 9 ft. on average.

Mahonia lomariifolia, which is one of the tallest, is also by far the least hardy of those mentioned here. Soil requirements are as for *M. japonica*, but except in the most favourable climates it needs all the shelter it can get. Nevertheless a hard winter rarely kills it, but severely mauls the naturally handsome foliage of this most decorative plant, which is slow to refurbish itself after a really bad winter.

Nyssa sylvatica (Tupelo) This dislikes being moved, so try to give it a permanent position and leave it there, in a moist, preferably lime-free soil.

Olearia (Daisy Bush) The hardy varieties are not at all faddy. Olearias are sun-lovers and do particularly well at the seaside, but not all are equally hardy.

Oxydendrum arboreum This needs a well-drained, acid soil and some protection such as may be afforded by surrounding shrubs.

Pachysandra terminalis (Japanese Spurge) Spreading, as it does, a dense carpet of dark green foliage rosettes beneath trees and shrubs even in deep shade, this is one of the most efficient of all forms of ground-cover. Mr Graham Thomas regards it as calcifuge, though this opinion does not seem to be widespread. I am unfamiliar with its behaviour under limy conditions, but in other respects it is singularly unfussy. It spreads somewhat slowly, especially at first, (usually looking rather a poor thing on arrival from the nursery), but will eventually blanket an unlimited area, even in the densest shade. In this garden it particularly enjoys running and suckering in the decaying leaf-mulch, which seems to speed up its spread.

The variegated *P. terminalis* 'Variegata' (or 'Silveredge') is a pretty, cool, pale green and white, but is so much less robust in its habits that it is considerably less useful as ground-cover than the species. Its tastes are similar, but it seems to thrive rather better in shady conditions than out in the open.

Paeonia suffruticosa (cultivars and other tree peonies) Spring growth of the *P. suffruticosa* varieties is so precocious that it is safer to plant these where they will get no sun until the afternoon. A backward position retards precocious growth, and protection from morning sun gives the young shoots a chance to thaw out after frost before the sun reaches them. Early October is the best time for planting, burying the graft union not less than 2 in. below the soil. They thrive on heavy clay and on rich, limy fare, disliking hot, sandy soils. Phosphates and potash are safe fertilizers to add to the soil where necessary, but nitrogenous fertilizers should be used sparingly, if at all, since the type of soft, lush growth it tends to encourage is more vulnerable to disease.

Since tree peony species such as *delavayi* and *lutea ludlowii* ('Sherriff's Variety') seed themselves freely, though with slightly variable results, the instructions regarding grafted plants do not of course apply to species grown from seed.

Paulownia This needs full sun and shelter from strong winds. I have not found it to thrive in a cold garden.

Phormium tenax varieties (New Zealand Flax) I have found these much less delicate than is commonly supposed. They enjoy rich soil and are generally said to prefer a moist one, but I have seen magnificent specimens growing in near-drought conditions. Most tolerate shade well, but the purple-leaved varieties need full sun both for good colour and because they appear to be less hardy than the rest.

Phygelius capensis (Cape Figwort) This seems to need the protection of a warm wall, or at least a sunny spot, in an average garden climate. When grown in the open garden it makes about 4 ft. of growth in suckering bush form, but will climb to quite a fair height against a wall. Much of the growth dies to the ground in winter in this garden, to reappear in spring.

Pieris All need a moist, acid soil. Varieties with brilliant scarlet spring foliage (as *formosa forrestii* 'Wakehurst' and 'Forest Flame') also require shelter from spring frost and wind. They appear to stand winter cold, but to be bud-tender, as regards both flowers and foliage, in early spring frosts.

Pterostyrax This is hardy in a cold garden, given a sunny position and good soil.

Rhododendron (including **Azalea**) The top of the root ball must be planted flush with the surface of the soil—not buried, and only lightly sprinkled with peat or leaf soil over the surface. Generally speaking the rhododendrons with the smallest leaves thrive in full exposure, whereas the largest-leaved species such as *falconeri, macabeanum, sinogrande* and their hybrids need plenty of shelter and woodland shade. All rhododendrons and azaleas are lime-haters, and most resent dryness at the roots.

The dwarf evergreen azaleas thrive in sun or in part-shade, but make much more compact plants in exposed positions. Flattish lumps of porous sandstone placed in a circle covering the root ball of these azaleas and of dwarf alpine rhododendrons are helpful in conserving moisture, and also for anchoring layered branches, which is to be recommended at planting time if any are long enough to layer without risk of breakage.

Robinia The brittleness characteristic of the robinias makes some wind protection advisable. They enjoy dry, sunny conditions.

Romneya (Tree Poppy) Full sunshine and a good depth of soil, preferably well-drained, are necessary for success.

Rose Roses should, if possible, be planted between the end of October and the end of November, whenever soil conditions are suitable. The point at which the graft has been made (the lump is easily detectable) should be positioned 1 or 2 in. below soil level. Roses like to get their flowering growth into the sun and their roots in the shade and they hate strong draughts and waterlogging. In the absence of that rare rose-growing commodity, 'ideal loam', it will be necessary to add some form of bulky organic manure to the soil when planting, e.g. well-rotted farmyard manure, compost, rose peat or decayed turves. Slow-acting fertilizers such as bonemeal are also suitable.

When transplanting old specimens cut the plants down to within a few inches of the base, removing all dead wood; then replant with the 'burl' (i.e. the swelling at the base of the woody stem just above the roots) just below the level of the soil.

Sarcococca Plant this strongly scented, dwarf, winter-flowering subject where it may be appreciated, near a much used path or entrance for instance. It is shade-tolerant in any good soil.

Silver-leaved Subjects Many are none too hardy and should be planted in spring, the most tender being the last to be planted, in mid-May (for detailed information see Mrs D. Underwood's catalogue). All demand rapid drainage and sun-baked situations. Wet feet are anathema. Two of the most coveted, *Artemisia arborescens* and *Convolvulus cneorum*, are unfortunately among the more tender outdoor kinds.

Skimmia The skimmias are particularly useful for shady situations, but are also good in sun. For berries plant a male form of *S. japonica*, or preferably the beautiful russet-red-budded, pink-flowered *S. japonica* 'Rubella' alongside a female form of *S. japonica* or 'Foremanii'.

Stewartia (Syn Stuartia) Being bad movers, stewartias should be carefully sited to avoid a later change of mind. They need a moist, acid, peaty soil and semi-shade.

Styrax (Snowbell) As for Stewartia. In my experience, the younger this delightful shrub or small tree is when planted the faster its progress.

Symphoricarpos orbiculatus 'Variegatus' (Coral Berry) Plant in exposure for good yellow variegation on this dainty foliage plant.

Vaccinium The evergreen species in particular are shade-tolerant, but deciduous types grown largely for autumn leaf colour (e.g. *arctostaphylos* and *corymbosum*) need more light. All are calcifuge.

Weigela japonica 'Looymansii Aurea' and **W. florida 'Foliis Purpureis'** The superb, large, butter-yellow foliage of the former does best with slight shade, whereas the purplish-brown of the latter only achieves a worthwhile colour with plenty of light, becoming dull and drab in anything less than full exposure. The weigelas have no soil fads.

Wisteria All require a good loamy soil, which should be incorporated in the planting hole in limy areas in particular. They may be trailed over large trees, grown as standards in open-ground positions, or trained as climbers against walls and other more orthodox backgrounds.

Zenobia pulverulenta This shrub, which is one of the most delightful for cutting, unfortunately insists on an acid soil and, moreover, prefers a moist one. It does best in semi-shade. On my naturally fast-draining, sandy soil the leaf-mulch evidently retains sufficient moisture for it to prosper, given the other two conditions.

Fruiting Trees and Shrubs

In case of possible confusion as to the use of the term 'fruits' in the shrub garden, without being over-technical one may say that they do not have to be edible, such as figs, apples, mulberries or currants, or even a crab apple grown for the beauty of its fruits rather than for utility. Flower arrangers will be thoroughly familiar with the use of the word 'fruits' in a somewhat similar context, in which it applies to almost any form of seed-bearing container, from a fir-cone or bladder nut pod to a rose hep or conventional berry such as the fruit of pyracantha, callicarpa, cotoneaster and the like. In many cases a female subject, such as the unsuitably named holly 'Golden King', requires a nearby male pollinator (the male 'Silver Queen' might as well complete this transvestite pairing!). Skimmia, pernettya and certain other genera include hermaphrodite or self-pollinating species, but in my experience both these and such forms of fruiting shrubs as are said to require no male co-operation bear heavier crops when grown in clumps of three or more rather than as single specimens.

Layering

Having based the operational sections throughout Part Three on a roughly chronological pattern, I was somewhat dubious about interrupting their natural sequence at this stage with apparently misplaced details of a practice most commonly thought of as a method of propagation. What follows does however form a logical sequel to the Planting section, since shrubs are in fact often layered at planting time or, if this is not feasible, as soon afterwards as they have developed shoots of suitable length and placement, in order to encourage sturdy growth. For me, therefore, the primary object of layering is to promote vigour and good looks in a young plant by increasing its root system, though among established shrubs it is also of course a simple and cost-free means of increasing stock on its own roots, which is usually much to be preferred to a grafted plant.

When the layers are allowed to remain *in situ* as part of the parent plant, shrubs of slightly suspect hardiness in particular, such as some of the dwarf evergreen azaleas, cistus, halimiums, helianthemums, dwarf brooms and so on, derive a considerable amount of extra protection from the outer circle of rooted growths and additional vigour contributed by the layers to the root system.

Layering of Pliant, Semi-mature Shrub Material Choose young branches which have not yet borne flowers, if possible—and the nearer they are to the ground the easier the job will be, provided they are long enough to allow for an adequate growing tip beyond the buried part of the shoot. Strip off leaves and any vestige of buds and other growth on the portion to be buried, so that this is entirely bare, but leaving any such growth untouched towards the tip of the shoot beyond the burial point; take out the soil at that point to a depth of several inches; half-fill the hole with moist peat or leaf soil, or a mixture of the two; push the branch firmly on to this filling, taking care not to snap brittle shoots under pressure; cover with 3 or 4 in. of the same filling, mounding it slightly over the layer for extra depth if necessary (i.e. in fast-draining soil and dry situations), and peg down with a heavy gauge wire 'hairpin' or woody crook (most easily cut from an inverted Y section of a ripe, branching bamboo cane, which is strong and slow to rot). A solid lump of porous stone (such as sandstone) placed over the layer on the soil covering it—the bigger and heavier the better, so long as its proportions fit its purpose—is effective as a means of retaining moisture in the soil beneath it, and it also helps to prevent the layer from shifting in case of accident.

If the business end of the layer will not stand upright unaided, tie it to a perpendicular stake to hold the elbow-bend in position underground in order to reduce the flow of sap from the parent plant to the far end of the shoot, thus inducing the layer to put down roots of its own at the point of blockage in a desperate bid for self-preservation. This, however, it will only be able to do if it is kept reasonably moist in the meanwhile.

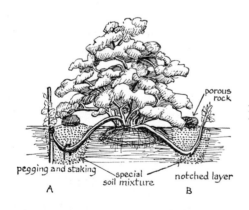

porous rock

pegging and staking   special   notched layer
                       soil mixture
        A   B

Fig. 8. Layering
A. Pegging and staking.
B. Notching.

'The meanwhile' can vary considerably, 12–18 months being about average for woody growth and rather less for softer young shoots. Layers intended to remain where they are should not of course be severed from the main plant except in cases where the centre growth has become sparse and leggy with time. If so, the whole plant may be lifted, the exhausted growth cut away, and the sturdier outer layers put back to take its place.

If a layer is to be transplanted, make sure that it has developed an adequate root system to sustain it before severing the umbilical cord through which it has hitherto received its nourishment. A mere sprinkling of spidery root hairs is not enough. A layer thus prematurely removed from its parent is no more likely to survive on its own than a premature infant abandoned on a doorstep without recourse to special medical care. Look for new growth at the tip of the layered branch as an indication that it has developed a root system to match; but if in doubt dig it up and have a look before irrevocably cutting it loose, putting things back carefully as you found them if not yet ready. If this sounds too much like digging up the pet tortoise in hibernation to see how it is getting on, it is none the less regarded as O.K. horticultural practice (from which the prospective layer is more certain to recover than the tortoise).

Where transplanting is intended it may be preferred to grow the layer into a flower-pot, rather than into a prepared hole, alongside the plant. If so, the pot should be buried in the empty hole and half-filled with moist peat or leaf soil, pressing the layer into the pot's contents. Then carry on as described, according to the woodiness or degree of pliancy of the intended layer, filling the pot and packing it snugly inside the hole with the peat mixture.

Layering of Woody Growth For instance, established specimens of rhododendrons, all kinds of azaleas, magnolias, viburnums, 'whipcord' hebes, hydrangeas, witch hazel, corylopsis, eucryphia, pieris, fothergilla, stachyurus, kalmia and any number of others.

When the wood or the bark of the intended layer is especially tough it may be advisable to prepare it in one of the following ways, before embarking on the drill already described.

a. Make an upward-slanting slit with a sharp knife on the underside of the limb, cutting into not more than half the thickness at the point where it is to be buried, wedging the tongue open gently if necessary with a matchstick or something of similar thickness.

b. Cut out a wedge-shaped piece of the wood at the operative point on the underside of the layer, again being careful not to exceed half the total thickness of the wood (see Fig. 8B).

c. Merely scar that part of the bark on the underside of the branch along the portion to be buried. Even a comparatively slight wound such as this is said to encourage rooting.

These devices are by no means always necessary, but the first two certainly make it easier to establish the all-important elbow-bend in an unyielding branch—and easier also to snap the vital shoot off altogether at this weak spot unless very carefully handled. Whether or not branches are pre-treated in some such way, subsequent procedure is the same as that already described.

Training Growth for Future Layering   In the absence of any suitably placed growth on a woody shrub it may be necessary to resort to longer-term persuasive methods by gradually coaxing some of the higher branches soilwards for future layering.

a. They may be forced downwards as far as they will go without breaking and anchored firmly to a stake as low down as may be risked.

b. They may be bowed into position with the aid of a strong wire hoop pressed deep into the soil on either side of the branch.

Fig. 9. Coaxing shoots downwards for future layering

A. Held down by attachment to stake.
B. Held down by hoop.
C. Weighted by large stone.

c. A weight may be attached somewhere about the middle of its length, but not too near the tip of the branch. To avoid breakage by the use of too heavy a weight try it first towards the thicker (i.e. lower) portion of the branch, gradually working up towards mid-length with it to gauge at what point its weight feels excessive for the strength of the supporting branch. If you feel obliged to stop before reaching midway the weight is obviously

too heavy. If on the other hand it will happily dangle from near
the tip it is too light.

In all these methods the down-drag should gradually be increased
as growth develops, until soil level is reached with enough to spare.
The process takes time, but by these means I acquired quite a
number of good plants for nothing in early days from other people's
gardens, where patience can be more easily practised when 'out of
sight' means 'out of mind' for at least some part of the waiting
period.

Layers from Horizontal Planting An unlikely type of layering
used for recuperative treatment on certain woody subjects may
appeal to the adventurous—but this is not for the lily-livered!
Long ago I bought a suspiciously cheap Ghent azalea graft which
for many years made such poor growth that I was advised by
Mr Haworth-Booth to dig it up, replant it with the root ball lying
on its side and layer as many branches as I could.

Now one does not write off a slow starter before giving it ample
time to do itself justice; and this particular runt, though poorly
equipped for vigorous growth on its single 'leg' (as distinct from a
shrubby cluster of basal shoots), was by then fully adult, with a
specially broad though shallow root system. The immediate effect
of so unnatural a practice was monstrous. A great half-moon of
exposed root ball jutted straight out of the ground—indeed, there was
rather more of it above ground than below, once all available
branches had been coaxed into layering positions. This tortured
thing, I thought, must surely die. But not a bit of it. The lump
gradually, but unaccountably, disappeared and once the branches
had rooted this travesty of a plant developed into a shapely bush
as well-furnished as any of its better-class relations in my garden.

Layering or Pegging Down of Softer Growth For instance,
heaths and heathers, helianthemums, ballota, santolina, the more
dwarf hebes, dwarf brooms and so on.

For certain sub-shrubs and carpeters it is only necessary to
spread-eagle the shoots with one hand while sprinkling moist peat
among them with the other. If they are disinclined to lie down
sufficiently to root into the peat, or if of rather woodier growth
(such as cistus or broom), peg the shoots down with coarse hairpins,
bent wire or split bamboo before dribbling in the peaty soil to

encourage the rooting which readily follows without the necessity for elbow-bends and the rest of the tricks applied to tougher subjects.

Any number of new plants may of course be obtained in this way, but the job is well worth doing purely for the sake of the extra-handsome top-growth resulting from the much increased root area.

Fig. 10. Wholesale pegging down of a dwarf shrub

Suitable Times for Layering As for the correct time of year for layer-making, I have found each one of the four seasons separately recommended by one or other of our professional horticulturists and, apart from the layering recommended at planting time or soon afterwards, I find I do a bit of it whenever it occurs to me, with a slight theoretical bias in favour of autumn, time permitting (which is unlikely). No matter how pressing the task on hand, putting down the odd layer or two is one of those countless beguiling jobs which invariably sidetrack the gardener with some other fixed aim in mind.

The methods described above by no means exhaust all types of layering, but most of those omitted serve purely for propagative purposes rather than to further the well-being of the parent plant and do not therefore concern us here.

Stakes, Ties and Labels

Stakes There is no obligation to stake a plant if you are satisfied that it can grow straight, strong and secure without support. The fewer the wooden stakes to be left rotting in the ground and the fewer the ties to threaten strangulation to imperceptibly swelling trunks or limbs the less the risk to the health of trees and shrubs. But where staking is essential it pays to do the job properly. Generally speaking, the taller, tap-rooted subjects such as tall genistas and brooms, many evergreen conifers whose wind-resistant bulk is liable to over-balance, and the fast-growing hardy eucalypts are the most likely to need firm anchorage, at least for a start.

If a wooden stake is to be used, make sure that it is a sound one, rather than just any mouldering old stick. It should be tapered to a point at the lower end so as to penetrate the soil more readily, and at least the portion to be buried should have been treated with a wood preservative harmless to plant life–or charred, for more short-lived protection. In areas where the killer honey fungus disease (which stems from rotting wood) is prevalent the rust-proof, painted metal type of tree stake now available would probably justify its rather high cost if a permanent stake were needed. Temporary wooden ones should of course be removed and burnt if beginning to disintegrate, rather than left to rot on the spot once their support is no longer needed, or replaced with a sound one if necessary.

Upright Staking   When an upright stake is to be used it should be placed on the side of the plant from which the prevailing wind blows and should be put into position at the start of the planting operation, ramming it well home into the more solid, undisturbed subsoil and firming it into the planting hole as the earth is filled in, with the plant roots carefully disposed around it, thus avoiding the damage caused by driving it in blind, as an afterthought. Some of the metal tree stakes are fitted with a stay-plate for extra stability.

Diagonal Staking   On windy sites a diagonal stake may be more practical than a perpendicular one, slanted into the direction of the strongest gales. It should be driven into the ground at an angle of about 60° at a suitable distance from the trunk to make contact with it at a convenient height for a tie. Since the stake will enter the soil beyond the perimeter of the newly planted roots it may safely be inserted after planting. To make doubly sure of firm anchorage a diagonal prop may be used in conjunction with an upright one, to which it must be securely bound at their junction before attaching the plant to each (see Fig. 11, No. 1).

Tripod Staking   Three strong bamboo canes will provide a sapling with a surprisingly stable support if driven into the ground diagonally and roughly equidistantly beyond the root-spread, and joined around the trunk wigwam-fashion near to their tips, so that the tree may be attached to all three. Because they take the strain in three different directions even comparatively slender canes are able to hold a young tree stable in gale force winds so long as they are firmly and sufficiently deeply embedded in the earth to resist being dragged out by the force of the wind (see Fig. 11, No. 3).

For a large specimen, three or four wire hawsers may be attached to the carefully protected trunk (as by threading the hawsers through rubber tubing at this point) and anchored at a distance from it with angle-iron stakes deeply buried in the soil slantwise, like tent-pegs, to take the strain. But this method carries a greater risk of strangulation, since the trunk must be pretty tightly gripped if it is to be effectively moored.

Ties   The life of a tie should, generally, correspond to that of its stake. That is to say, a very temporary form of twist-tie will suffice to attach a slender young stem to a bamboo cane for its first season or two, whereas if a tree is likely to need permanent anchorage it may pay to invest in one of the commercial brands of tie specifically designed for strength, long life and non-constriction.

Twist-ties   For pencil-slim stems or shoots the twist type of tie made of paper-covered wire in various lengths up to 18 in. is immensely handy. At least one maker describes his product as 'permanent', but the more significant part of the blurb is that which says 'A twist of the fingers and the plant is tied *for the season*'—the italics are mine. It would be safest to regard these quick and easy ties as no more permanent than this. They should be only loosely fastened in the first instance, and kept under observation if allowed to remain for more than a season; for it should be remembered that by the time the partially weather-proof paper covering has disintegrated the plant stem will have thickened, and is therefore in danger of being cut into by the tightening grip of the now naked wire.

The recently introduced Nu-Twist Plant Tie, made of wire-reinforced plastic ribbon, is more durable and more hygienic than the paper-covered variety, but something longer than the 4–6 in. ones available at the time of writing would be more useful to the shrub gardener.

The new Sylglas Garden Tape, which has some 'give' in it (see pp. 79 and 151), is particularly suitable for attaching small plants to their supports.

Durable Tree Ties   The commercial products are made of long-lasting and, in most cases, expandable materials such as plastic, rubber or webbing, usually with a 'spacing collar' to prevent chafing, and with adjustable fastening to allow for growth. It is not difficult to improvise an almost equally durable home-made substitute with a piece of plastic or rubber tubing long enough to encircle the trunk with some to spare, through which is threaded a still longer piece of stout, many-stranded wire. Only the non-abrasive tubing comes into contact with the bark, its ends being crossed over between trunk and stake to provide a form of 'spacing collar'. The naked wire ends should be long enough to be bound securely round the post (see Fig. 11, No. 2).

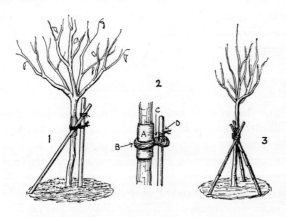

Fig. 11. Stakes and ties

1 Diagonal staking used in conjunction with perpendicular stake.
2 Home-made tree tie:
    A. padding round trunk;
    B. tie made of rubber tubing threaded with stout wire;
    C. twist or knot in tie, as buffer between tree and stake;
    D. stake.
3 Tripod staking.

Laddered nylons are much to be recommended as plant ties for their elasticity, strength, durability, soft texture, rapid drying properties and (usually) self-effacing earthy hues. They may be cut into strips or, where considerable strength is needed, cutting the legs from tights or using stockings whole.

Wire, String and Protective Wraps Trunks should be loosely wrapped at the point of attachment to their stake with a strip of rubber (e.g. a piece of old hot water bottle), felt, carpet, hessian or, again, nylon stocking, to protect the bark from any kind of tie liable to cut or chafe, such as naked or plastic-coated wire, tarred string, rope and so on. In my view the rubber or the nylon stocking make the best buffers, since these dry out rapidly after rain, whereas most other materials remain soggy in wet weather.

Whatever the form of tie used, the bark should not be in direct contact with the stake, even if only separated from it by a fat knot or twist in the tie.

For training and tying in against wall supports, see *Accommodation for Wall Plants and Climbers*, pp. 154–55.

Finally, since the greatest strain on stakes and ties comes with winter gales and heavy snowfall, it is advisable to check that those in use are sound and firmly anchored before the onset of hard weather catches us out.

Labels The choice of a suitable label depends on one's objective. If, for the edification of a visiting public, labels need to be ubiquitous, eye-catching and clearly legible from lawns and paths, so as to deter avid culture-vultures from trampling among the shrubs to read their names or helping themselves to sample shoots for identification. Labels intended only as a private *aide-mémoire* may be much more unobtrusive, but should nevertheless be durable and permanently legible. The job should, moreover, be treated as urgent on receipt of the plants, before the names on the nurseryman's paper tags are obliterated for good.

The rather expensive Dymo labelling kit is perhaps something of a luxury, but is uncomplicated to use, does a very tidy job and may also be put to various domestic uses. It prints permanent, clearly legible, embossed, self-adhesive name-strips on a variety of background colours and with a choice of letter sizes. The strips stick firmly to any smooth, dry surface, including the plastic markers supplied with the set.

For a more rough-and-ready job the comparatively cheap Hartley's metal labels are convenient and easy to write on. A bluntish pencil point will engrave fairly permanently on the specially treated surface of these labels, of which there are several sizes, all made with a tapering tail and a hole at one end, through which to thread a tie. The lazier way of twisting the tail round some part of the plant almost always causes bark damage and, even when properly attached, the tie should be checked periodically to ensure that the growing branch is not being throttled. With very soft young growth I prefer to wind the tail of the label round a small cane to be stuck into the ground alongside, to avoid damage to the plant; but the stick needs to be pushed firmly in to a fair depth to prevent dislodgement by birds, babies, dogs and mowing machines.

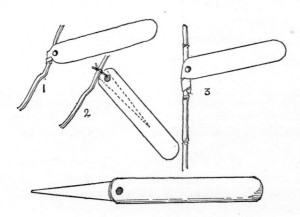

Fig. 12. Metal label and methods of attachment

1 Winding tapered tail round branch (not recommended).
2 Tie threaded through hole and loosely attached to branch, turning tapered tail back on underside of label, as shown by dotted line.
3 Tail of label wound round bamboo stake to be pushed into soil alongside plant.

A very cheap but serviceable waterproof label may be devised with a strip of paper bearing the plant name enclosed between lengths of the transparent green plastic Sylglas Garden Tape, which somewhat resembles a more durable, transparent Sellotape in appearance and, being slightly elastic, may be attached to the plant without fear of damage. When used to cover the plant name on the original nursery tag its life is as least as long as that of the label and the name will remain legible until the paper label itself disintegrates. Sylglas Garden Tape is furthermore one of the least harmful means of attaching any form of label to a branch.

Mulching

Objectives The Royal Horticultural Society's *Dictionary of Gardening* defines a mulch as 'a layer of material spread on the soil above the roots of plants with the object of (1) supplying 'food' for the plant, (2) conserving soil moisture, or (3) preventing sudden fluctuations in temperature'. Whereas an odd assortment of 'materials' such as spent hops, lawn mowings, coconut fibre, spent mushroom compost, garden compost, peat, straw, sawdust and bracken, *inter alia*, are commonly recommended for the purpose, fallen leaves applied fresh (as distinct from leafmould) more rarely get a mention. Nevertheless, an annual mulch of fallen leaves is more natural and, to my mind, more valuable than any other for trees and shrubs, achieving a good deal more than all that the Dictionary asks of it.

1. It enriches the topsoil by slowly rotting down to a fine, flaky leafmould on the surface of the soil, whence the small particles are drawn underground by the good offices of the earthworm.

2. The leaf cover delays the rate of evaporation of moisture from the soil which, if exposed in its nakedness, rapidly becomes parched during periods of drought, persistent wind or strong sunshine.

3. It not only helps to keep the roots cool in hot summers but also keeps so much of the frost out of the ground in winter that except in the very hardest weather the soil is usually workable beneath the leaves.

4. Perhaps its principal virtue is to ensure that shrub gardening is indeed labour-saving, because it keeps the ground between the shrubs virtually free of weeds. This cuts out the need for any hoeing or forking of the soil among the roots, which most trees and shrubs greatly dislike. Even such weeds as may occasionally defy the mulch may be tweaked out by hand with the greatest of ease.

Leaves Certain large, coarse leaves which tend to become soggy (e.g. sycamore and horse chestnut) and slow-rotting evergreen foilage such as laurel or holly are unsuitable for mulching purposes. Most others will serve well enough, but beech and oak are best because of the good, flaky texture of the resulting leaf soil.

Supply If these are not available on the premises or in the wild nearby, in many districts it is possible to order leaves by the lorry-load from the local Council when road-sweeping starts in the autumn. It is advisable to put one's order in as soon as the leaves begin to fall, especially if stipulating a preference for beech and oak. What once used to be a free, unmarketable commodity is nowadays delivered in this district at a charge of 50p for a large load (at the time of writing). A free-will offering to the drivers helps to foster good relations for future seasons and may reduce the damage to grassed or gravelled approaches and plantings adjacent to the dump, though the new-style jumbo sweepers are so cumbersome that a trail of ruts, skid-marks and broken branches in their wake can hardly be avoided in a circumscribed area. Even so I would far rather endure some minor havoc than forgo this precious commodity.

Leaves from Trees and Shrubs Grown on Lime It is not generally understood that, no matter what the tree or shrub, if growing in an alkaline soil its leaves will have a limy reaction; so it is as well to know where one's leaves have been. If your garden is in the heart of a limy district presumably you will have no choice in the matter of venue, but watch out if you grow lime-haters in suitably acid soil on the fringe of an alkaline area, because even beech and oak will, if grown on lime, make an unacceptable mulch for calcifuge subjects.

Method of Application The easiest way I know of conveying the leaves to different parts of the garden is to line a deep wheel-barrow diamondwise with one of the immensely useful $5\frac{1}{2}$ ft. square hessian carriers mentioned on p. 57, pile the leaves into it and fold the corners over the load to prevent loss en route. The frontal parts of the borders can be mulched by the handful direct from the barrow, after which the lightened load can be hauled in the carrier into the more inaccessible back parts. If a stooge can be found to fill sacks these are even more portable among dense plantings, but for a single-handed operator sack-filling is much more time-consuming than filling the carrier-lined barrow.

The leaves should be fairly tight packed, about 5 in. deep when freshly applied, but keep them away from the ankles of trees and shrubs, because if they are piled against the stems they may induce a

Fig. 13. Carriage of leaf mulch
Barrow-load of leaves, packed in hessian carrier, ready for distribution.

basal rot or softening of the bark which lays the plants open to disease.
If applied when wet they will not take off with every puff of wind
before they have settled. In very windy areas, or in very naked new
plantings, it may be found necessary to lay a few stems of bracken
on top of the mulch to prevent it blowing about, or even to scatter
it very lightly with earth or sand, remembering that the leaves must
on no account be buried. Contrary to popular belief, a properly
applied leaf-mulch does not blow all over lawns and paths, provided
it is hemmed in behind the dwarf shrubs of the front rank. If the
leaves are placed too close to the edge of the border some are,
however, bound to be scattered by untidy blackbirds in their
search for food. Most of the carpeting plants soon suffocate beneath
a pall of decaying leaves which the larger shrubs find so delectable,
so all verge plantings should be kept free of fallen leaves, whether
from the trees and shrubs overhead or from the mulch. A rubber
rake is the least damaging tool for the job, when this is on a scale
beyond hand-picking. A finer mulch such as moist peat for the
verges will smother weeds while keeping the carpeting plants
happy.

Timing It is advisable to get the mulch distributed as soon as
possible after delivery in the autumn in order to get the maximum
goodness from the leaves and to retain what warmth remains in
the soil before hard frost has a chance to penetrate. However, if

severe frost occurs before the job is finished, wait until the ground has thoroughly thawed rather than mulch on to a frozen soil.

Alternative Forms of Mulch

Peat In districts where suitable leaves are not to be had, in gardens small enough to keep the cost within reason, and also for dwarf or verge plantings, moist peat makes an excellent mulch, is easily handled and good-looking to boot. Naturally acid bracken peat, sometimes available from local deposits, contains potash and other plant foods, whereas the usual commercial brands are said to be non-nutrient. Here I can get the natural screened peat direct from a local 'mine', and therefore have little experience of the bagged or baled product, but any described as 'rhododendron peat' or 'shrub peat' should be suitable for use among calcifuge as well as other shrubs. Irish moss peat is, to my mind, of a more convenient texture, being less lumpy and more fibrous than 'rhododendron peat'. Alexpeat is also excellent for general shrub garden use.

Dry peat acts like the moisture-retaining substances sold for flower arrangement in that it sucks up a surprising amount of moisture before giving any away. Whether for planting, mulching or topdressing it must, therefore, be well moistened before use. If there is time to let the weather do the job, spread it out to be rained on, turning it occasionally to ensure that it is wetted right through. If dry when wanted for immediate use it must be artificially moistened by the bucket- or barrow-load, or by hosepipe, and then squeezed if necessary, like bulb fibre, until it stops dripping. A depth of 2 in. or so is enough for most mulches, other than the more bulky, freshly fallen leaves.

Bracken Bracken itself makes a nourishing, lightweight mulching material and is especially useful for dwarf shrubs, but when gathered and applied in the russet brown stage it rots down to vanishing point much too fast for convenience. It is richest in potash if cut just before the young green fronds are fully unfurled, and those strong-minded enough to turn their backs on television throughout the Wimbledon fortnight—or sooner, in early districts—to gather, chop and administer it in peak condition should later reap their reward. Once the green croziers are fully expanded they start passing the plant foods down to the black, juicy roots, or rhizomes, for storage. Consequently these too provide a rich source of plant foods if dug up, lightly smashed to release the white juice and spread over the roots of trees and shrubs. Instead, these highly nutritious food parcels are all too often thrown on the bonfire as a useless nuisance when bracken land is cleared for a garden-in-the-making.

Garden Compost   The only other form of mulch of which I have personal experience is garden compost, which is widely recommended for the purpose, but I confess that my own heaps are so carelessly put together that the end product defeats one of the main objects of mulching. Whereas weeds are almost or entirely absent from areas well mulched with leaves or peat, and are discouraged by a bracken mulch for as long as it lasts, topdressings of my home-made compost never fail to produce a pestilential rash of weed seedlings in no time at all. And so, valuable though mine is to me for improving my poor soil when buried in planting holes, I would not recommend any but the most conscientiously made compost for a surface mulch, for fear the usual crop of weeds may sprout with all the exuberance of cress on a damp flannel.

Other Mulches   Almost any form of mulch is better than none, but some have built-in dangers.

Hop manure is one of the best, being not only safe and passable in appearance, but also nutritious. Spent hops, which are said to have little food value, are also recommended as a surface mulch.

Mushroom compost usually consists largely of horse manure with added chalk and is, therefore, unacceptable for lime-haters. Gypsum, which is neutral in pH value, is sometimes used instead of chalk, however, and it is worth finding out about this before deciding against it.

Weathered sawdust was not a great success on rose beds in a local garden where I have seen it used. It must not be (and was not in this case) applied fresh.

I suspect that sawdust may have the same drawback for mulching purposes as fresh lawn mowings, both being liable to become dangerously soggy in wet weather, but are better than nothing in dry spells. Lawn mowings should be free of seeding weeds if possible and should not be applied thickly enough at any one time to allow of heating up. Grass from areas recently treated with weedkiller should not be used for mulching purposes.

It is a heartening thought that each year, as it becomes more and more difficult to circulate among the close boscage of the shrub beds with the annual mulch, the need is continually diminishing, for the reason that the trees and shrubs yearly make a larger contribution of their own in this respect until at length they provide an adequate leaf-mulch without our intervention.

Pruning – General

Before dealing with the subject in detail, it may be helpful to clarify some of the horticultural jargon applied to pruning operations which are liable to confuse the beginner. The line drawings in figures 14–26, illustrating pruning terms used in the text, seem to me the clearest way of putting their meaning across. Verbal definitions of most of these terms are also given in this section.

Whereas instructions for the pruning of individual subjects are set out in the appropriate seasonal sections of the Working-calendar, here I intend to give as much general information as I can think of, because I feel sure that for the beginner instructions are only foolproof when they leave nothing whatever to the imagination. It seems that doubts about how and when to prune are one of the biggest problems for the inexperienced and may well scare off a prospective shrub gardener of diffident make-up, but I can assure them that no great mental effort is required to grasp the objects of the exercise, and that even the most unintelligent pruning is rarely downright fatal.

They may also be encouraged by the fact that although many shrubs should receive regular pruning there are a whole host of others which require none at all, as well as a number which benefit from only occasional reduction. It is however important that, regardless of any such categories, dead or diseased wood should, for reasons of hygiene, be promptly removed whenever it appears, and that plain green shoots on variegated plants should also be cut right out to their point of origin without delay at any time, because if left unchecked these will eventually take over. Among those most commonly affected in the latter respect are:

Acer negundo 'Variegatum' (variegated Box Elder)
Elaeagnus pungens 'Maculata'
Euonymus (various)

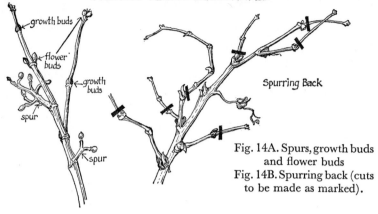

Fig. 14A. Spurs, growth buds
and flower buds
Fig. 14B. Spurring back (cuts
to be made as marked).

Fig. 15A. Correct pruning cuts
1 Clean, well-angled cut just above a
bud
2 Unwanted side-shoot removed flush
with main stem.
Fig. 15B. Incorrect pruning cuts
1 Jagged cut
2 Snag left by removal of side-shoot.

Fig. 16. Double leader at
the top of a conifer.

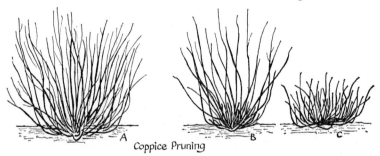

Fig. 17. Coppice pruning

A. Before coppicing
B. Partial coppicing
C. Fully coppiced 6-in. stool (scale of C rather larger than A and B).
N.B. Pollarding of trees: Same principle as in C of Coppicing, but
reducing top growth to within about 6 ins. of trunk.

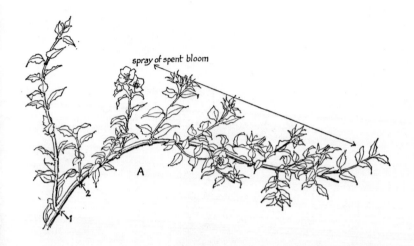

spray of spent bloom

Fig. 18A. Well-grown branch ready for pruning, having finished flowering.
Cut back to 1 (good strong shoot) if available. If not, a smaller growth, such
as 2, will have to serve.

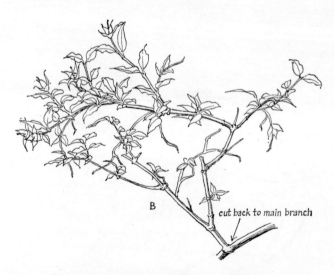

cut back to main branch

Fig. 18B. Muddled, twiggy growth from same shrub
Cut away, to its base (not worth preserving).

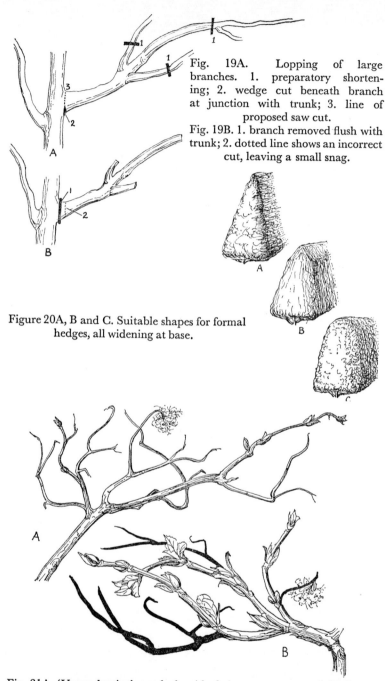

Fig. 19A. Lopping of large branches. 1. preparatory shortening; 2. wedge cut beneath branch at junction with trunk; 3. line of proposed saw cut.

Fig. 19B. 1. branch removed flush with trunk; 2. dotted line shows an incorrect cut, leaving a small snag.

Figure 20A, B and C. Suitable shapes for formal hedges, all widening at base.

Fig. 21A. 'Unproductive' wood: devoid of vigorous new growth buds.
Fig. 21B. 'Productive' wood: strong, well-budded growth, requiring only removal of dead wood (shown in black).

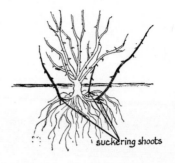

Fig. 22. Pinching out
Remove tip of shoot (shown in black) between finger and thumb nail.

Fig. 23. Suckering of roses
Suckers from the rootstock (shown in black) to be removed at point where they join roots.

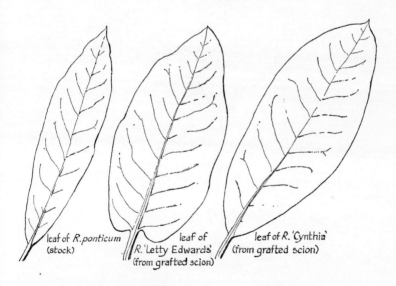

leaf of *R. ponticum* (stock)

leaf of *R.* 'Letty Edwards' (from grafted scion)

leaf of *R.* 'Cynthia' (from grafted scion)

Fig. 24. Detection of sucker growth in grafted rhododendrons
Foliage of *R. ponticum* stock is usually darker in colour as well as narrower than that of scion grafted upon it.

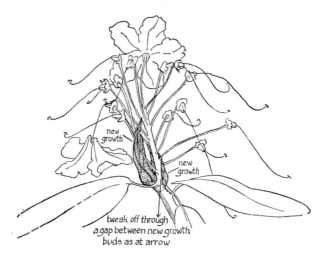

new
growth

new
growth

tweak off through
a gap between new growth
buds as at arrow

Fig. 25. Deadheading of rhododendrons

one dead bloom in a
flowering truss

a

new shoot

b

Fig. 26. Deadheading of roses

Remove individual dead blooms to *a*. When whole truss is spent cut back to
b, from which good new growth is springing.

Hedera helix 'Gold Heart' (a small-leaved ivy with a bright yellow centre, often incorrectly listed as 'Jubilee')
Kerria japonica 'Variegata' ('Picta')
Symphoricarpos orbiculatus 'Variegatus' (yellow and green variegated Coral Berry)
The variegated form of rue

No pruning   The following list of plants which need never be pruned, unless to remove a badly placed shoot occasionally, does not pretend to be exhaustive, but it includes many of the most commonly grown within this category:

Abutilon vitifolium
Actinidia
Amelanchier (Snowy Mespilus)
Arbutus (Strawberry Tree)
Aucuba (Spotted Laurel)
Azalea
Azara
Berberidopsis
Camellia
Caragana
Cercis siliquastrum (Judas Tree)—except as a wall shrub
Choisya (Mexican Orange Blossom)
Cistus (Rock Rose)
Clerodendrum
Cornus (Dogwood)—tree types, but not those grown for coloured bark
Cotinus (syn. Rhus, Smoke Bush)
Cotoneaster—except against walls
Daphne
Decaisnea
Desfontainia
Elaeagnus
Embothrium (Chilean Fire Bush)
Enkianthus
Eucryphia
Exochorda
x Fatshedera
Fatsia
Fothergilla
Gaultheria

Griselinia—as open-ground shrubs
Hamamelis (Witch Hazel)
Hedera (Ivy)—small-leaved types in particular
Hibiscus syriacus (Tree Hollyhock)
Hoheria
Hydrangea petiolaris (Climbing Hydrangea)
Kalmia
Laurus nobilis (Bay)
Ledum
Leiophyllum
Leptospermum
Ligustrum ovalifolium 'Aureum' (Golden Privet)
Magnolia—especially deciduous types
Mahonia—most
Pachysandra
Parrotia
Parthenocissus quinquefolia (Virginia Creeper)
Pernettya
Phormium (New Zealand Flax)
Pieris (syn. Andromeda)
Poncirus (syn. Aegle, Japanese Bitter Orange)
Prunus, most shrubby types
Pyracantha (Firethorn)—except as wall shrubs
Rhododendron
Schizophragma
Skimmia
Styrax japonica (Snowbell)
Trachelospermum
Vitis coignetiae
Yucca
and, finally
Trees.

Almost anything growing on a single, clean trunk is better left unpruned, so trees have only had a mention in the above list when they also exist in shrub form (i.e. with a number of growths springing from ground level) such as some of the *Cornus* and *Magnolia* species.

Occasional Pruning   Common examples of others which benefit from no more than *occasional* pruning, mainly to reduce overcrowded growth or to maintain a shapely (but not topiarized) appearance, are given below. Individual instructions for these will be found in the Working-calendar.

Abelia
Arundinaria and other bamboos
Berberis, evergreen and most deciduous
Callicarpa
Clethra
Corylopsis
Danae racemosa (Alexandrian Laurel)
Escallonia, open-ground shrubs
Garrya elliptica (Tassel Bush)
Hippophae rhamnoides (Sea Buckthorn)
Mahonia japonica
Neillia
Ribes (Flowering Currant)
Rosa, species
Rosmarinus (Rosemary)
Stachyurus
Staphylea (Bladder Nut)
Stranvaesia
Vaccinium
Viburnum, most deciduous varieties.

Regular Pruning Although shrubs which demand annual pruning may be expected to deteriorate in vigour or in beauty and abundance of bloom if neglected over a long period, it should nevertheless be stressed that when in doubt, even for the plants in this category, and certainly for those in the two previous ones, it is wiser to leave well alone rather than to hack at them without understanding why, when, and how to set about it. Practical experience is the quickest teacher; for instance, if one removes potential flowering growth on a shrub grown for its berries the absence of these later on will suggest that the baby has been thrown out along with the bath water. Brooms and genistas are outstanding examples of those which rarely recover if early pruning is neglected, but most others will come to little harm if left unpruned for a season or two. At worst one may later have to sacrifice a season's bloom on an overgrown shrub which calls for more drastic pruning than usual to put matters right.

Having this book on the stocks, I recently attended one of the practical demonstrations on the pruning of hardy shrubs held annually at the Royal Horticultural Society's Garden at Wisley and took my notebook with me. Instructions were so clear and helpful that any but the most widely experienced Fellows would surely find this a spring afternoon well spent, and for the novice it would be infinitely valuable. The demonstrator's theme was that once one understands the 'Why' of pruning the 'When' and the 'How' also begin to make sense, and much of what follows is based on my rough notes made on the spot.

Reasons for Pruning

The 'When' and individual aspects of the 'How' are taken care of in the Working-calendar, so here our main concern is with the 'Why'. This is determined by one, some or all of the following aims: (a) to keep the plant healthy; (b) to keep it well shaped; (c) to fill its allotted position; and (d) to achieve its maximum effect.

Health Because air-borne fungus diseases enter into the plant tissues through dead or damaged wood, it is important to remove this as soon as it is noticed, at ground level if wholly dead or, if partially live, cutting back to a bud or a joint in the sound growth, leaving no jutting snags to cause die-back. To obtain the cleanest possible cut one should try to approach it from a suitable angle— that is, one which allows the blades to cut flush with the joint when cutting back to a main limb or, if cutting back to a live bud, to make a slanting cut tapering off just above the bud (see Fig. 15). It follows that one needs to move around a shrub to prune it properly and even so the position of adjacent shoots may interfere with the correct approach. In this case any snags left by an awkward cut should be pared flush with a razor-sharp pruning knife.

If a large branch has to be removed an incision should first be made on the underside of the proposed cut to prevent the weight of the falling branch tearing the trunk or leaving a jagged 'hat-peg' (exceptionally heavy limbs may be removed in sections). The branch should be taken off flush with the trunk or main limb from which it grows and the wound trimmed smooth with a sharp knife, because bark cannot grow over bumps or hollows (see Fig. 19). Any wound of more than ¾ in. in diameter should be painted with one of the antiseptic bitumastic compounds such as Arbrex, which have the advantage over white lead paint in that they contain fungicides. Wounds of more than 6 in. across will need to be repainted periodically because they take more time to heal. If you find it necessary to employ outside help for major tree surgery, check on the operator's credentials before engaging him, so as to ensure that you get an efficient tree surgeon and not a mere botcher or butcher.

If a tree has to be got rid of altogether, it is far better to remove roots and all rather than to fell to a stump, because of the risk of honey fungus invading the rotting wood as a base for its lethal activities among live plants (see Diseases, pp. 117–29). If this is impossible the stump should be treated with a brushwood-killer such as SBK a few days after felling, preferably between January and March.

Shape Pruning to induce or maintain a good shape is most often necessary for evergreens from time to time, when the removal or shortening of a runaway shoot is required for the sake of symmetry. Certain young conifers in particular have a tendency to develop a double leader, which later results in splitting (see Fig. 16). One of the competing shoots should, therefore, be cut out and the other gradually trained into an upright position by tying it to a cane.

It is possible to control the shape of both deciduous and evergreen subjects by pruning in such a way as to stimulate new growth just where it is wanted. To avoid a huddle of crowded growth or an ill-balanced framework and to direct the vigour of the plant into a smaller number of healthy and well-placed shoots it may be necessary to cut out some of the new wood (as well as some of the older, more unproductive growth), which is contrary to normal pruning practice; so it is as well to have a fairly clear idea of what one is trying to achieve before experimenting (see Figs. 21A and B).

In pruning to obtain a pleasing, balanced shape one should, wherever possible, cut a shoot back to a growth bud pointing in the direction in which expansion is wanted. And, since shortening a shoot has the effect of encouraging growth, the opposite result can only be obtained by removing it at the ground line.

Filling of Allotted Position For any plant intended for a permanent position–i.e. most trees, and such shrubs as are bad

movers—it is important to have some idea of its probable proportions 20 years hence before deciding whether it can comfortably be
accommodated. A live warning to the improvident may be seen in
a street of small, semi-detached villas on the outskirts of Reading,
where in each tiny strip of front garden a robust 30-year-old
cherry—the ubiquitous 'Kanzan'—is now trying to stuff its pink
fingers in at the bedroom windows all along the line, except where
one or two have been ruthlessly pollarded into ugly knob-heads.
The moral is clear. Then again, if plants ultimately outgrow their
permanent positions much weak wood will result from overcrowding, increasing the amount of pruning required. And since the
shortening of shoots usually peps up growth still further, a good
deal of wood will need to be cut right back to the base in order
to make any effective reduction in the space occupied by an over-
sized shrub. Though I, personally, favour what many regard as
overcrowding, I must admit that there is more dead wood to be
removed among my shrubs where branches have become densely
interlaced than in gardens where they are more widely spaced.

Maximum Effect Maximum flower power is not one's sole
concern in the shrub garden, where colourful bark, ornate fruits
and fine foliage colour and design also play their part.
   As regards colour in bark and leaf, maximum effects (other than
autumn foliage hues) are usually confined to the new growth
stimulated by pruning. Examples of the former are to be found
among certain dogwoods and willows, which need to be cut hard
back coppice-wise to achieve their spectacular clumps of yellow,
orange, scarlet, crimson, maroon, purple or violet wands (see
Fig. 17), and of the latter among the purple-leaved berberis, or in
hardy eucalypts such as *Eucalyptus gunnii* or *E. perriniana*, in which
the juvenile foliage differs in form as well as in colour from that of
the adult leaves. Foliage effect may also depend upon the production of vigorous new shoots on which the finest leaves are borne
(e.g. *Rosa rubrifolia*, *Philadelphus coronarius* 'Aureus', *Weigela florida*
'Variegata'), in which case pruning back to strong and suitably
positioned growth buds and removing weak, muddled twiggery
will give these scope to develop (see Fig. 18B).
   Pruning for berries or other fruits amounts to much the same
thing as pruning for floral effect, since one cannot have the one
without the other, but in this case one must be careful not to remove
spent flower shoots when ornamental fruits should follow.

To turn to the problem of achieving maximum floral effect, as already mentioned, a great many shrubs will regularly cover themselves with bloom year after year without any pruning at all, but *if* pruning is necessary to achieve the most effective display of any one of the attributes with which we are concerned, then it usually needs to be a regular yearly operation. Such plants as benefit from regular annual pruning fall into four categories—three deciduous and one evergreen. Details for individual treatment have been given at appropriate seasons in the Working-calendar, the instructions which follow being of a more general nature, bearing in mind that, in general, strong cutting induces vigorous growth, whereas lighter pruning makes for greater abundance of bloom.

I am all too well aware that, when attempting to carry out pruning instructions, it seems that the plants themselves are none too familiar with the rules. Where one cannot track back, for instance, to an unequivocal 'strong new shoot' behind the spent flower portion (see Fig. 18A), one must just do the best one can, either cutting back to a punier side-growth or removing the shoot altogether if there is not enough vigorous new greenery to be worth preserving.

Deciduous Shrubs Flowering in Winter and up to mid-April

Beginners are often baffled, as I was, about the distinction between shrubs which flower on the old wood and those which do so on the current season's growth. One must be able to sort out this conundrum if one is to make a rational approach to pruning; but common sense will come to the rescue if one gives it a moment's thought instead of struggling to memorize lists of either kind, parrot-fashion. In the case of plants which bloom in the earliest months of the year —say up to mid-April—it stands to reason that there simply has not been time for new wood to have developed since the start of the winter, so that it is physically impossible for them to flower on the current year's growth—growth, that is, which has not yet been made. It follows, therefore, that if such shrubs need to be pruned at all the sooner they are relieved of their spent flower shoots the longer the new growth will have to ripen and so produce flower buds for the following year. The most common examples in this category are forsythia, winter jasmine and the early-flowering forms of shrubby spiraea.

Deciduous Shrubs Flowering from mid-April to Mid-summer These, too, flower on the wood formed during the previous season, for the reason that most of the new growth will not yet be sufficiently mature to bear flowers. In this group it is usually rather easier to decide where to cut, since the new growth will be identifiable, even though not yet fully developed, by the time pruning is due. Here again, this should be done (if required) as soon as possible after flowering, shortening the flowered shoots back to a strong new growth where possible (see Fig. 18A). Where it is not, unproductive old wood (i.e. bearing few strong new shoots, see Fig. 21A and B) may be cut right out at ground level, or to the lowest point at which a good new shoot arises. At the same time, all the thin twiggy bits which contribute little or nothing and only crowd the centre of the bush are better removed to let in more light and air (see Fig. 18B). Examples include deutzia, weigela, kolkwitzia (Beauty Bush) and philadelphus (Mock Orange).

Deciduous Shrubs Flowering after Midsummer Reason again suggests that the shrubs in this group will by now have had ample time to ripen wood on which to bear flowers during the current year. Generally speaking, these are the ones we must refrain from pruning, if pruned they need to be, until spring, when the coming season's growth can be detected. Examples include *Buddleia davidii* varieties (Butterfly Bush), caryopteris, the late summer-flowering deciduous *Ceanothus* 'Gloire de Versailles' and *Spiraea* x *bumalda* 'Anthony Waterer'.

Evergreen Flowering Shrubs Evergreens of all sorts mostly need little regular pruning beyond the removal of wood damaged by frost and wind as soon as possible after the risk of severe frost is past. Late April or early May is the time to cut out damaged wood, when new growth is just beginning. It is not a good thing to cut into live wood on evergreens in winter (though we all do it without compunction for Christmas decoration and, it seems, without very serious results). Those which flower in the earlier part of the growing season (e.g. spring-flowering ceanothus, some escallonia, rosemary) may be cut back to new growth after flowering, whereas the later-flowering evergreens such as *Ceanothus* 'Burkwoodii', shrubby hypericums (St. John's Wort) and so on should be left until the spring.

Overgrown Shrubs Just as neglected spring-cleaning may pass unnoticed for a year or two but will eventually betray itself in dingy paintwork, grubby furnishings and overflowing drawers and cupboards, so also in the shrub garden neglect will only gradually become evident in the tell-tale accumulation of dead wood, crowded, unproductive old growth and the slowly dwindling floral spectacle. In either case it is rarely disastrous, but does somewhat tarnish the beauty of one's environment, whether indoors or out.

I have already mentioned that a badly overgrown shrub may often be restored by drastic pruning at the appropriate season in order to encourage fresh growth from or near the base, but in the case of flowering subjects any floral display will usually be sacrificed for at least one season if all top growth is drastically reduced in one operation. The job may therefore, if preferred, be spread over several seasons, cutting part back to base each year over a period of, say, three years, for the sake of keeping some bloom during the process.

Trimming

Although trimming is, of course, a form of pruning, I hesitate to include it under this head lest it be taken as a licence for indiscriminate use of the shears, especially in the untrained hands of the jobbing gardener. Unless one happens to fancy an assortment of domes, drums, parachutes and footballs in the shrub borders it will be wiser to forbid him the use of the shears except for intentional topiary, for formal hedge-clipping and perhaps, where time presses, for cutting back certain dense, feathery subjects such as heaths and heathers. Shears are sometimes recommended for clipping over the larger brooms and genistas, but unless they are exceptionally sharp they tend to chew rather than to cut cleanly, and the whiskery growth is better reduced with sharp secateurs. One-handed sheepshears make quite a good tool for clipping heaths and heathers.

Informal Hedges

There is little purpose in planting a flowering hedge if lack of room dictates a close-clipped finish, but where space permits the use of flowering shrubs for an informal hedge, they will need pruning shoot by shoot, much as for similar single specimens, if they are to flower effectively. Pruning will, as a rule, consist of cutting spent shoots fairly hard back to a suitable new growth or growth bud after flowering (e.g. evergreen berberis, escallonia).

Formal Hedges

By formal, I mean hedges kept close-clipped to a definite shape—and the shape itself is important. An inverted V shape is ideal, not only preventing snow damage but also allowing light to reach the basal growth, which will become bare if deprived of light by the overhanging upper leafage. The strictly triangular pattern may be varied by giving it a rounded top or by angling the topmost part of the slope more steeply than the lower portion, so long as a general outward slope from top to bottom is preserved (see Fig. 20). As soon as the newly planted hedge shows any signs of new growth, density should be encouraged by frequent light clipping in its early years. It is important to prevent the young plants from shooting up too fast until a well furnished base has been established, since a scrawny one is almost impossible to correct at a later stage. Mature hedges mostly need only one or two trims annually, and may get by with even less.

Evergreen types   Some kinds of formal evergreen hedge such as yew, holly, box and certain conifers may make do with one annual trim, for which August is the best time. But others such as privet and *Lonicera nitida* very quickly become untidy and may need trimming as many as three or four times a year. If drastic reduction of an overgrown hedge becomes necessary, leave this until April. Whenever I read, as one so frequently does, that broad-leaved evergreen hedges must always be trimmed with secateurs rather than shears, to avoid mutilating the foliage, I am reminded of a Nigerian proverb: 'Slowly, slowly, a well may be dug with a needle'. Surrounded as I am by tall boundary hedges of common laurel I cannot spare time for all that needlework, yet find no fault with the neat appearance of my laurels after shearing—the secateurs being used only on wood too tough for the clippers.

Deciduous types   Non-flowering types of deciduous hedging such as beech and hornbeam, for which a once-yearly trimming suffices at maturity, look better if this is done in August, which gives them an opportunity to make some fresh growth before winter. Otherwise they may be trimmed at any time during the winter except in frosty weather.

Pinching Out

This is a form of pruning for which no tool is required. It consists of nipping out the soft young tips of new growth with the thumb and finger, being careful not to pinch out flower buds instead of growth tips, in the case of flowering shrubs (see Fig. 22). In my experience certain plants such as cistus and halimiums respond much better to repeated pinching out during the growing season than to actual cutting, while others such as the evergreen ceanothus and *Senecio greyi* may benefit from both. The object is to induce bushiness, particularly where there is a natural tendency to legginess, and roughly corresponds to the practice of 'stopping', as applied to broad beans, wallflowers and the like. The denser growth which results is especially desirable for plants of doubtful hardiness in a cold garden. Pinching out should not however be continued after early August, because new growth formed in late summer and autumn will not be sufficiently hardened to withstand the winter.

Suckers

Plants on their own roots are usually dearer than grafts, but are often the better buy because of their greater robustness, let alone the absence of undesirable sucker growth. Grafting consists of joining a shoot (or scion) of the plant required on to the rooted portion (or stock) of another—usually at or near ground level in the case of shrubs—in such a way that the two fuse to make a single plant. Naturally, therefore, any shoots springing from below the join will be alien suckers, which are an unmitigated nuisance in that they deprive the true plant of nourishment and will eventually overpower it if allowed to develop. Some of the worst of the gardener's sucker troubles come from roses which, alas, are all too rarely available on their own roots (see Fig. 23), and from grafted rhododendrons and azaleas. Rhododendron suckers are easy enough to spot because the foliage of the *ponticum* stock is usually narrower, and often differently shaped and darker in colour than that of the scion (see Fig. 24). Suckers from grafted rose stock are not always so readily recognizable, but they can differ from the true growth in the number, size and colour of their leaflets, the number, shape and colour of their thorns, and the colour and texture of their shoots. Other grafted plants given to suckering include lilac, witch hazel, tree peonies, some elaeagnus, viburnums and chaenomeles (Japonica), also robinia and a number of other trees.

Suckers springing from the stock should be removed at source as soon as they are discovered, but because many garden shrubs on their own roots are of a naturally suckering habit one must first make sure that the suspect shoot is not a valuable new growth from the base of the true plant. To do so, it may be necessary to find out from the nurseryman who supplied it whether the plant is grafted or on its own roots.

To trace a 'wrong un' back conscientiously to its point of origin on the rootstock below the soil is a tiresome business, but it is not a bit of use skimping the job by removing it at ground level or thereabouts, since this will only multiply the sucker crop. The younger they are the easier they are to eradicate, and the stronger they are allowed to become the more they weaken the plant. Opinions differ as to whether they should be cut cleanly away with a sharp knife or pulled away, but what is chiefly important is to remove the sucker at the point where it springs from the root.

Hoeing, raking or forking among trees and shrubs with metal tools is one of the surest ways of stimulating tiresome sucker growth, which springs most readily from abraded or otherwise damaged roots—yet another point in favour of mulching.

Deadheading

Deadheading differs from that form of pruning proper which consists of shortening spent woody flower shoots (as in the case of forsythia or deutzia, whose flowers are borne in sprays extending along a shoot for much of its length) in that it usually concerns either quite a large single bloom or a truss, (that is, a number of short-stemmed flowers combining to form a cluster upon one main flower stem, of which rhododendron and pieris are examples). It is recommended not only for appearances' sake, but also because it directs the plant's vigour into the formation of new growth instead of into seed production. It follows, therefore, that the longer dead-heading is delayed after flowering the less its benefits will be.

Often it is best done with finger and thumb, holding the branch firm with one hand and using the other to give the main stem bearing the dead bloom or truss a sharp sideways tweak. In the case of rhododendrons and azaleas, for example, one must be careful to aim the break towards a gap in the new growth buds forming at the base of the stem of the truss, so as not to snap these off at the same time (see Fig. 25). By the time the older specimens outgrow one's reach they should be vigorous enough to prosper without further attentions. Though one cannot keep pace with the dead-heading of the small-flowered species and varieties of either after their first few years, I have nevertheless found that they grew more rapidly if the dead flowers were removed for as long as one could cope. In the case of the exuberantly flowered evergreen azaleas, which afterwards remain shrouded in a mass of browned corollas, roughly combing through the bushes with one's fingers, claw-wise, will remove the majority of the dead heads, much improving the appearance of the plants, though not of course preventing them from setting seed.

No doubt we all deadhead our roses. But although the easiest way is to pick off individual dead blooms by hand, we should, correctly, cut the flowered stem back to a new growth a little lower down the shoot when the whole truss is spent, taking it farther back in late summer than in the early part of the season (see Fig. 26). Certain rose species need no deadheading, either because of their ornamental heps, or because they are naturally so floriferous as to make the job impracticable. *Rosa moyesii* is an example of the one and *R.* x *cantabrigiensis* of the other.

Whereas it is undesirable to let the lacecap types of hydrangea set seed, it is better to leave the mophead types alone until the spring in cold gardens, since they help to protect the new buds lower down from frost. Inflorescences affected by botrytis should not, however, be allowed to remain festering on the plant.

Disbudding

In the shrub garden disbudding is chiefly to be recommended in the case of very young plants equipped with comparatively large, fat flower buds, such as rhododendrons and camellias. Though some gardeners are disappointed to receive young specimens devoid of flower buds the fact is that if a small new plant is sent out from the nursery well budded up it is wiser to pick these off, so that its undivided energies may go to build up growth. The sacrifice of a few disproportionately large and comparatively ephemeral blooms, even for more than one season, is not a high price to pay for speeding up the growth of the infant shrub to a more suitable flowering size; and it is always excusable to allow just one or two buds to flower in order to satisfy one's curiosity or whet one's appetite for future enjoyment.

Mature rhododendrons also benefit from some disbudding if a number of flower buds are crowded in a cluster at the tip of a shoot. In this case all but one bud should be removed.

Fig. 27. Pruning tools

A. Anvil-type secateurs.	B. Scissor-type secateurs.
C. Short-armed pruner.	D. Long-armed pruner.
E. Pruning saw, scimitar-shape.	F. Pruning knife.

Pruning Tools

Essentials in the shrub gardener's armoury are: secateurs, a pruning saw, a pruning knife, a short-armed pruner and, probably, at a later stage, a long-armed or tree pruner. The outlay can, however, be spread over a number of years when making a new shrub garden, the secateurs and the knife being adequate for a start, with a gradual build-up to the more powerful tools as woody growth and plant heights develop.

Secateurs   The commonest are the two which have a scissor or anvil action. The first is self-explanatory and the second has a single blade which cuts against a broader strip of metal like an execu-

tioner's axe on the block. Whichever way one's choice falls it pays
to buy a reliable brand of strong constitution, to reserve it for one's
own exclusive use, and to cherish it—that is to say, keep it clean,
dry, sharp, well oiled at the joints and refrain from wrenching it
to hack through tough wood beyond its strength. As far as possible
the cut should be made with the base of the blades to reduce the
risk of forcing, and the tool should be used the right way up.
Makers of good quality secateurs are usually able to renew spare
parts so that, no matter how dilapidated, they can often be
miraculously restored (at a price, and in some cases not without
rather long delay).

Pruning Saws These may be scimitar-shaped, straight and
tapered, single-edged, double-edged, or with a straight blade
folding into a handle. I find the scimitar shape handiest for getting
into confined spaces and awkward angles, the one I use having a
tapered blade about 15 in. long. The same type in a smaller size
would also be valuable, if such exists, in place of the small, straight-
bladed one I make do with for lesser jobs. I have no experience of
the double-edged saw, but it is already so hard to avoid abrading
the bark of adjacent shoots with the top side of a single blade that
a two-edged tool could, I feel sure, only add to one's difficulties.

Pruning Knives The experts are pretty fussy in their choice of
a knife, even to the point of distinguishing between right- and left-
handed models, and ensuring in particular that the boy scout
handle is stout and rugged enough to provide a firm, comfortable

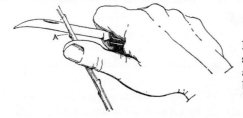

Fig. 28. Knife-pruning

Note thumb used to support
shoot, *not* as anvil for blade,
as cut is made just above
bud, at A.

grip. For those who get the impression, from watching a professional at work, that the thumb serves as an anvil for the knife blade,
I should point out that the thumb is in fact used to brace the shoot
only, the cut being made immediately *above* the supporting thumb,
in a one-handed operation, while the other hand steadies the shoot

higher up, if necessary. In my experience the average amateur is happier–and safer–with other pruning tools for making the actual cuts and I suspect that, like throwing a cricket ball, males are congenitally better than women at wielding the knife.

But even if one has no intention of pruning with it one should in fact possess a pruning knife for paring smooth the surface of rough saw cuts, and so on. One is enjoined to trim cuts made with any tool other than the knife, but I wonder how many of us find time for such a counsel of perfection unless the original cutting has been done with blunted tools. In particular, I am constantly amazed at the clean precision of the cut made by a well cared for short-armed pruner, and cannot believe it would be improved by further trimming with a knife.

Short-armed Pruners Variously called short-armed, long-armed, long-handled lopper and other names, the most useful of the various sizes measures about 19 in. to the start of the 3 in. blades of maxi-scissor-type secateur design. With its strong leverage it cleanly and effortlessly severs any branch which can be gripped in its open beak–that is, something around 1 in. in diameter. If well cared for it will perform with the greatest efficiency a number of tough jobs otherwise tackled with difficulty by, and often damage to, secateurs, or more laboriously and roughly done with a pruning saw. For anyone who finds stooping disagreeable, the long arms make comparatively easy work of removing tough old or dead wood at ground level in the dense heart of a shrub. Mine was bought in a guilty fit of extravagance, but for me it has moved out of the luxury class and into the category of indispensables.

Long-armed, or Tree Pruners Here again some confusion exists regarding the name of the tool, which varies from one maker to another, some of them using 'long-armed' for the tool just described, which I prefer to call 'short-armed'. The long arm may be had in various lengths from 6–12 ft. and is topped by a hook-beaked cutting device operated by pulling on a lever-handle near the lower end of the arm. As in the case of the short-armed pruner, the powerful leverage makes it possible to cut through a fair thickness of branch without difficulty.

All cutting tools should be kept sharp, clean and dry, and if used on diseased wood should be sterilized with a disinfectant when pruning is finished.

Pests and Diseases and their Control

A. PESTS

In a well-ordered shrub garden serious disease problems are few, but even the healthiest of trees and shrubs may suffer damage from a variety of harmful insects and other pests unless we are reasonably assiduous about keeping them under control.

Biological Pest Control

Those who hold that we are upsetting the balance of nature by destroying the pests which would otherwise fall a prey to friendly predators will not have much use for what follows. But so often Nature seems unaware of her responsibility in a man-made garden. Though long periods of enforced neglect in this one have given the birds, ladybirds, toads, hedgehogs and other reputedly beneficent creatures ample opportunity for justifying our expectations, the sucking and biting insects and the voracious slugs remain just as numerous as ever, while tits, bullfinches and sparrows continue to decimate the spring blossom, blackbirds and others to steal autumn berries, and squirrels to chew branches bare of their bark.

Non-chemical versus Chemical Controls

The case against chemical warfare in the plant kingdom has been persuasively dealt with in a number of pamphlets issued by the Henry Doubleday Research Association (see Recommended Reading, in Appendix One). While respecting the views of his disciples and other gardeners who prefer to rely on antidotes of natural origin such as nicotine (though surely it cannot be necessary to boil cigarette stubs collected from pubs and cinemas in order to obtain supplies?), or the stewed leaves of rhubarb, elder and such like, I feel that the majority of modern gardeners are more disposed to put their trust in horticultural chemicals for the control of pests and diseases with maximum efficiency and a minimum of time and trouble.

As I understand the problem, it is not the comparatively infinitesimal quantities of chemical poisons used in the average private garden, but their wholesale application on vast tracts of agricultural land, commercial orchards and so on, which may make for a 'silent spring', or be thought to constitute some risk to human health. Products which have been approved by the Ministry of Agriculture, Fisheries and Food as safe for human use, as well as efficient for their purpose, are marked with a capital A topped by a crown. Preparations which are toxic to bees, fish, humans and other animals carry a warning to this effect on the label, and all should be kept out of reach of young children. When applying dusts it is wise to wear a gauze mask to prevent inhalation, and gloves save the hands from any possible harm from contact with chemicals. The makers' instructions should be scrupulously followed, and in this connection it should perhaps be mentioned that spray ingredients sold in powder form, to be dissolved in water, must not be confused with the horticultural dusts actually intended for dusting. Shopkeepers stocking horticultural sundries as a sideline are not always themselves aware of the distinction, and I have on a number of occasions been offered wettable powders in all good faith for use as dusts.

Modern Garden Chemicals

Scientific developments crowd so thick and fast upon the gardener's world of today that familiar remedies are constantly being superseded by a multitude of products claiming to be more effective or more labour-saving than our old-fashioned pharmacopaeia. The choice is bewildering for those amateur gardeners who lack a chemical education, and for my part I look to the Journal and other publications of the Royal Horticultural Society and to other reliable horticultural periodicals for guidance, and also to the gardening correspondents of our leading national newspapers, who do a particularly useful job in keeping abreast of developments and passing on their findings. I am personally much indebted to the compilers of the R.H.S. booklet, *Gardening Chemicals*, not only for much valuable information, but for the immensely helpful layout and cross-referencing which makes it surprisingly easy to find the answer to even the most difficult problems. It is to be hoped that so useful a work will be revised often enough to keep pace with the latest developments.

Without wishing to confuse the reader with a bewildering choice of remedies, I have usually given one or two alternatives, for the reason that the average local ironmonger-cum-horticultural sundriesman will only stock the products of a very few firms.

SOME COMMON PESTS OF ORNAMENTAL TREES AND SHRUBS AND THEIR TREATMENT

Slugs These rank among the chief of garden nuisances, munching away through summer and winter alike, mostly at night, with an appetite out of all proportion to their size. They are, perhaps, most damaging in spring, when there are so many tender young shoots to be mown down and succulent new leafage to be riddled with holes. But although winter offers less variety, the diet of shrubs and ground-cover is still well above the slug's subsistence level and it is a mistake to suppose that they hibernate.

Treatment   In horticultural drug warfare enemy corpses are to be preferred to walking wounded. Whereas the earlier metaldehyde-based anti-slug preparations usually produced only a temporary knock-out, the new methiocarb (e.g. PBI's Slug Gard, or Draza from Baywood Chemicals Ltd and from Boots) is a killer. These mini-pellets also give a wider coverage than the larger ones hitherto available, one pellet per 5 in. being the recommended rate of application. Stale beer is claimed to be a sure-fire remedy, which may appeal to the anti-chemical gardener, though there must be practical difficulties about its wide distribution in the open garden. Reliable reports quote greenhouse experiments in which 300 slugs were lured to a drunkard's death by drowning in shallow pans of beer, as against 28 poisoned, probably only temporarily, by metalde-hyde baits in identical circumstances!

Moles   Although the most noticeable mole damage in gardens is to lawns, in the shrub borders they cause a lot of disturbance, even tunnelling clean through the dense root balls of large rhododendrons, for example.

Treatment   The commonest remedies are mole 'smokes' and 'fuses' (e.g. Topvil or Fumite) and, of course, traps. Trapping works if you know how to do it without alerting the mole in the process, but he must not be able to smell your fingers or recognize human inter-ference with his premises. More folksy measures abound, most of which seem to work for some and not for others. One which has more popular support than most is to plant numbers of *Euphorbia lathyrus* (Caper Spurge) where moles are troublesome, but this is slow to take effect, if at all. Moles are, however, officially registered as pests, so if in serious trouble the best solution may be to ask the Local Authority to send along a professional mole-catcher to do the job, for which I think most use the smokes or fuses.

Other Fur-, Hide- or Feather-clad Pests   Unlike a number of its predecessors the recently introduced and entirely harmless repellent, Curb, really does appear to fulfil the maker's claim to repel pecking birds and inhibit chewing and similar animal nuisances, from squirrels, deer, hares and rabbits to mice, and also dogs and cats. So far as I have been able to test it as yet, two or three applications during the winter saved much spring blossom, and the spraying of entrances and hedge-bottoms kept away boisterous, bumbling dogs (which do so much damage among the smaller shrubs) at least until a heavy fall of snow, beneath which the dog-repellent smell apparently ceased to give offence.

It is especially important to repel bark-gnawers in the shrub garden, since branches and even whole trees may be killed by ring barking—that is, stripping the bark off completely round a trunk or limb at any point. Branches may be sprayed and trunks painted or sprayed with Curb to prevent bark-gnawing, but although it has been used successfully in commercial orchards, amateur gardeners will be limited to what they can reach with ordinary equipment— and the squirrels anyway can reach a lot higher than most of us. Whereas rabbits, hares and even deer may be kept out with a close-mesh fencing, and the lower parts of tree trunks protected from them with a collar of wire netting, only a very tall, prickly hedge, well furnished to the ground, will present much of an obstacle to the air-borne squirrel. Squirrels are said to move on elsewhere if their dreys are broken up, but these are not easy to find, or to reach, high up in the trees.

Before leaving the subject of Curb, which I have been mixing according to the hot water recipe for longer durability, I should mention that it had hitherto tended to clog the sprayer unless *very* thoroughly mixed; but the makers (Sphere Laboratories, see p. 250) assure me that this problem has now been overcome. In any case careful subsequent cleansing of the sprayer is important. The aerosol container in which Curb is also available of course avoids any such risk, but is not practical for large-scale application. Wear gloves for operating the aerosol.

Control of Sucking Insects

Insect damage is usually caused either by chewing or by sucking. From the shrub gardener's point of view clay-coloured and vine weevils, caterpillars and earwigs are examples of some of the most tiresome chewers; and of the suckers, aphids such as greenfly and blackfly, leaf-hoppers, leaf-rolling sawflies, scale insects, thrips, capsids and froghoppers (which produce cuckoo-spit) are among the worst.

While we may be prepared to put up with a certain amount of disfigurement to flowers or foliage it should be realized that most of the sucking pests will at the same time be causing more serious, if less easily detected damage in sapping the plant's vitality, and may also be a means of spreading disease as they pass from one host to another.

Treatment Generally speaking the sucking pests are most easily controlled by the modern systemic type of insecticide which is sprayed onto the plant or watered onto the soil beneath it, to be absorbed into its system, thus making the sap poisonous to such insects as feed on it. Although caterpillars are chewers rather than suckers they, too, usually succumb to systemic insecticides. A strong point in favour of this method is that because the liquid is taken up within the plant it cannot be washed away by rain and therefore needs less frequent application than the external types of insecticide (e.g. malathion, BHC), which kill on contact with their victims but do not prevent fresh infestation, nor are they rainproof. As a rough guide systemics may be expected to last three or four weeks and contact sprays about half as long, or less, depending on the weather and other factors.

Systemics specially formulated for roses (e.g. PBI's Toprose Systemic Spray) are said to provide one of the best means of defeating the rose leaf-rolling sawfly and the equally difficult customer, the tortrix caterpillar, which are not only particularly damaging and dis- figuring to the foliage, but are also especially difficult to exterminate once they have ensconced themselves in the rose leaflets within which they roll or wrap themselves so tightly that the foliage can no longer function properly. Inhabited leaflets may be picked off by hand if not too numerous, and starting to spray or dust with BHC or Sevin (carbaryl), or the new liquid substitutes for DDT, during May, or immediately the first sign of their presence is spotted, before the leaves are too much distorted for external sprays or dusts to reach their inner surfaces, may ward off serious attacks of either.

Although in the shrub garden roses seem to attract more of the sucking pests than any other shrub, and greenfly in particular, it is a mistake to suppose that the latter confine themselves to a diet of rose sap. One should keep a general look-out for aphids, both green and black, in the spring—greenfly being most commonly found also on the young shoots of camellias, evergreen magnolias, hydrangeas and honeysuckles and on the flower stems and buds of clematis; blackfly, which fortunately has comparatively few hosts in the shrub garden, mainly infests *Euonymus europaeus* (Spindle), certain viburnums (especially the Snowball Tree) and sometimes also cherries. Where just

Fig. 29. Rose foliage attacked by leaf-rolling sawfly

Fig. 30. Tortrix caterpillar damage

the odd few greenfly are spotted these may be fairly gently pinched to death *in situ*, between finger and thumb; and if only isolated shoots are more heavily infested quite dense colonies may be knocked off into the palm of one hand by holding the shoot over it and tapping it vigorously, the resulting handful being then exterminated by squeezing between both palms. While on the subject of greenfly, it is not always recognized that the tiny, fine, white threadlike mites often seen on likely hosts are in fact greenfly not yet hatched.

General purpose systemic insecticides should take care of more wholesale attacks by these aphids, whether green or black. For quick and easy application, particularly for small colonies of sucking insects as distinct from heavy infestation, against which the more tediously precise mixing of a spray in large quantities will not be wasteful, the Metasystox Aphid Gun is remarkably handy and accurate in its aim. For those who regard this product as dangerous, even when correctly used and despite the Ministry's approval, the dust form of malathion contact insecticide is one of the most effective for the same purpose. The Gard Pest Pistol (PBI) puffs out a general purpose insecticide dust with a fair accuracy of aim; and the other dust forms of more familiar products such as BHC and nicotine are still convenient for quick application to sucking insect pests, if dispensed from an efficient powder blower (see Fig. 36) rather than from the manufacturer's erratic puffer pack in which they are mostly sold. Refill packets for the latter are naturally cheaper than the puffer pack itself, so that the low cost of the Acme Blower is soon recouped (see Equipment, p. 129).

Control of Chewing Insects

Given a powder blower with an easy, reliable action, dusting is convenient in that it can be done at any time of day and needs no preparation. To me it is a much more congenial job than spraying, which requires such precise measuring and thorough mixing, followed by careful cleaning of the apparatus. When faced with a choice between wet or dry formulations I therefore tend to favour a dust from sheer laziness, though the white powdery coating may be somewhat unsightly and may soon be washed away in wet weather.

In my own shrub garden the clay-coloured and vine weevils rate among the most malicious of the biters, chiefly because of their ravages among certain rhododendron species which I greatly treasure for the splendour of their rusty-backed, silver-lined or glaucous foliage. I doubt whether they seriously undermine the constitution of strongly growing specimens, but they ruin their appearance by gnawing great jigsaw chunks out of the tender young leaves, mainly along the margins. Although they also attack other shrubs including roses and ornamental vines, to my eye the results are, at least aesthetically, less disastrous. (The treatment prescribed throughout the year for control of these weevils should also keep rhododendron bug and rhododendron white fly from damaging rhododendron leaves.)

In late summer earwigs are also troublesome, one of their nastiest habits being that of nipping out the petals at the heart of a flower, causing them to fall prematurely. Large-petalled blooms such as roses, romneya (Tree Poppy) and clematis (the latter is also nibbled into holes) seem to be their favourite victims.

Fig. 31. Weevil damage to rhododendron foliage

Treatment   One is advised that both earwigs and weevils in the adult stage may be trapped in rolls of sacking or paper laid beneath the plants overnight and emptied of the catch next morning, but hitherto I have found DDT dust the most effective and labour-saving form of control for both. Now that DDT is being withdrawn on health grounds the Murphy Chemical Co. have already introduced a substitute in the form of Sevin dust, which claims to destroy caterpillars, weevils, flea beetles, leather-jackets, woodlice and so on, and I would expect that it also takes care of earwigs. Still more recently the same firm have produced Fentro (fenitrothion), which appears to be the first of the promised replacements for liquid DDT. BHC is one of the existing controls for earwigs and for weevils. Either Sevin dust or BHC should be applied to the ground around rhododendrons periodically from midsummer to February or March to deal with weevil larvae which overwinter in the soil, and light dusting of the foliage (being careful not to let it clot thickly on the ornamental undersides of the leaves and so spoil the colour), from early spring to September, will cover the chewing period of the adult weevils. In the case of earwigs both the surrounding soil and the affected plants should be lightly dusted with BHC or treated with one of the new DDT substitutes. Earwigs are chiefly troublesome in late summer.

Caterpillars are various and ubiquitous, but on the whole they tend to keep out of sight (and out of reach) among the trees and, short of investing in the orchard type of spraying equipment, I am on the whole resigned to their presence, so long as it remains well overhead. Those not beyond the reach of a long-armed spray are mostly taken care of together with the other pests destroyed by systemic insecticides, despite the fact that they live by chewing rather than sucking. Those that attack precious foliage plants are sprayed with systemic insecticides.

Compatible Sprays

For some time past it has in fact been possible to achieve the same kind of double kill by making up one's own brew of 'compatible' insecticides and fungicides (i.e. chemicals which may be mixed together) for application in a single spraying operation, which has been particularly time-saving in the case of roses, for example. Thus black spot and mildew could, for instance, be controlled simultaneously with various rose pests, so long as one was careful to combine only such chemical substances as were declared compatible by the makers. To these a third element may now be added in the form of a foliar feed, which is dealt with in more detail in Section 9, under Feeding, p. 136 (see also Principal Diseases of Roses, pp. 127–28).

B. DISEASES

A catalogue of such diseases as may possibly attack ornamental trees and shrubs might look formidable enough to deter the prospective shrub gardener, but because most trees and shrubs are able to build up a natural resistance to infection when growing conditions are to their liking disease is not much of a problem in a reasonably well kept shrub garden. Sensible cultivation, including the control of strength-sapping pests, avoidance of extremes of drought or waterlogging, a respect for each plant's special fads, if any, the regular removal of dead or unsound wood and the painting of wounds with an antiseptic pruning compound such as Arbrex therefore combine to provide the best insurance against disease.

I think it is true of most of us that, the less our experience, the more we tend to imagine disease where none exists, so first let us dispose of one or two of the non-diseases which most often cause unnecessary concern.

Flowering Problems

As a rule there is nothing whatever the matter with a flowering tree or shrub which refuses to bloom for a number of years after planting. Indeed, it will almost certainly make stronger and faster growth when not consuming its youthful energies in premature flower and seed production. Some subjects are much slower to mature than others, certain magnolias, for example, taking as long as 20 years to flower for the first time. On the other hand, if a plant not by nature notoriously slow in this respect remains obstinately flowerless on reaching maturity (that is, after several years at least, the length of time varying from one kind of shrub to another), it may merely be wrongly sited or otherwise incommoded by its growing conditions. For instance, although partial shade is usually recommended for eucryphias and kalmias, for 10 years or more they failed to flower here until I tried them in full sunshine, with spectacular results. It seems that in a cold garden they need all the warmth they can get in order to ripen their flowering wood. Sometimes a plant may be jolted into action by a move, but having put up with a totally flowerless *Rhododendron yunnanense*, jolts and all, for 16 years here I feel this one is overdue for the bonfire, especially since the species is said to be very free-flowering by nature.

Plants which bear a fine flower crop one year and then almost none for several successive seasons may also cause anxiety. For this our British climate is usually to blame. *Cornus florida* is an example of those which must have a good, warm summer in which to ripen flowering wood for the following year. And in wet and sunless summers the late-flowering *Koelreuteria paniculata*, campsis, and the hardy hibiscus hybrids, among others, will drop perfectly good flower buds unopened. Then again, plants which originally received as much light as was necessary to encourage flowering may, in time, have become so much overshadowed by the increasing spread of trees or tall shrubs nearby as to inhibit flowering in such circumstances.

Physiological Discomforts

Even when obviously unhappy, a plant is not necessarily diseased. Unless disease symptoms are unmistakable, we should first look for some physiological cause of distress such as unsuitable soil or aspect, excessive dryness or moisture, or perhaps simply a draught funnelled through a hole in a hedge or fence. Distorted foliage, often thought to be infected, may be the result of drought or frosting in an early stage of growth, or of attack by some sap-sucking or leaf-rolling insect. Nor is there anything sinister about the disastrous-looking rolling of rhododendron leaves in frosty weather, this being merely a useful defence mechanism. Some browning of eucalyptus foliage in a hard winter is also fairly common and need cause no alarm. Trees and shrubs are commonly given up for dead if affected by an untimely leaf-drop, while others, whose leaves have unaccountably withered and yet refuse to fall, cause less concern; but it should be the other way about. The first may well be due to some physiological factor which may be quite easy to rectify, whereas there is usually something very seriously wrong when dead foliage remains clinging to the branches (except in the case of hedging beech).

SOME COMMON DISEASES OF ORNAMENTAL TREES AND SHRUBS AND THEIR TREATMENT

While it is only prudent to keep a sharp look-out for early signs of ill-health, amateur diagnosis may often be dangerously wide of the mark. So unless the symptoms are unmistakable it is safer to seek professional advice before taking remedial action. One of the many valuable services offered to Fellows of the Royal Horticultural Society is diagnosis and advice regarding treatment of ailing plants, samples of which should be sent to their Wisley laboratory in a dry plastic bag, accompanied by full pertinent details.

Not only am I prejudiced against inexpert diagnosis of plant ailments, but I also anticipate that currently available products for treatment of individual fungus diseases will largely be superseded quite soon by the systemic fungicides on which work is well under way (systemics for general garden use are at present available only as insecticides). I therefore propose to deal individually only with the recognition and treatment of such diseases as are either so easily identifiable, without any education in plant pathology, or so dangerous, or so generally troublesome as to warrant special mention. Of most included here I shall speak from personal experience and it should be encouraging to note that they are comparatively few. Among those outside this category honey fungus (*Armillaria mellea*) is capable of causing such sudden and widespread death among trees and shrubs that I feel compelled to mention it here, though I am not at all sure that it has caused me any losses in this area of high infection. And although I have had no fire blight, this also has a mention because of its disastrous consequences to commercial orchards if the disease is allowed to fester unchecked on an ornamental crab apple or some such in a nearby garden. Silver leaf is included for much the same reason.

Azalea Gall

This debilitating and unsightly disease confines its attacks to the dwarf evergreen, or semi-evergreen (sometimes called Japanese) azaleas, as distinct from the larger, deciduous types which are, happily, immune.

It reveals itself in obscene, fleshy swellings and distortions, mostly on the new foliage in spring, but occasionally also on the flowers. These grotesque growths are usually of an even paler green than that of the young leaves, though sometimes tinged with red or pink, all at a later stage developing a powdery white coating of fungus spores which spread the infection. Bad attacks weaken the plants, inhibit flowering, spread rapidly if left unchecked and will ultimately kill.

Fig. 32. Azalea gall (a bad case)
a Leaf swelling
b Swellings at base of new shoots
c Swelling on calyx
d Swellings on corolla
(dotted areas indicate swellings)

Treatment   In gardens subject to previous attacks it is undoubtedly sound policy to prevent a recurrence if possible, rather than to try to cure an established outbreak. In this garden, which has been badly affected in the past, I have found spraying with Dithane (zineb-based, PBI) to give the best protection. It should be applied as a preventive measure immediately before the vulnerable new foliage is due to sprout in spring. If this treatment should fail, or is neglected, further periodic spraying of infected plants as soon as any swellings are detected should keep a check on the disease. It is in any case important to look these dwarf azaleas over frequently for signs of the gall and to pick off and burn the bloated growths before they reach the white-coated stage, at which time the disease begins to produce spores to infect fresh shoots and leaves. Even though only one leaf in the cluster on a young shoot appears to be affected, the whole of that new shoot should be nipped out, when picking off diseased parts by hand, since the remaining leaves and stem will almost certainly develop the symptoms in their turn. Indeed, the swellings often begin, almost imperceptibly, at the base of new shoots, before the leaves themselves are affected. Some varieties of evergreen azalea seem much more susceptible than others (or so I find in my garden, where the comparatively large-flowered *kaempferi* x *malvatica* hybrids are among the worst affected). The trouble is likely to be most concentrated where the back branches are crowded beneath neighbouring shrubs and thus deprived of light and air—one of the penalties, no doubt, of exaggerating close-boscage practice.

Bud Blast

Only rhododendrons suffer from bud blast (azaleas, which are also, strictly speaking, rhododendrons, being excluded in this instance) and in my experience the hardier hybrids are most liable to infection.

Next year's flower buds begin to turn brown or grey-brown in autumn and by midwinter have enveloped themselves in a hairy, black fungus growth, each tiny bristle ending in a pinhead tip. Affected buds fail to open, as do those killed by frost, but the latter are easily distinguishable in that they are brown and brittle, and devoid of the hairy fungus.

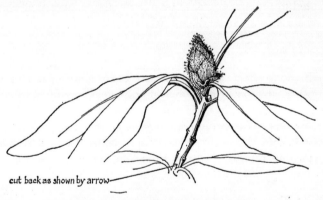

cut back as shown by arrow

Fig. 33. Bud blast of rhododendrons

Treatment There is as yet no cure for bud blast, but the spread of infection may be arrested by removing diseased buds, together with a short length of stem, and burning them. The trouble may be indirectly controlled by waging war on adult leafhoppers, which are thought to provide a means of entry for the fungus spores through tiny slits made in the bud scales for egg-laying purposes. It may, therefore, be thought worthwhile to spray or dust specially treasured specimens with BHC, Sevin, Fentro or other substitutes for DDT during the egg-laying month of July, when these insects are busiest.

Chlorosis

This most often stems from physiological causes, the commonest being some form of mineral deficiency, as suffered by plants unable to assimilate iron when grown in limy soils. Although calcifuge subjects are worst affected by such growing conditions, chlorosis may occur in a large variety of shrubs, such as roses, hydrangeas and others, the leaf colour becoming abnormally pale green or sickly yellow, the latter often being especially pronounced between the veins.

Treatment For lime-haters growing in alkaline (and possibly neutral) soils spray the ground or water the plants (or do both) with Murphy Sequestrene, in late winter or early spring for preference. An annual application is usually, but not always, necessary. There is no difficulty whatever about testing soil for acidity or alkalinity (see Soils pp. 37–44), but if the symptoms of chlorosis cannot be attributed to liminess it would be safer to seek expert advice rather than to attempt amateur diagnosis and treatment.

Clematis Wilt

Though said to affect clematis of 2 years old and upwards, in my case this most troublesome disease has almost always confined its attacks to very young plants, in their first or second season. Leaves begin to sag and wither in early summer, creating an appearance of the direst distress. Whole shoots, or even whole plants, droop and collapse with startling rapidity, wilting from the tips of the shoots backwards.

Treatment The cause seems to baffle the experts, as does a specific remedy, though some of the specialists believe that the use of captan helps to control it. Each of the professional growers has his own theories about prevention, which are aired in their catalogues (see clematis specialists in the Nuserymen's List in Appendix Two). Once the symptoms appear, the wilting shoot must in any case be cut right back to its base or, if the whole plant is infected, all must be razed to the ground. Thereafter the remaining growth or, at worst, the apparently vacant site, must be repeatedly and copiously watered throughout the growing season whenever the soil might otherwise become dry. I can personally testify that scrupulous attention to this seemingly fruitless task often results in the emergence of new shoots at ground level. Protection from slugs, rabbits, dogs and other marauders is particularly important at this stage, for if this brave bid for regeneration is frustrated the plant will almost certainly curl up its toes for all time and refuse to try again.

It is perhaps worth mentioning that deaths sometimes blamed on clematis wilt are in fact due to undetected damage to the very fragile stem of a young plant. The portion near ground level therefore needs to be carefully tied in several places to a firm cane or other support before surrounding all in a collar of wire netting at the base, until such time as the maturing trunk is strong enough to withstand kinking or breakage.

Fire Blight

In the shrub garden ornamental crab apples (*Malus*), pears (*Pyrus*), hawthorns (*Crataegus*), japonica (*Chaenomeles*), firethorn (*Pyracantha*), whitebeam, rowan etc. (*Sorbus*), and *Stranvaesia davidiana* are among the chief victims and, therefore, spreaders of this disease. Ordinary pears, particularly the cultivar 'Laxton's Superb', and apples are also commonly attacked.

First symptoms are blackening flowers and leaves and sodden, oozing patches of slime on the branches just beneath the bark in spring, the bark taking on an unhealthy, grey-black hue. As the moist stage dries up later in the season the leaves turn brown, as though scorched by fire.

Treatment There is not yet a cure for fire blight, which is of such serious significance to commercial fruit growers that one is legally bound to report known or suspected infection on one's property to the Ministry of Agriculture. If suspect symptoms appear, it would be advisable to write at once for the free leaflet on the subject issued by the Publications Branch of the Ministry of Agriculture, Fisheries and Food, Government Buildings, Tolcarne Drive, Pinner, Middlesex. Now that the law no longer requires that all infected trees must be grubbed out and burned, the cutting out of infected parts under official supervision is often permitted in the less serious cases. Tools used for the job should afterwards be sterilized.

Honey Fungus

One of the swiftest of killers, attacking a wide assortment of plants, from trees and shrubs to bulbs and vegetables, is the disease variously known as bootlace fungus, collar rot fungus, honey fungus and shoe-string fungus. The Latin name *Armillaria mellea* is used no less freely than any of the nicknames. Bootlace and honey are the most familiar of the latter, the one describing the stringy black parasitic growths (rhizomorphs) which creep underground from their host in dead tree stumps and other decayed wood to attack the roots of living plants, and the other relating to the usual colour of the rather conical-capped toadstools which often appear above ground in the region of the rotting wood or from unseen rhizomorphs. The 'bootlaces' can travel many feet from plant to plant, causing rapid and apparently unaccountable devastation when they attack the roots.

Treatment The presence of this disease sometimes does no damage but, more typically, offers such a serious threat to so many different kinds of vegetation that the Plant Pathology Department of the Royal Horticultural Society recently staged an educative, if spine-chilling exhibit at the Chelsea Flower Show (May 1970), demonstrating all stages of the disease and its effects. A leaflet available from the Society at the same time describes in full the symptoms and habits of *Armillaria mellea*, lists plants thought to be the most resistant to attack, together with a list of those most highly susceptible, and details 12 different precautions or remedial measures. The leaflet is free to Fellows, and the information too lengthy to be summarized here. It may, however, be encouraging to repeat, as is stressed in the leaflet, that well cultivated plants in good health are more resistant to this as to other forms of disease, and that the less rotting wood there is available for the fungus to live on, the less opportunity it has to flourish. As always, dead plants should be dug up and burned—and, here again, Fellows are advised to send specimens of diseased plants to the Wisley laboratory if uncertain as to the cause of death.

A more optimistic side to the picture is supplied by Mrs Victoria Bray, author of *Ensnared with Flowers*, in which she describes how, some years ago, she set about working out her own salvation on most unusual lines in her Surrey garden, which had suffered heavy losses from honey fungus disease. In an attempt to sterilize some badly infected trees she applied refined creosote, neat, to the base of the trunks, the upper roots and the surrounding soil, and was later

amazed to find the hitherto moribund trees putting out fine new
growth which, she says, has remained healthy ever since. The
success of such unorthodox measures has recently aroused much
interest in horticultural circles, but because the chemical constitution
of ordinary creosote varies so widely it has been thought necessary
to standardize a non-variable creosote-based preparation for use in
the control of *A. mellea*. This product which, she tells me, has the
blessing of the Royal Horticultural Society and is in use in Kew
Botanic Garden, has now become available under the name of
Armillatox (see Appendix Three).

I wonder if Mrs Bray has heard of the gardener who, recently sus-
pecting silver leaf on a plum tree, removed branch after branch as the
infection spread, until only the stump and an odd stem or two
remained. Having plastered the stump with creosote to prevent the
disease spreading he waited until spring to remove it. By this time one
bright green shoot was springing from the base, soon to be followed
by more from the centre of the stump. The owner now reports
'groups of thick long branches coming from all over it'—and not a
sign of silver leaf. From his account it was clearly evident that he
knew nothing of Mrs Bray's experiments with creosote in relation to
honey fungus.

Hydrangea Botrytis

This seems most likely to attack plants growing in light, hungry soils,
particularly in dry conditions and also, possibly, if the roots were
cramped during the planting process. The first symptoms are a few
unsightly brown blotches on the flowers, which spread rapidly so
that whole sections of the flower heads or entire blooms wither, the
relevant portions of the flower stems becoming extraordinarily
tough and wiry. A number of the leaves also develop soggy brown
patches, and a grey mould may appear on the surface of the patches.

Treatment If poor root action is suspected, the application of
foliar feeds at about fortnightly intervals from spring, when the first
leaves appear, to midsummer if necessary, may help to forestall
attacks which may otherwise develop later in the season. At the
first signs of blotching the diseased florets should be picked off, or
larger areas of infection cut away, and the plants sprayed with a
captan, thiram or zineb fungicide, though the latter is said to leave
a fairly thick deposit on the blooms.

Leaf-curl

The fungus causing leaf-curl is to be found in the shrub garden mainly on various *Prunus* species such as ornamental cherries, almonds and peaches. As mentioned earlier, infestation by sap-sucking insects may cause many kinds of leaves to roll, curl or become similarly distorted, but the symptoms are in this case readily distinguishable in the change of colour in the diseased foliage, which first turns yellow, then pinkish or red, and at the same time becomes conspicuously puckered, blistered or swollen. If the trouble is allowed to recur from one season to another, whole trees may in time succumb to it and die. Less severe infection causes die-back of shoots and branches.

Fig. 34. Leaf-curl

Treatment Arrest the spread of the fungus in the early stages by picking off diseased leaves or, if beyond hand-picking, cutting out and burning all infected growth, painting the cuts with Arbrex or some other wound-sealing fungicidal preparation. Further attacks may be forestalled by spraying with Bordeaux Mixture or lime-sulphur just before the buds are due to open, in late winter or early spring and again in autumn just as the leaves start to fall, and immediately leaf-fall is completed.

Peony Wilt or Blight

Unfortunately the shrubby tree peonies are no less susceptible to peony wilt than are the herbaceous kinds, and in this garden, where

frequent late spring frosts and the naturally acid, sandy soil conditions seem to suit tree peonies least of all my shrubs, they evidently
lack the stamina necessary to ward off infection, which is most
prevalent in spring and early summer, unless precautionary measures
are taken. One of the most tantalizing features of the disease is that
not only the new, leafy side-shoots but also young flower buds
suddenly turn limp and hang their lifeless heads, often just in time
to deny us the superlative beauty of the promised bloom. At the
same time the pinkish tinge of embryonic growth buds turns brown
and lifeless on the lower, woody parts of diseased stems, which may
develop a coating of grey mould. Brown patches may also later dis-
figure the more mature foliage.

Fig. 35. Tree peony infected by peony wilt

A First cut back to A, which may be a healthy bud, but if wood
B shows a brown, diseased core cut right back to B at base of shoot.
C Cross-section of diseased wood, showing browned pith.

Treatment For tree peonies fungicide sprays based on zineb (e.g.
Dithane, as recommended for azalea gall), thiram or captan are
considered by the Royal Horticultural Society's plant pathologists
to be more effective than dusts in protecting plants liable to attack,
applied at the first signs of leaf growth in early spring and repeating
fortnightly until they come into flower. Further spraying after
flowering in mild, damp seasons may be necessary to keep the foliage
in a healthy condition.

If, despite these precautions, symptoms of peony wilt should appear, surgical action should be taken without delay. Drooping shoots must be cut right out to the base, also any woody parts found to contain a discoloured brown core in place of healthy cream-coloured pith, and the painting of even small cut surfaces with Arbrex is, I think, advisable wherever the disease is prevalent. In similar circumstances picking off foliage showing brown patches and collecting and burning all tree peony leaves as soon as they begin to fall should also help prevent disease spores overwintering in the garden.

Powdery Mildew

Attacks are seen during the summer on roses, clematis and various other ornamental trees, shrubs and climbing plants, as a superficial, whitish powder coating on leaves, stems, buds and young shoots. In small doses it is not very harmful, but bad attacks cause deformities and stunting and are generally debilitating. Still, humid air en courages the growth of the fungus, especially when the soil is dry, so that it often proves particularly troublesome on certain climbers and other plants grown against walls and solid fences, where the ventilation space between these and the plant may be inadequate. Beds at the foot of house walls, though providing most valuable shelter and support for all manner of semi-tender subjects in particu-lar, are notoriously dry as a rule because overhanging eaves or the direction of the wind tend to prevent the rain from reaching them.

Treatment Once established, it is difficult to cure, so although it is most prevalent in late summer, preventive action should be taken early in the growing season, as it sometimes appears as early as May or June. Fortunately, periodical applications of special rose fungi-cides containing copper, dinocap, folpet, captan and so on will simultaneously take care of black spot and powdery mildew on roses. Boots or Murphy's Rose Fungicide, Gard (PBI) and General Garden Fungicide (ICI) are among those which claim to control the trouble together with certain other forms of disease. In other circum-stances Karathane (dinocap) in dust or spray form is an effective mildew specific, for application at intervals from late spring to autumn. In mild, damp spells weekly dusting with Karathane in between the fortnightly spraying of roses with other fungicides may prove necessary for really effective control.

Roses, Principal Diseases

The commonest of these are black spot, mildew and rust.

Black Spot We are all, alas, familiar with the circular, blackish, fringed spots which quickly spread over almost the entire surface of a leaflet and sometimes also affect the stems, resulting in yellowing and premature leafdrop, and seriously weakening the plant. The lowest leaves are often the first to succumb to the spores which over-winter in the soil on old leaves and stem debris, and are splashed over the foliage by rain, spreading thence upwards throughout the plant. The disease is more prevalent in the clean air of country districts than in towns and industrial areas, where sulphur is present in the atmosphere. Among a number of roses which are, happily, immune to black spot are the Polyantha Pompon types and some of the tall, shrubby species and their garden forms and hybrids e.g. *Rosa* x *cantabrigiensis, R. moyesii, R. rubrifolia, R. rugosa.*

Mildew See Powdery Mildew, p. 126. Most Polyantha Pompon cultivars are especially susceptible.

Rust This disease tends to occur in late summer, but may appear from the end of May onwards. The most characteristic symptom is the appearance of dark, orange-brown, raised spots on the under-surface of the leaves. These later become powdery and turn black, so that there may be both orange and black spots present at the same time. The stems are also occasionally affected in the same way. The spores produced from the black spots can overwinter on fallen leaves, and it is these which give rise to a fresh infection in the following season.

Treatment of the Above-mentioned Diseases of Roses

Black Spot and Powdery Mildew Boots and Murphy's Rose Fungicides make reliable claims to defeat two of the three diseases under discussion, since each contains recognized black spot and powdery mildew specifics—and the Murphy Chemical Co. spray does more besides.

Much time and trouble may be saved by mixing compatible insecticide and fungicide sprays together in a single operation, and

those that will also combine with a foliar feed are even more welcome. To take Murphy's products as an instance, not only is their
Rose Fungicide compatible (i.e. mixable) with their own brand of
systemic insecticide, but also with their immensely effective foliar
feed sold as Murphy's 'FF', which is absorbed through the leaves
into the plant's system. In my view this company deserves con-
gratulation upon one special form of advertisement apparently
designed to clarify customers' difficulties rather than to coax their
money from them. Their clearly tabulated and annually revised
Pests and Diseases Chart advises what to use and when, and what
for, and includes a most helpful mini-chart showing which of their
products are compatible and the few which must not be mixed–all,
to me, a deal more persuasive than any amount of superlative-laden
sales-talk.

Rust Specific controls for this disease are thiram, maneb or zineb.
Among those manufacturers who have received the Ministry's
approval for all three of their sprays based on these chemicals are
Bugges, their maneb and their zineb (the latter selling under the
name of Dyblite Wettable Powder) being effective against black
spot as well as rust.

The disease is not very troublesome in this garden where, if
necessary, I use zineb (PBI's Dithane) of which I need to keep a
stock on hand for the treatment of persistent azalea gall (which it
does with more success than other remedies I have tried).

Certain of PBI's Toprose range, again including a foliar feed, may
similarly be combined to demolish most rose pests, together with
black spot, rust and mildew. And no doubt other reputable manufacturers do a similar job equally well; but few that I have come
across give sufficient information in their style of advertising to guide
the ignorant amateur's choice in their direction.

When fungicides are only required in small quantities it is useful
to keep a powder blower of the bellows kind charged with captan in
dust form for isolated attacks of black spot and another with
Karathane (dinocap) dust for mildew.

So much for the prevention and cure of rose diseases during the
growing season. Winter hygiene includes ridding the ground of
latent disease spores by collecting and burning the fallen rose foliage
and stems and afterwards watering the soil with Jeyes Fluid or, if you
prefer, Bordeaux Mixture in late winter, to destroy spores of black
spot and rust. Prunings should also be collected and burned.

Silver Leaf

The most usual victims are eucalyptus, laburnum, various *Prunus* species including Portugal Laurel, rhododendrons, and poplar (also edible fruits such as apples and plums). Except in the case of rhododendrons, affected leaves take on a silvery sheen and, if cut into, the wood shows dark internal staining. Finally, typical purplish bracket fungus growths appear on the dead wood, turning brown as they desiccate. Either the entire plant or parts of it are killed as the disease progresses.

Treatment Until fairly recently one was obliged by law to cut out and burn infected wood on apples and plums before mid-July, and although the law has now been relaxed it is obviously unwise to neglect this disease in the shrub garden. Since the fungus makes its way into the plant tissue through wounds in the bark the painting of cuts with some fungicidal substance is important. (The last paragraph under Honey Fungus (p. 123) may be of equal interest or curiosity value in the present context.)

Sooty Moulds

Quite a number of ornamental trees and shrubs are liable to disfigurement by deposits of sooty moulds.

The sticky honeydew excreted by aphids, scale insects, rhododendron leafhoppers, rhododendron white fly and other sucking insects invites the growth of an unsightly black film on foliage deriving from sooty mould fungus. The trouble is more uglifying than dangerous, but the black deposit does deprive the plant of light, and prevents the stomata (breathing pores) of the leaves from transpiring water vapour.

Treatment Nothing can be done except to exterminate the insect sources of the honeydew, and to sponge or spray all badly affected leaves forcefully. The culprits are mainly sucking insect pests, and can be dealt with by the remedies recommended for this type of pest on pp. 110–13.

Equipment for the Application of Horticultural Chemicals

Sprayers There are already so many different modern types of spraying apparatus on the market, with new ones constantly being added, from large and expensive back-pack equipment to finger-operated, pint-sized models, that choice must largely depend on the amount of spraying to be done and on what one can afford. For the average garden I find that the compressed air sprayer of about 8-pint capacity, equipped with a long-armed nozzle, combines a minimum of effort with high efficiency. No kind of sprayer will, however, operate satisfactorily unless the contents are very thoroughly dissolved and the apparatus carefully cleaned each time after use, according to the maker's instructions.

Powder Applicators   There is no such freedom of choice among horticultural dust dispensers. Popular though it may be, I find the maker's 'puffer pack' in which dusts are mainly sold infuriatingly inefficient, either puffing to excess in fits and starts or not at all. (The DDT puffer pack produced by PBI is an outstanding exception, and although DDT is banned for use by the private gardener any other puffer pack which may be marketed by the same company will no doubt operate equally smoothly.)

There is, however, one form of all-purpose dust dispenser which is exceptionally efficient. This is the inexpensive Acme Powder Blower (available from the Acme Chemical Co., 2 Lindsey Street, London, E.C.1), intended for use with all kinds of horticultural dusts, which are distributed in fine clouds by means of a bellows action operated by a waggle of the wrist. (To work efficiently the cylinder

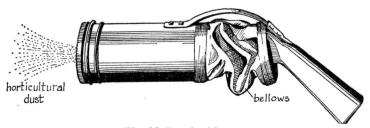

horticultural
dust   bellows

Fig. 36. Powder blower

must not be more than half-filled.) The small initial cost of the blower is soon recouped by the saving on the cheaper packets of dust intended as refills for the other type of puffer pack. I find it convenient to keep several Acme Blowers on hand for use with different dusts, attaching temporary labels to each to remind me as to their contents.

SUMMARY OF TREATMENTS FOR MAIN PESTS AND
DISEASES
(For the correct time of year for application of the remedies, see the
Working-calendar)

PESTS

Birds, most kinds of chewing animals, dogs and cats: Curb.

Moles: traps, smokes or fuses. Alternatively ask for
                    action by the Local Authority.
Slugs: Draza or Slug Gard.
Sucking Insects: systemic insecticides, malathion or BHC.
Chewing Insects: BHC or recent substitutes for DDT (e.g. Sevin,
                    Fentro).

PESTS AND DISEASES

Compatible insecticides and fungicides. Check on what these
products do or do not control.

DISEASES

Azalea gall: zineb (Dithane, PBI, or Bugges's Dyblite Wet-
                    table Powder).
Bud blast: insect-induced; malathion, BHC, or DDT sub-
                    stitutes.
Chlorosis: Murphy Sequestrene if caused by presence of
                    lime in the soil; if not, seek professional advice.
Clematis wilt: remove diseased parts to their base; apply
                    captan; water copiously; protect stem base
                    when young.
Fire blight: no cure. Remove diseased parts or grub out
                    altogether if necessary. Paint wounds with
                    Arbrex.
Honey fungus: Armillatox.
Hydrangea botrytis: captan, thiram or zineb. Foliar feeding may
                    also help.
Leaf-curl: Bordeaux Mixture or lime-sulphur, also hand-
                    picking of infected leaves and removal of
                    affected growth.

Peony wilt:	zineb, thiram or captan in spray form, and cut out diseased wood if necessary.
Powdery mildew:	Karathane (dinocap) or certain Rose Fungicides.

Some Rose diseases:

Black spot and mildew:	Murphy's or Boots Rose Fungicide.
Black spot only:	captan.
Mildew only:	see Powdery mildew, above
Rust:	thiram, maneb or zineb.
Silver leaf:	remove infected growth at once and paint wounds with Arbrex.
Sooty moulds:	insect-induced; systemic insecticides, or spray forcefully or sponge badly affected leaves.

If some find this chemical-ridden section somewhat formidable, I beg them to lose no sleep over it. Generally speaking, the treatment of insect pests poses no very difficult chemical conundrums. And as for the diseases, when in trouble remember that so long as you have joined the Royal Horticultural Society you are entitled to consult the experts at the Wisley laboratory, sending diseased specimens there for diagnosis and advice as to treatment.

No doubt it is heresy to admit that, despite all this pious clinical talk I myself too rarely practise my own precepts, and yet the garden remains prosperous and pleasurable to look at. I have already mentioned that the majority of diseases are not usually rife in the shrub garden, so long as some effort is made to grow suitable subjects in reasonably suitable conditions and to care for them adequately in certain other respects. My own most persistent troubles come from tree peonies and Floribunda and other roses of this kind, both of which are ill at ease in my soil and climate, and from azalea gall, which has gained a hold through sheer neglect earlier on. So far as my own experience goes, therefore, I was none too well equipped to handle the section on diseases and their remedies—indeed I have only been able to attempt it with the help of much valuable expert criticism and advice supplied by my publishers.

Only the perfectionists will aim to leave nothing undone. And while they lie awake fretting over their omissions the rest of us might as well turn over and go back to sleep on the resolve to attend to first things first, then fitting in just as much more as time permits.

Watering

The nourishment required by trees and shrubs is assimilated from the soil by fine, somewhat hair-like feeding roots, which pass it up to other parts of the plant in soluble form through a network of arteries and veins. Even in a poor soil a shrubby plant will absorb enough food, at least for subsistence, so long as adequate moisture is present to convert it into liquid form. Too much moisture is as bad as too little, since the feeding roots will drown for lack of aeration in water-logged conditions; if the earth is parched, no matter how much rich nourishment may be stored away in it, trees and shrubs growing in it will before long starve to death unless artificially watered. In other words, watering is a good deal more important than feeding, when circumstances require it.

It is not possible to be very precise in defining such 'circumstances'. Ten days without rain is sometimes said to constitute a drought, but in well mulched borders the majority of trees and shrubs will manage for a great deal longer than this without watering, the length of time depending upon such factors as the nature of the plant, structure of the soil, and amount of humidity in the atmosphere. Arid conditions which would be anathema to hydrangeas, for instance, are actually enjoyed by silver-leaved subjects, and by cistus (Rock Rose), helianthemums (Sun Rose), halimiums, brooms, genistas, rosemary and other natives of sun-baked Mediterranean slopes; light sand and chalk drain much more rapidly than heavy loams and clay; persistent hill fog or sea mist may help thirsty plants through rainless periods; tender new growth and recently planted evergreens, in particular, are at risk from the kind of drought created by the searing winds of spring and early summer; overhanging eaves or other impedimenta may deprive plants at the foot of house walls of their share of rain-water, even when the rest of the garden needs no watering. The latter fact is particularly well demonstrated in house beds mulched with peat, which will be light in colour and bone dry, even after rain, within 1 ft. or more of the walls, when the much darker colour of the rest shows it to be thoroughly well moistened. One can only play this by eye, but the eye soon learns to pick up the distress signals. Above all one should ensure that newly planted trees and shrubs never go short of water during their first growing season—and the next, if this is not asking too much.

It is however a mistake to water unless the need is real, because once one starts there must be no letting up until adequate rainfall restores the balance. If watering is necessary, two gallons per medium-sized shrub at any one time should be the absolute minimum. A thorough soaking at longer intervals does much more good than watering little and often, allowing the water to percolate deep down where it is wanted, whereas a piddling daily sprinkling will only attract the feeding roots towards the surface in search of moisture, with increased risk of parching. On steeply sloping sites a heavy downpour rarely results in the good soaking one might expect. Though the heavens may have opened, near-drought conditions may still persist as the water courses down the hillside, barely wetting the topsoil, instead of gradually seeping into the parched earth as in spells of gentler and more beneficent rainfall.

Gentleness is no less necessary when watering by hand, and the flow will certainly not be gentle if poured from a height or sloshed on from a bucket. Much less care is, however, required when watering on to leaf-mulched surfaces, beneath which the soil will remain undisturbed, even though roughly deluged from a bucket or can. The water should be aimed over the root area and should not in any case be applied overhead in bright sunshine unless one is prepared to carry on until sundown, because once the watering stops the heat of the sun on the droplets scorches the foliage—or so they say.

For calcifuge subjects it is an advantage to store as much rain-water as possible, because even in acid-soiled areas the mains water supply is likely to be hard (i.e. limy), but when supplies of rain-water give out I believe in using tap water for lime-haters along with the rest, rather than letting them go thirsty. In my experience, those in the open ground show no signs of resentment, whereas one of my camellias in the narrower confines of a garden vase appears rather less tolerant of the limy mains supply. Rain-water stored in butts or tanks in the open has the further advantage that it takes its temperature from the atmosphere, in contrast to the shock of cold tap water. Do not forget to lag stand-pipes against freezing, and empty water butts made from wooden barrels or metal drums, which are liable to be burst by expanding ice in severe winter weather.

When dependent on the mains supply for extensive watering, a flattened plastic hosepipe, perforated on one side only (and available, I believe, in different lengths) is a godsend. With the perforated surface placed uppermost it rains a fine spray fanning upwards and outwards in a wide strip along its length or, if the holed side faces downwards, a gentle trickle of water at ground level seeps into the surrounding soil. The latter action is especially valuable in periods of prolonged drought, since it can safely be used during the daytime, even in strong sunshine, to give large areas a soaking sufficient to last for several weeks.

Among trees and shrubs which resent arid conditions are:

Acer (Japanese Maple types)
Actinidia kolomikta
Aesculus splendens
Camellia
Campsis (Trumpet Vine)
Carpenteria
Clematis
Cornus kousa
Davidia (Pocket-handkerchief Tree)
Desfontainia
Embothrium (Chilean Fire Bush)
Eucalyptus, in early years
Eucryphia
Feijoa
Fuchsia
Hydrangea
Kalmia
Lithospermum *diffusum* vars.
Magnolia
Metasequoia (Dawn Redwood)
Nandina
Paeonia, tree species and hybrids
Pieris
Raphiolepis
Rhododendron (including Azalea)
Sambucus (Elder)
Stewartia
Styrax (Snowbell)
Taxodium
Vaccinium
Viburnum
Vitis (ornamental grape vine)
Wisteria
Most foliage plants with cream or white variegation

The efficacy of watering against late spring frost damage is less generally appreciated than that of high summer water requirements, but this is one of the most important uses to which the sprinkler hose may be put. This form of emergency frost protection is dealt with in detail under that heading (see pp. 153–54), for fear the instructions might be overlooked at a time when they are most urgently applicable.

Feeding

Fertilizers no doubt rank high in importance in kitchen gardens and herbaceous borders but are, or should be, of much less general concern to the shrub gardener. People are often surprised to find that even on my naturally thin, pale mauve sand I rarely use any except in the first instance, at planting time, and even then do little or nothing to improve the soil for ascetics such as the silver-leaved subjects and other natives of the arid *maquis* country, which thrive on a minimum of food and drink, abhorring manure and revelling in fast-draining, sun-baked near-desert.

The fact is that, given a good send-off, most trees and shrubs do not require a rich diet. Indeed, many flowering subjects in particular make a better show on fairly spartan fare, because feeding tends to encourage luxuriant leafage rather than freedom of flower. Over-rich soil conditions will also make for lush, sappy growth which, except in the case of bone-hardy subjects, will be very vulnerable to winter damage and to a more rapid spread of fungus diseases. What may start as abnormally poor, 'hungry' soil will gradually build up a top layer of fine leaf soil if kept regularly mulched with fallen leaves, and this provides quite as much nourishment as is good for most trees and shrubs, except for the greediest feeders. Where there is no such build-up of leaf soil the older trees and shrubs in particular will benefit from some form of annual feeding.

Manures and Organic Fertilizers

These differ from inorganic (that is, artificial or chemical) fertilizers in that they are of animal or vegetable origin, deriving from such natural sources as animal excrement, seaweed, and decayed garden waste. When available, such natural products are much to be preferred to artificial fertilizers in the shrub garden because of their more lasting benefits as improvers of the soil. With such a wide variety (both organic and inorganic) to choose from, I propose to discuss only those of which I have personal experience or which are likely to be of most value to the shrub gardener.

Bonemeal Though one of the most widely used of plant tonics, bonemeal (15–32% phosphoric acid) is regarded with suspicion by some shrub gardeners, for fear that its calcium content should be unpalatable to lime-haters. I doubt, however, whether the risk to calcifuge subjects growing in a suitably acid soil need be taken seriously in the case of such a slow-acting fertilizer. As often as not, bonemeal and hoof and horn are regarded as interchangeable, with nothing other than the lime content, or lack of it, to distinguish the one from the other. There is, however, a far more important difference, in that each contains quite different nutrients, with correspondingly different results in terms of plant growth. Bonemeal is mainly beneficial to the roots, on account of its highly phosphoric content, whereas hoof and horn, which consists almost entirely of nitrogen, is most useful in promoting the growth of shoots and leaves. Obviously, therefore, the one cannot be regarded as a substitute for the other. Bonemeal is especially useful at planting time—that is, generally speaking, in late autumn and winter, when dormant trees and shrubs are most likely to absorb phosphorus into the root system, which is the only part of the plant likely to be active at this season.

Since it is possible to contract salmonella infection from untreated bonemeal it should be bought in the safe sterilized form in which it is usually now sold.

Bracken Bracken country provides a free store of valuable plant foods and of potash in particular, not only in the half-opened green fronds, but also in the fleshy black roots (or rhizomes) to which the plant foods are passed down by the summer foliage for storage throughout the winter. I imagine that trees and shrubs get better value from the succulent winter rhizomes when these are crushed to release the nutritious white juices, before applying as a mulch, but when starting on the transformation of virgin ground, densely overgrown with bracken, brambles and tough grass tussocks, into the proposed garden, I could spare no time for refinements of this sort, so my winter bracken roots were applied straight on to the soil, where they dried out on the spot without attempting to root or to sprout afresh. Both young fronds and mature rhizomes serve as a tonic for the sickly, and ginger up reluctant growth when used for individual mulching purposes.

Dried Blood   Dried blood (12% nitrogen) is a fast-acting, powerful stimulant for use in spring or early summer, to be carefully mixed into the surface of the soil, without disturbance to the roots, at the rate of 2 oz. per sq. yd. It provides a valuable source of nitrogen for limy soils in particular.

Farmyard Manure   Where something really meaty is required, as on the most miserably infertile soils, I would put farmyard manure (cow, horse or pig) at the top of the list, for those who can get it (and can pay for this increasingly rare and expensive commodity). On such exceptionally light, thin soils most trees and shrubs except those referred to in the first paragraph will appreciate a forkful or two of well rotted manure buried out of the immediate reach of the roots at planting time, finishing off with a surface mulch of it. But the richer the soil by nature the less even such an initial boost will be necessary. Pig and cow dung are said to be best for light soils and horse dung for heavy ones, though I have not been aware of any marked difference in results in this garden, where I have occasionally had to accept horse instead of cow. Farmyard manure is usually fairly fresh on arrival and should be stored beneath a waterproof cover, if possible, until well rotted.

Poultry droppings also have their uses, but are particularly liable to cause damage in a fresh state and are therefore more safely incorporated in the compost heap.

Fish Manure   The interment of fish corpses in the garden is less handy than applying fish manure, but both are highly nitrogenous. The dried product is an effective and quick-acting nutrient containing balancing additives. For the application of a fertilizer with such rapid action it is advisable to follow the instructions supplied with proprietary brands, unless one is thoroughly versed in its use. Spring application is most beneficial, and it should not be used after July, because the late growth promoted by its rapid effects will not be frost-resistant.

Garden Compost   Home-made compost is the most economical form of organic manure, and is especially valuable for mixing with soils of poor quality at planting time, as well as for topdressing (when sufficiently well made). If it is to be buried it should have rotted to a crumbly, dark consistency in which its components are no longer identifiable. For surface application it must be free of weeds and viable weed seeds, which requires more attention to the task of correct compost-making than it commonly receives (see Compost Heaps pp. 160–65).

Hoof and Horn   Some attempt has already been made to establish the important differences between bonemeal and hoof and horn, in order to disprove the widespread fallacy that the one is a substitute for the other. Both are slow-acting organic foods, but whereas the one consists mainly of phosphorus, the other–hoof and horn–is almost entirely nitrogenous; that is to say, it benefits growth of woody plants above ground, as a stimulant to shoots and leaves in spring and early summer, whereas bonemeal is an underground winter worker used to encourage root development. Hoof and horn bears some affinity to dried blood, in that both are nitrogenous tonics for young growth, but the former is far more gentle and slower to take effect. Its use is limited to the early part of the season, when new top growth of trees and shrubs is being formed, serving little purpose during late autumn and winter after leaf-fall, and during winter rains which tend to leach the nitrogen out of fast-draining, sandy soils in particular. Recommendations of well-known gardeners vary as regards rate of application from '1 generous pinch' per shrub to 2 oz. (i.e. 1 male handful) per sq. yd. Perhaps the safest ratio would be something between the two, with a bias towards meanness. Fortunately this is one of the slow-acting organics in which dosage need not be tremendously precise.

Hop Manure   Where neither animal farms nor bracken wastelands abound, hop manure may be easier to come by. It should not be confused with spent hops, which are useful enough as a moisture-retaining, weed-smothering mulch, but lack the food value contained in hop manure.

Peat   Most of the moss and sedge peats marketed in bags and bales are valued for their moisture-retaining properties rather than for their nutritive content, but where a source of natural, acid bracken peat is available this will be rich in potash and will contain other plant foods. It is therefore doubly valuable, both for incorporating in the soil and as a topdressing. Of such packaged brands as I have sampled Alexpeat and Irish Moss Peat are personal favourites for general purposes on my light Surrey greensand. Possibly the coarsest grades might be more profitably mixed with clay.

Seaweed   Although seaweed in its natural state makes nutritious mulching material, having a high potash content and a full quota of trace elements, most gardeners will find processed seaweed products more convenient to use, whether in powder or liquid form. These have the same properties as raw seaweed, and are particularly effective on light soils.

Lime

Since lime does not fit very neatly into either of our chief categories it may serve as a convenient link with the next main subject (in-organic fertilizers).

While shrub gardeners with limy soils have no choice but to endure them or to treat them specially with chemicals such as iron seques-trene (see Soils p. 42), those on acid soils would be ill-advised to lime any part of their garden in which they are ever likely to grow trees and shrubs, whether lime-tolerant or calcifuge; for, if at some future time they should decide on a reshuffle, artificially limed patches would then have to be avoided in the re-siting of calcifuge plants. Having made this point I must confess to having tried a localized scattering of lime around my tree peonies, which appear to need not only a richer, but a more alkaline diet than I have to offer. They are, however, the only shrubs which seem positively to resent the acid conditions characteristic of my garden soil. This might be interpreted as not so much the faddiness of the *gourmet* as the frustration of the undernourished *gourmand,* since the tree peony is known to be a 'gross feeder'.

It is advisable to check on the analysis of any bagged and branded product sold as an organic fertilizer (e.g. composts, processed animal manures, and so on) in order to ensure that it does not contain lime in harmful quantities.

Lastly, a warning about bonfire or wood ash, which is markedly limy, even when the plant material from which it derives has grown on acid soil.

Inorganic Fertilizers

Inorganic fertilizers (i.e. chemical or artificial fertilizers) such as sulphate of ammonia, sulphate of potash and so on, are used more widely for short-lived crops than for trees and shrubs, their purpose being to provide temporary sustenance for the plant itself, rather than to enrich the soil from which the plant derives its nourishment.

There are, however, a number of proprietary tree and shrub fertilizers which will chiefly be of benefit to gardeners who object to leaf-mulching. Where this is practised annually the resulting leafy topsoil which gradually builds up in depth provides all the enrichment that is good for the majority of trees and shrubs, except for the greedier subjects, and overfeeding is positively discouraged as an inducement to over-lush, leafy growth, often at the expense of flower production.

Rose Foods   Proprietary rose fertilizers are one of the most useful of the inorganics, being made up of ingredients specially balanced to meet the plant's needs. Applications should be given during spring and early summer (but not after July), following the maker's directions, and in particular keeping the fertilizer clear of the stems.

Foliar Feeding   This is perhaps the best of all forms of chemical feeding, where feeding is needed. Because in nature plants obtain their nourishment through their roots, foliar feeds, which are absorbed through the leaves, are particularly beneficial whenever the soil remains parched, waterlogged or otherwise in poor condition for any length of time, when the feeding roots have suffered sufficient damage to interfere with their proper functioning, or for plants weakened by pests, diseases or any other cause. They also help to give a young weak plant a good start where climate, environment or other growing conditions are against it, and are a convenient source of nutriment for plants grown in containers. Foliar feeds (of which FF (Murphy) is one of the best) combine various essential plant foods such as nitrogen, iron, potassium and magnesium in the form of a spray applied to the foliage, and since a variety of compatible insecticides and fungicides may be mixed with them, much time may be saved when spraying roses, for example, by making up a single mixture to supply essential foods, to destroy insect pests, and to prevent or control disease. Foliar feeds are most effective in the early part of the growing season, from spring to late June, and are best applied in the early morning or late afternoon. Although I have only mentioned roses by name under the heading of Foliar Feeding, it should be understood that this form of feed may be used indiscriminately in the shrub garden wherever it is likely to be of benefit.

Before leaving the subject of inorganic fertilizers I should perhaps mention that in addition to those discussed here there are any number of proprietary tree and shrub fertilizers on the market.

A Few Precautions

At a time when hazards to human health from the use or abuse of modern chemicals are under close examination we are apt to overlook the risks attaching to some of the more natural fertilizers such as that of tetanus (lockjaw) from animal manures (which is said to be on the increase) and of salmonella from bonemeal. Inoculation offers immunity from tetanus, but I wonder how many of those who use dung in the garden, or even handle soil which has at some time been manured, have failed, as I have, to take this wise precaution. The wearing of hole-free, impermeable gloves for gardening must at least lessen the risk from this and a number of other sources, since tetanus can only attack through cuts and abrasions. I understand that salmonella infection occurs only through the mouth and that the health authorities are now doing their best to prevent the importation of untreated bonemeal. To be on the safe side, one should buy only those brands advertised as sterilized, such as that sold by PBI.

Whether organic or inorganic, fertilizers should not come into contact with the trunk or stems of trees and shrubs when spread on the soil above their roots. This caveat is not always respected in the case of artificial fertilizers such as rose foods, which should not come within about 2 in. or so of the bark for fear of scorching, thus making way for the entry of canker and other diseases. Fresh animal manures must be kept from direct contact with roots as well as trunks and stems. And granular chemical fertilizers should not be inadvertently scattered on growing leaves, which will erupt in brown patches wherever the fragments lodge.

Perhaps most important of all, one should never resort to guesswork regarding rates and methods of application for any kind of chemical. No matter how small the print or how inconveniently calculated the dosage, the maker's instructions must be carefully studied and followed to the letter.

Winter Protection

In the most rugged of garden climates the shrub grower has little choice but to concentrate on plants of iron-clad constitution; but for most of us this does not rule out an occasional gamble on an especially desirable but less dependable subject. No matter how cold or how mild our garden may be, there is always the temptation to try something just a little beyond the safety limit. And for plants such as these it is prudent to provide some sort of winter protection.

In the coldest gardens it is not always in the hardest winters that casualties are most numerous. A wet and sunless summer—or, worse still, a series of them—produces such soft growth on woody plants that they may lack the stamina to withstand winter conditions of only moderate severity, whereas they often survive worse winters without much damage when plentiful warmth and sunshine during the preceding summer have ripened their wood to the requisite degree of toughness. However this may be, one cannot afford to wait and see. And even though all our protective devices should prove to have been unnecessary, few of us will begrudge the insurance against the disaster that did not happen.

Garden trees and shrubs are normally able to withstand occasional short-lived frosts of some severity, even when of only border-line hardiness, but I aim to give these doubtful doers what protection I can before they are faced with prolonged spells of frost and snow, which is standard winter weather at Hindhead, in Surrey. For safety my protective contraptions must, therefore, be in position by mid-December. Hitherto they have mostly been made from straw, wood straw or withered bracken loosely sandwiched between two layers of chicken-wire and are tailor-made to fit individual needs. More recently I have been experimenting, so far most successfully, with a $\frac{1}{4}$ in. mesh windbreak type of featherweight plastic netting, which is very much easier to adapt to odd shapes and sizes.

Frost

Overhead Protection   It is surprising how much frost protection is afforded by a canopy of bare branches, even of the most 'see-through' design. After a frosty night in this garden few signs of frost are evident at the lower end, which is now rather too full of trees whereas the exposed kitchen garden on the same latitude next door will be thickly blanketed in rime. Thus an ornamental cherry, Japanese maple or robinia, which may earlier have made its seasonal contribution to the garden scene, may do double duty by warding off frost damage to nearby shrubs in winter, though it should be borne in mind that few flowering shrubs are able to do themselves justice in really dense overhead shade.

A more solid anti-freeze roofing may be contrived from a length of the wire netting sandwich with a loosely packed filling of straw, wood straw, bracken or some such. The canopy should be firmly bound to the tops of cane supports pushed into the ground around the plant or, in the case of wall plants, given cane legs at the front and attached to the wall trellis at the back. This kind of structure will also take the brunt of fairly heavy snowfall, so long as it is brushed off from time to time to prevent collapse, and also to avoid the cold drip of melting snow during a thaw. In the worst of weathers the sides may be enclosed by a fine plastic or nylon windbreak netting (see pp. 147–48).

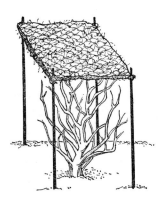

Fig. 37. Overhead frost protection. Canopy of wire netting packed with wood straw

Protection at Ground Level   Fallen leaves, bracken, straw, wood straw and similar litter, or loose gravel, chippings or weathered ashes offer a variety of useful mulches to be piled over the roots of certain half-hardy plants which die to the ground in winter. Bracken is, however, said to be unsuitable as a blanket for fuchsias because their roots find it so much to their taste that they are attracted to the surface in search of it, thus increasing the risk of frost damage which the mulch was intended to prevent. Weathered ashes (i.e. ashes which have been exposed to the weather for several weeks at least) give effective protection to such fuchsias as receive no natural blanketing from evergreen carpeters such as *Hebe* 'Pagei', helianthemums and lithospermums. Given this much protection a number of fuchsias bearing no guarantee of hardiness have come safely through the testing winter conditions in this garden for many years. These include *Fuchsia magellanica* 'Versicolor', 'Coachman', 'Duchess of Albany', 'Lena', 'Marinka', 'Mrs Rundle', 'Royal Purple', 'Rose of Castile Improved', the rather hardier 'Mme Cornelissen', and, of course, the exceptionally sturdy 'Margaret'. Even in less cold areas such fuchsias will probably need protection at least for a year or two, until their roots have reached a safe depth in the soil.

Non-vegetable mulches should be removed in spring, once the danger of severe or prolonged frost is past, just before the new shoots are due to emerge.

Plants in Tubs, Garden Vases, etc.   The soil in such containers naturally freezes much more readily than that in garden beds, since there is only a comparatively thin casing of wood, stone, earthenware, lead, plastic, fibre glass or similar material between it and the outside air. Irrespective of its degree of hardiness, no plant suitable for British gardens will enjoy being frozen solid at the root for long spells in winter, as would have happened to a hardy camellia in a garden vase on my open-sided porch, unless given some kind of protection. On the advice of the Royal Horticultural Society I had a wooden box made to take the container with a little room to spare to allow for a packing of sawdust beneath and all round the pot up to its rim. The plant is watered the day before, and once it is in its box the soil and the sawdust packing is covered with polythene to keep the roots moist and the sawdust dry. The vase goes into the box (which is painted to match the front door and therefore not unsightly) towards the end of November, emerging probably in late March just in time to flower, both vase and plant having thus come through many a cruel winter unscathed.

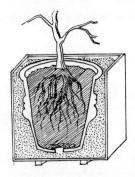

Fig. 38. Cross-section of wooden box packed with sawdust to take garden vase

If boxing is unacceptable, tubs or vases may be thickly swaddled with sacking, straw or bracken to insulate them against frost, though this method is rather less reliable than the other. An outer covering of polythene would, I think, make for extra safety by preventing the wrapping becoming rain-sodden and then frozen, but it would need to overlap the rim of the container in order to keep the padding dry.

In gardens where such containers are extensively used they are commonly planted with bulbs, annuals or greenhouse subjects for spring, summer and autumn display and left empty in winter. If they contain more permanent plants it is usual to move them into a frost-proof house or shed at the onset of winter. In my own case no such accommodation was available for my potted camellia, which has now spent many comfortable winters in its sawdust box on the porch.

Frost and Wind

When planning a group of shrubs for a cold or windy district it should be remembered that slightly tender shrubs will benefit as much from the shelter of their immediate neighbours as from the protection of overhead branches, so long as the planting is not too sparse and contains a fair proportion of evergreens. For instance, *Hoheria lyallii* and *H. glabrata*, though usually thought to be of slightly suspect hardiness, have never caused any anxiety here, where evergreen shrubs of about 3 ft. in height grow at their base to protect the young trunk.

Where greater protection is necessary, it is a mistake to under-estimate the damage done by wind. Even where there is nothing to fear from freezing temperatures, tender young plants, and ever-greens in particular, may need shelter from winter gales and from the searing winds of spring during their infancy, especially in the deceptively mild but windswept coastal areas.

Screens, Tents, and Cages The kind of loosely packed wire netting sandwich already described (see p. 144) may be up-ended to form a barricade against frost and wind, supported by canes threaded through the wire mesh with their ends pushed firmly into the soil around the shrub. This should not be completely encircled by the screen, because frost may be trapped inside unless some outlet is provided, the south side being the safest for the gap, bearing in mind the direction of the prevailing wind. For small plants the screen should be rather higher than the plant itself, but for young trees a 12–18 inch-high shield at the base of the trunk on the north and east sides is often adequate, and is particularly useful for young eucalypts, whose trunks are said to be vulnerable to frost and icy winds at or close to ground level.

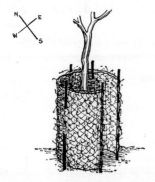

Fig. 39. Frost and wind shield for a young
tree trunk. Materials as in Fig. 37

A lean-to shelter made from the same materials may be preferred for the smaller subjects. In this case the padded wire netting is supported on sloping canes in the form of half a wigwam without a top, surrounding the plant on three sides, with the south side open. Extra protection will result from bending the shelter over and inwards slightly at the top. Windbreak netting may suitably be substituted if preferred.

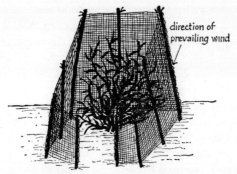

direction of
prevailing wind

Fig. 40. Frost and wind protection
Lean-to shelter made from ¼ in. mesh Windbreak netting.

For a small temporary shelter a tent-shaped bower of evergreen branches pushed into the ground around a plant and meeting above it is quick and easy to fix, but little light will reach the plant, so it should be dispensed with as soon as possible (see Fig. 41).

Some of the new nylon and other ¼ in. mesh products designed for wind protection, such as Rokolene Windbreak (made by Roko Containers Ltd, Field Lane, Litherland, Liverpool L21 9LZ), or the rather dearer but better known Netlon Plant Windscreen, appear to provide excellent winter protection from frost as well as from wind. I have recently tried Rokolene Windbreak only, which can be very quickly assembled into a tent shape gathered by a tie at the top of a strong cane support rather taller than the plant and pushed into the

Fig. 41. Live evergreen bower for temporary winter protection (or summer shading) of small new shrubs

soil near its centre, pegging the netting down at ground level a little wide of the plant's perimeter, so as to create a slight gap between the two. So long as a few canes are placed so as to protrude slightly above a plant to prevent direct contact as far as possible and to take the weight of snow, any dwarfish shrub can be even more simply draped with the netting, no matter what its shape, again pegging down the covering at soil level. These materials have the advantage of being waterproof and thus free from frost in freezing temperatures and are also very light in weight.

I should perhaps point out that both were designed merely for *wind* protection and that my own tests with them for anti-frost coverings are limited to one winter's experience, during which results have so far been most encouraging. In the worst of winters one might perhaps be tempted to use them doubled, for safety's sake.

Whatever form the construction takes it is important that the wind should be able to filter through it, rather than be forced up and over the top of a wind-resistant obstacle, only to cause fiercer turbulence on descending into the enclosure designed for the plant's protection. For this reason screens of loosely woven hessian and wattle hurdles are also recommended, whereas more solid wind-proof substances such as plastic sheeting, corrugated iron and solid wood are unsuitable for protective windscreens.

For some none-too-hardy subjects it may be necessary in very severe winters to envelop them in plastic bags (the extra-lightweight ones from the cleaners are better than any), or in polythene sheeting, providing some ventilation holes to prevent the trapping of stagnant air. Alternatively, it may help to tuck bracken or wood straw loosely in among bare branches, but this will need a little teasing out occasionally if impacted by heavy rain or snow, since soggy or frozen wads may do more harm than good if allowed to clog the limbs for long.

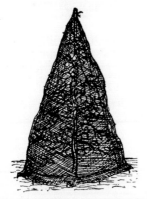

Fig. 42. Frost and wind protection Tent of ¼ in. mesh Rokolene plastic Windbreak netting.

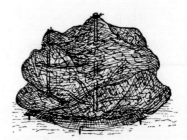

Fig. 43. Frost and wind protection Half-hardy plant blanketed in ¼ in. mesh plastic Windbreak netting.

Snow

Prevention of Damage A blanket of snow is a good deal more snug than is generally supposed, especially if it falls on unfrozen ground and does not itself freeze, so it is usually wiser to leave it undisturbed except where its weight is likely to cause damage. Evergreens, which naturally collect more snow than plants with leafless branches, and tap-rooted subjects which are less securely anchored than others, are most at risk. Examples are the tree kinds of genistas, dense, twiggy brooms, ceanothus, tree heaths, the upright-habited *Escallonia* 'lveyi,' youngish eucalypts, and conifers of pyramidal form, which may be so badly bowed or spread by the weight of snow as to remain either permanently misshapen or actually split apart.

Sound stakes and ties help to some extent to prevent snow damage, but the more accident-prone subjects should be relieved of their snow-load periodically, when falls are heavy or prolonged. If roughly jostled or banged with a metal-ended garden tool bark may be abraded or branches broken, but a long-handled, soft-bristled house broom may safely be used for gently tapping, rocking or joggling trunks or branches.

Pyramidal shrubs (e.g. tree heaths and some conifers) may need some precautionary netting or tying in, girdling the plant at intervals to prevent splaying. In some cases it may only be necessary to tie in a few individual branches.

Though mostly tough enough to survive the winter without cosseting, the tall, snow-trapping evergreen leaf blades of the phormiums (New Zealand Flax) never regain their poise once their stiff backs have been broken by the weight of snow, and it is a long wait until the plant's stately demeanour is restored by the matured shoots of the coming season. They may, however, come through the winter with little or no damage if four strong canes are stuck into

Fig. 44. Phormium trussed for protection from snow and frost

the ground around the clump and tied round at intervals with old nylon stockings, finishing with one as close to the top of the leaves as possible. The canes should hug the plants closely, reaching a little higher than the tallest leaves. The stocking is broader, softer and more yielding and yet stronger than string for girdling, leaving no scars on the foliage, while providing firm support. This contraption serves to hold the outer leaves erect and keeps the rest so closely bunched that they brace one another against heavy snow and keep out frost at the same time, which, I believe, may have been responsible for their recent increased flowering in this garden.

Dwarf shrubs in particular are usually best left undisturbed beneath a snowy eiderdown, but I find it difficult to decide what is best for dwarf evergreen azaleas. The more compact varieties rarely suffer much breakage, and since some are not too hardy they are probably better off when blanketed by snow against freezing temperatures and icy winds; but the more loosely branched types tend to split badly at a fork when weighed down with snow, so that if one decides against uncovering these one must be prepared for a good deal of repair work directly a thaw sets in.

Winter Repairs

Frost   Recently planted trees and shrubs should be re-firmed in the soil as soon as it has thawed if they have been pushed upwards and loosened by frost.

Wind   Any plants which have keeled over in the winter gales or have been wind-rocked to form a hollow in the soil around the base of the trunk must be staked upright and made secure before their roots suffer any worse tearing. The hollow collar in the soil must also be filled in with dry soil and made firm, so as to prevent rain and snow collecting in this funnel-shaped depression to rot the basal bark.

Though strong winds may tear away branches, snow is responsible for the greater number of splits and breakages, which have therefore been dealt with under the next heading.

Snow   My own treatment for split forks among evergreen azaleas and other dwarf shrubs is to attach the partially severed branch to a cane or canes stuck into the ground in such a way as to return it to its original position, with the split surfaces pressed as closely together as possible, before binding firmly. Hitherto I have used insulating tape for binding splits, but for a small fracture I now prefer the new, transparent green plastic Sylglas Garden Tape, which has some 'give' in it, to allow for expansion as the plant grows. It is self-adhesive, waterproof, rotproof and for plant repairs it is easier to handle than insulating tape. Supporting struts should be left in position until the split has knitted together, or longer, since the joint will remain weak for several seasons.

It helps to relieve the strain on a deeply split fork under repair if the upper part of a break-away limb is tethered to a strong one higher up or on the opposite side of the plant. Old nylon stocking ties are recommended for taking the suspended weight of damaged branches on larger trees and shrubs, especially if the threatened fracture is beyond the reach of crutches to provide extra support from below.

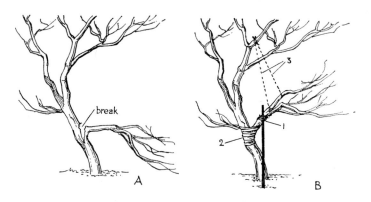

Fig. 45. Repair of breakages from weight of snow and other causes

A. Showing torn branch.
B. Threefold type of repair:
   1 propping the split branch back into position.
   2 firm binding at the point of the break.
   3 easing the strain by attaching to a suitably placed branch higher up.

When a sizeable limb is torn away altogether the wound should if possible be trimmed flush with the trunk or point of origin and, if more than ¾ in. in diameter, painted with some form of wood preservative (see Fig. 19).

The directions for wind-rocked plants on p. 151 apply equally to those overbalanced by the weight of snow.

Emergency Measures Against Late Spring Frosts

At some point I should have drawn a distinction between ground frost and air frost. The former, occurring chiefly in spring and autumn, is literally confined to ground level and therefore does little or no damage to trees and shrubs, nor does it last long. Air frost, of the kind most often experienced in midwinter and frequently long-lasting, is the one to beware of. And even one night's air frost in spring in particular can do untold damage. In the shrub garden early autumn air frosts are perhaps more disappointing than damaging, because the soft, immature growth of late summer will not in any case survive the winter in most districts, but an air frost in late spring is quite another matter. It will scorch tender young foliage, turn myriads of unfolding flowers to a brown pulp overnight, wither buds that were to provide colour in summer and autumn and kill soft new growth back to ground level.

Overnight Precautions   Shrub gardeners in low-lying or cold districts should keep in touch with early evening weather bulletins in late spring, so as to be able to cover up the most vulnerable sub-jects when night frost is forecast. Almost any kind of covering will serve in an emergency, from newspaper to old net curtains. The new plastic windbreak netting such as Rokolene, of $\frac{1}{4}$ in. mesh, is especially practical for the purpose, being very light and yet easy to anchor when thrown over a shrub in a hurry. It should be borne in mind that such emergency measures may have to be repeated several nights running, so they need to be thoroughly practical and time-saving and yet reasonably secure.

Plastic bags or sheeting, though safe enough for evergreens, are unsuitable for protecting tender young growth such as that of the precocious tree peony, for example, because the young shoots take such a bashing from the polythene as it slaps to and fro if the wind gets up that the result is almost as punishing as frost damage.

Early Morning Salvage   Some time or other one is almost bound to be taken unawares; and then one must beat the sun to it with hosepipe or watering cans in the early dawn, drenching flower buds and tender new growth with cold water to thaw them before the sun reaches them—for it is an inconvenient fact that the day usually dawns bright and sunny after night frost in late spring. It is, I think, a waste of time to attempt to salvage fully open flowers, though buds showing petal colour may be saved. An effective and more com-fortable alternative to the chilly and frenzied operations at first light is to play a sprinkler hose on the shrub borders all night when frost threatens, but it takes a lot more sprinkler piping than most of us possess to protect even a small shrub garden, in which case we can but use it as far as it will go and resign ourselves to watering the rest at daybreak if needs must.

Accommodation for Wall Plants and Climbers

Walls of all sorts, and house walls in particular, are of unique value in the shrub garden in that they afford the shelter without which one could not attempt to grow many half-hardy subjects out of doors except in the mildest climates. And house walls are best of all, because they escape the down-draught to which walls in the open are subject in windy areas, they retain some warmth from within during the winter, and they offer a choice of four different aspects, to suit sun-lovers, shade-seekers and a whole host of plants in between.

It is, therefore, sheer lunacy to girdle a house with paths or paving right up to the walls, as this one originally was. However, it was not too difficult to prise it all up and cart it away in order to make beds for shrubs and climbers all round the house, siting any necessary paths much more conveniently beyond the perimeter of the new beds. But the earth at the foot of such walls is often full of lime, builders' rubble and other rubbish: and, since it will need to be replaced by a good soil rich in humus in order to conserve as much moisture as possible in these naturally dry situations, gardeners in limy districts may seize the opportunity to exchange the original soil for an acid, peaty mixture in which to grow some of the choicest lime-haters. Plantings are a great deal more effective when the beds are made wide enough to accommodate climbers and tall plants at the back (as far as windows and so on allow), and dwarfer ones in the front rank—that is to say, the bed would need to be not less than about 4 ft. wide. When planted against a wall the roots should be at least 1 ft. away from it and fragile stems should be guided carefully back towards the permanent framework on which the plant is to be trained so as to avoid kinking, as so often happens to clematis in infancy. The possibility of growing two climbers on the same wall space is discussed under Spacing (see p. 50).

Many shrubs which enjoy the shelter of house walls will, of course, grow in such positions without support (e.g. cistus, choisya, *Hibiscus syriacus*), whereas others (e.g. ceanothus, pyracantha, chaenomeles) can be better trained to fill their allotted space when tied to some sort of framework. For the majority of true climbers this is essential, except for those equipped with suction pads like Virginia creeper, or with clinging aerial roots like ivy, *Euonymus fortunei* or

Hydrangea petiolaris, and even for the latter kinds some support may at first be needed before they are able to cling to the wall surface unaided.

For climbers it is not a bit of good bunching a fistful of trailing shoots together like a horse-tail and tying them to an odd nail or two, or to a single strand of wire, as is so often the fate of clematis. No matter how puny a young plant may seem on arrival it is worth while (though increasingly costly) to cover the whole wall space which it is ultimately to fill, right at the start, with a non-collapsible wooden trellis made to measure, or with large-mesh, plastic-coated wire netting available in various colours, of which brown is the most self-effacing against ordinary brickwork and the crude blue-green the most unnatural for any garden purpose. Some form of pre-fabricated framework is much to be preferred to wires stretched on nails or vine-eyes; if stout enough to serve its purpose the wire will be almost impossible to pull taut, and if not it will soon come to grief beneath the stress of growing plants. Trellises should be fixed so as to stand an inch or so clear of the wall, to allow for the circulation of air necessary to combat the threat of mildew and to facilitate tying in.

Training in the early stages usually consists of spreading the shoots fanwise; but where space permits, the young growth of climbing roses (other than true ramblers) should be gently arched over horizontally to encourage new shoots to break all along the new canes. Tempting though it may be to dodge the trouble of tying by twining climbing plants in and out of the trellis, it is usually wiser to tie in wandering shoots on the outward side of the framework, because the slim young growth may one day thicken to the point where it becomes constricted by the trellis, or its increasing girth tears the latter from its moorings. And even if none of this comes to pass, we are merely blocking the ventilation we have been at pains to contrive with battens or vine-eyes if we fill the space between wall and trellis. Training to cover the allotted space should be regularly attended to throughout the growing season.

Aspects

For South Walls The following plants are most likely to need the maximum sunshine and shelter provided by a south wall (or possibly a west one—see p. 157) in all but the most favourable garden climates, either to flower abundantly or for the sake of winter protection, though most of the wall shrubs may also be grown in the open in mild areas. For other less tender subjects suitable for a south wall bed see the list of plants for any aspect (p. 158).

Actinidia kolomikta
Artemisia arborescens
Campsis (Trumpet Vine)
Carpenteria
Ceanothus
Cercis siliquastrum (Judas Tree)
Chimonanthus (Winter Sweet)
Cistus (Rock Rose)
Clematis armandii, C. florida 'Sieboldii' (*bicolor*) (being rather more tender than most). Others are also suitable, provided the roots are well shaded
Convolvulus cneorum
Cytisus battandieri
Euphorbia characias, E. veneta (*wulfenii*) (Giant Spurge)
Fatsia japonica 'Variegata'
Feijoa sellowiana
Fremontodendron (syn. Fremontia)
x Halimiocistus
Halimium
Hibiscus syriacus varieties
Jasminum officinale (Common White Jasmine), *J. primulinum*
Leptospermum
Lonicera japonica 'Aureoreticulata' (variegated form of Honey-suckle)
Magnolia grandiflora varieties
Passiflora caerulea (Passion Flower)
Phormium (New Zealand Flax)
Phygelius capensis (Cape Figwort)
Salvia officinalis varieties (Ornamental Sage)
Schizophragma (any aspect, but more floriferous in sun)
Senecio cineraria varieties
Solanum crispum, S. jasminoides
Teucrium fruticans (Shrubby Germander)
Trachelospermum
Viburnum macrocephalum
Vitis vinifera varieties (ornamental grape vines)
Wisteria
Yucca

For West Walls   The preliminary remarks under 'South Walls' also apply here.

Actinidia kolomikta
Camellia japonica varieties, *C.* x *williamsii* hybrids
Carpenteria
Ceanothus
Chimonanthus (Winter Sweet)
Clematis
Coronilla glauca
Cytisus battandieri
Euonymus fortunei 'Silver Queen'
Euphorbia characias, E. veneta (wulfenii) (Giant Spurge)
x Fatshedera
Fatsia japonica
Hedera canariensis 'Variegata' (Canary Island Ivy)
Hydrangea macrophylla varieties and others
Jasminum officinale (Common White Jasmine), *J. primulinum*
Leptospermum
Lonicera japonica 'Aureoreticulata' (variegated form of Honeysuckle)
Mahonia lomariifolia
Pileostegia
Schizophragma (any aspect, but more floriferous in sun)
Solanum crispum, S. jasminoides
Tree peony, Japanese hybrids
Vitis vinifera varieties (ornamental grape vines)
Wisteria

For North Walls   Any of those plants listed under 'Any Aspect' may serve here, the following being particularly suitable:

Camellia japonica varieties, *C.* x *williamsii* hybrids
Clematis montana varieties and the more vigorous large-flowered hybrids (e.g. *jackmanii* varieties)
x Fatshedera
Fatsia japonica
Garrya elliptica (Tassel Bush) (plant the male form for much longer catkins than the female)
Lapageria, in mild areas

Hedera (Ivy), various, except *H. canariensis* 'Variegata'
Hydrangea macrophylla varieties and others
Hydrangea petiolaris (Climbing Hydrangea)
Hypericum 'Hidcote' (form of St John's Wort)
Itea ilicifolia
Jasminum nudiflorum (Winter Jasmine)
Mahonia 'Charity', *M. japonica*
Pileostegia
Pyracantha (Firethorn)
Tropaeolum speciosum (Flame Flower)

For East Walls   As for north walls, except for camellias, whose
flowers are less liable to frost damage when not exposed to early
morning sun. Clematis of most kinds and wisteria may be added to
the list.

For Any Aspect

Chaenomeles (Japonica), especially *speciosa* and x *superba*
varieties
Cotoneaster
Euonymus fortunei 'Variegatus' ('Gracilis')
Forsythia
Garrya elliptica (Tassel Bush) (see note in previous list)
Hedera (Ivy), various, except the none-too-hardy *H. canariensis*
'Variegata'
Hydrangea petiolaris (Climbing Hydrangea)
Lonicera (Honeysuckle), except 'Aureoreticulata', which needs
sunshine for the yellow leaf colour
Parthenocissus
Polygonum baldschuanicum (Russian Vine), rampant
Pyracantha (Firethorn)
Roses, mostly for sun but some for each aspect, including north
Schizophragma, but flowers better in the sun

Climbers in the Shrub Borders

Certain plants of naturally trailing or clinging habit will happily
scramble through trees and shrubs in the open, and are particularly
useful in livening up winter-flowering subjects throughout the spring
and summer. Clematis, *Tropaeolum speciosum*, *Jasminum nudiflorum*,

ivies, parthenocissus and wisteria are all suitable for inclusion in the shrub borders, and *Vitis coignetiae* and *Hydrangea petiolaris* may also be grown through large and vigorous host trees. Ivy does not throttle its host plant as is commonly supposed, but honeysuckle may do so, and wisteria must be prevented from getting a stranglehold on a live support. Clematis, *Tropaeolum speciosum* and *Hydrangea petiolaris* all enjoy a cool, moist root run and should therefore be planted on the shady side of the host plant, whence the top growth will find its way towards the sun, or so we are always told. In the case of clematis I am inclined to disagree, finding that in such circumstances some make little effort to seek out the sunny side, so that, once entwined in the leafy centre of a tall, dense support, they lack sufficient light to flower freely. Planting nearer to the sunnier side of the host in the shrub borders presents little difficulty as regards shade at the roots and, in my view, is therefore to be recommended.

Weeding

There is one kind of garden visitor I heartily despise—the sour puss (usually female, alas) who gleefully inquires of her pal: 'Do you see what I see? Isn't that a weed?' For my part I should be infinitely more mortified if she were to spot dead wood, neglected disease, suckers and other evidences of bad husbandry (which she is more likely to overlook!). As for the weeds, I fully expect that you will detect a few along the verges of my borders—indeed I have never claimed that my garden is *entirely* weed-free, but only that the mulch makes it sufficiently so to save me the trouble of weeding wherever it has been properly applied. In a shrub garden kept adequately mulched with fallen leaves weeds will nevertheless be virtually non-existent and, apart from the dandelion type of tap-rooters, most of those that may creep in are so loosely anchored in the leaf soil that they may be pulled up with the greatest of ease. But before pulling *anything* up make sure that you recognize it for what it is and are not uprooting a valuable self-sown seedling from one of your trees or shrubs.

In such gardens weeds are most likely to appear among newly planted ground-cover and other dwarf plants along the front of the borders, where leaf-mulching is impracticable. If the dwarfs and carpeters are planted with a 4 in. surface layer of moist peat and kept topdressed with it thereafter this, too, should reduce weeding to a minimum. Such plants should however be hand-weeded for as long as it takes them to thicken up as ground-cover, because perennial weeds will be almost impossible to eradicate once they get a hold among dense carpeting growth.

The shrub gardener should have no use for the hoe, which disturbs and damages surface roots. Among the larger shrubs it is considered safe to use the paraquat weedkiller sold as Weedol, if necessary, which does not harm woody trunks and stems, but must not be allowed to come in contact with the foliage or soft green shoots of ornamental plants, which it will kill as indiscriminately as the green growth of annual weeds (and, incidentally, the self-sown seedlings of trees and shrubs), and the top growth of most of the less tenacious perennial weeds, except those with creeping roots, like couch grass, horse-tail and ground elder. Paraquat may be watered on the weeds from a can fitted with a rose or with a special bar sprinkler and since it has no effect on the soil itself planting may safely take place immediately after application. Certain horticultural writers state it to be capable of eradicating even the really stubborn, creeping-rooted couch grass, ground-elder and horse-tail 'after several applications', but it seems probable that 'after repeated applications over a number of years' would be more realistic in this context. When combating couch grass, ground-elder, horse-tail and other demon weeds as persistent as these, we would no doubt do better to use the new weedkiller containing dichlobenil and sold as Casoron G, which also shows considerable promise for use amongst certain shrubs; but it is most important in this connection that the maker's instructions are strictly honoured.

New gardeners should, I think, be on their guard against encouraging even the most engaging wildings in the shrub borders. Only the comparatively controllable wild primrose remains welcome in this garden, where the tenacious-rooted wild violet, the irrepressible Welsh poppy, the Male and Lady Ferns, wild foxgloves and bluebells, and even lily-of-the-valley, all of which were originally welcomed, have become a real nuisance, seeding or insinuating themselves everywhere and smothering dwarf shrubs.

Compost Heaps

Most gardeners are content—as I admit I am—to pile refuse for composting inside an open-fronted wire netting enclosure, and the less tidy-minded will probably dispense with even this refinement, which keeps the heap neat but does nothing to conserve the inner heat necessary for the manufacture of weed- and disease-free compost. Those whom the cap fits will need to put a fair amount of time and energy into turning sides to middle to get rid of the outer weed crust, and even the middle is almost certain to contain viable weed seeds unless the ingredients have been very carefully selected as seed-free and the heap very rapidly built to generate sufficient heat to kill those which find their way in. The latter condition is not easy to fulfil in a well mulched shrub garden where weeds are rare but, on a naturally poor soil in particular, a supply of home-made compost is so valuable that it is worth while making what one can, with kitchen and other household waste to supplement the garden rubbish.

The best people build their heaps within wooden frames, either of do-it-yourself construction or ready-made commercially, and are fanatical about recipes and 'cookery' methods. Those bent on counsels of perfection will wish to study the subject in detail (see Recommended Reading, in Appendix One); but among all my gardening acquaintance I know of only one such perfectionist and therefore assume that the following less arduous compromise stands a better chance of acceptance by most of us.

Site

Having something of a shanty-town air about it, the composting area needs to be tucked away out of sight, requiring a flat, sheltered site to take a heap 4 ft. square, plus working space and room to turn the heap. As a rule a patch of dry shade beneath trees may most easily be spared, and this suits compost-making well enough, though some watering of the heap may be necessary in dry summers in order to keep the 'activator' activating. Compost heaps should be built up on an earth base rather than on concrete or other impermeable surfaces and should not be made in a pit.

Construction Materials

The recipe, which is roughly based on instructions for the Henry Doubleday Research Association's 'Bocking Box', is for a heap 4 ft. square. Unless a great deal of material were available at any one time heat would be lost in a larger one, which would take too long to complete.

2 stakes, 5 ft. each
2 stakes, 4 ft. each
2 stakes, 3 ft. 3 in. each
34 ft. approximately of 2 in. mesh rabbit-wire, 3 ft. wide
24 bricks, approximately
Wood preservative
Staples
Strong, tarred twine or plastic-coated wire
Cartons and/or newspapers

For the cover: Corrugated iron sheets fixed on a wooden frame slightly more than 4 ft. square.

Method

The 5 ft. stakes are for the back corners of the 4 ft. rectangle and the 4 ft. ones for those at the front. Treat the ends to be buried in the soil with wood preservative before ramming them in 4 ft. apart and about 1 ft. deep. Cut off about 25 ft. of the wire netting to make a double wall round three sides of the enclosure, leaving the front open and keeping the stakes sandwiched between the two thicknesses of netting. Staple both layers of the wire netting to the stakes and pack the hollow walls with flattened cartons or newspapers.

Make a 'front door' by stapling a double thickness of wire netting to the remaining stakes (the shortest pair) so that the lower edge of the wire is about 3 in. from the bottom. Bind the double length of wire netting together along its lower edge with tarred twine or other non-perishable material and pad the pocket thus formed with flattened newspaper. This makes an easily movable barrier to be placed across the front opening to keep the heat in, while the 3-in. gap at the base provides ventilation.

Further ventilation is obtained by laying two double rows of bricks, on their broadest side, inside the enclosure with a space of 2 ft. between them. The lines of brick forming each double row are spaced 1 in. apart and run from back to front of the enclosure with their ends protruding under the 'front door' so as to let the draught in under the heap.

The corrugated iron canopy is chiefly required to keep the rain off in winter. Because it has an undesirable cooling effect if laid directly on the heap it is tilted from back to front by the extra height of the back pair of stakes on which it rests, so as to prevent direct contact with the compost material. A covering of polythene may seem a great deal easier, but is said to cause excessive condensation, to keep the slugs in, and the air out.

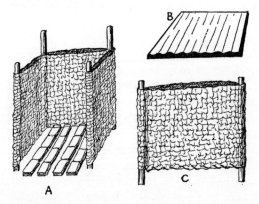

Fig. 46. Construction of a simple compost heap

A. Open-fronted enclosure made from padded double wire netting, with bricks for ventilation.

B. Corrugated iron roof, to slant downwards from back to front of the heap (note taller poles at back of enclosure on which it rests).

C. Movable 'front door', also made from double thickness of wire netting enclosing padding.

The Filling

To start the heap use rough, twiggy hedge clippings or coarse rubbish of some kind immediately on top of the bricks, so as not to defeat the object of the latter by impeding the passage of air. The lists of materials which follow apply equally to any kind of compost heap, no matter how slapdash its construction.

Unacceptable Materials   In certain cases the suitability of an ingredient rather depends on how quickly or slowly the heap is built. Although the best-made ones are said to generate enough heat at their centre to kill off disease spores and weed seeds few of them are as well made as all that, so it will probably be safer to ban seeding weeds and diseased material from the average heap. Despite the fact that twiggy bits have been recommended for the bottom layer to assist ventilation, it should be emphasized that really woody prunings, dead wood, wood shavings, and even sawdust (except in very small amounts) are unsuitable as composting materials. Other items to be avoided are unrottable substances such as plastic, nylon and other synthetic materials, rubber, metal, cinders and coal ash, broken china and glass, flower-pot crocks, oil, grease and noxious chemicals, and bread, cheese rinds and other non-vegetable food scraps likely to attract vermin.

Suitable Materials   With the exceptions mentioned above, most forms of garden waste may be composted, coarse stems and fleshy roots being first chopped or otherwise broken down as necessary. Bracken rhizomes are splendid if dried in the open before adding, and chopped green bracken is also first class. Very fine-textured substances such as lawn mowings should only be added little by little or well mixed up with other textures. Among household waste anything of vegetable origin such as tea leaves, coffee grounds, fruit skins, vegetable pods and parings and so on are all grist to the mill, as are carpet and floor sweepings, hair combings, non-synthetic rags, straw, feathers and small pieces of paper.

I have it on the best authority that, contrary to common belief, grass mowings which have recently been treated with a hormone weedkiller are a permissible ingredient, so long as the compost is thoroughly rotted before use—that is, it should have an agreeable, earthy smell, be teeming with earthworms, no single ingredient should be identifiable, and the whole reduced to a moist, crumbly, dark brown substance likened by Miss Sackville West to rich chocolate cake. But if it has contained hormone-treated grass cuttings, please make certain that your cake is well and truly cooked, slaphappy composters!

Garden compost has a natural tendency towards acidity and the gardener specializing in shrubs for acid soils may not be aware that, despite the limy nature of bonfire ash, a sprinkling will be beneficial in adding potassium to the heap, while not appreciably affecting the acidity adversely, since over-acidity *can* disagree even with the limehaters if so pronounced as to stop the action of bacteria.

Building the Heap

The assorted rubbish goes on to the heap in 8 in. layers, putting the coarser materials such as orange peel and chopped cabbage stalks towards the middle. The first layer is covered with farmyard or other organic manure, or scattered with fertilizer of animal origin such as dried blood, hoof and horn meal or fish manure. The second layer should be treated with some sort of proprietary activator, the simplest being in powder form, such as Marinure, made from dried seaweed which, though perhaps of particular interest to the anti-chemical fraternity, contains such a wide range of valuable minerals and trace elements as to recommend itself to gardeners of all persuasions. These two forms of sandwich filling are repeated alternately between the layers of rubbish.

The latter should not be trodden down or otherwise compacted, and the heap-in-the-making should be covered with sacks or something of the sort to keep the heat in. Ideally it should be built up very quickly, that is, within a week or two, but I confess I have never reached anywhere near this target. If our compost is less weed-free than it ought to be, there will be many of us who may take comfort in the fact that any old heap of suitable rubbish will in time rot down to provide useful humus for tree and shrub planting purposes, even if too disreputable for topdressing, always provided that it is thoroughly decayed to the moist chocolate cake stage when mixed with the soil in planting holes.

Turning the Heap

Those prepared to turn their heaps will get better results, since the outsides will rot down to match the hotter centre portion when sides are changed to middles. A second enclosure adjoining the original heap simplifies the turning process, but all that is strictly necessary is to have space available to build the remade heap alongside, as the old one is taken apart, putting the less decomposed material from the outside into the centre of the new pile. The inside of the original heap is likely to be dry if it has heated up as well as it should and will therefore need some watering during the turning process.

Stocktaking and Inspection

Stocktaking   Though high in order of importance, this Section has been left until last in the hope that its message may linger in the mind.

This is in fact a non-operation at least as ultimately productive as the most frenzied activity, so long as decisions are noted on the spot and not trusted to memory. Have you ever noticed how much the spread of a deciduous tree or shrub is reduced during dormancy,

after sloughing off the considerable weight of its leaves? If so, you
will appreciate that winter is no time for planning additions and
alterations to the shrub borders, when a likely-looking gap will
persuade even the more experienced of us that there is room for some
plant that we are anxious to winkle in somewhere, only to prove us
wrong when summer foliage closes in around the interloper,
smothering it and depriving it of light.

Critical assessment should therefore be confined to the late spring
and summer months, when the garden is in full leaf as well as in
flower and, incidentally, when the weather will be more appropriate
for the comparatively static business of contemplation. As far as
possible one should resist the temptation to depart from decisions
made at this time when giving effect to them in winter, for the
reasons already mentioned.

Colour combinations should be assessed for timing and for
harmony or shock value as they come into bloom; contrasts of shapes
and textures critically examined; any seasonal imbalance of flower
power noted for readjustment; new positions considered for plants
unfavourably placed, whether for their satisfaction or for ours; and in
gardens planted on close boscage principles any detrimental overcrowding, as distinct from intentional interlacing growth, should be
marked for appropriate action later on.

Only by planning future developments as early as possible in the
growing season are we able to order exactly what we want, with
every chance of getting it—and of getting it whenever delivery suits
us—with the further advantage of knowing what we propose to do
with it when it arrives.

Inspection

Stocktaking and inspection are by no means the same thing, despite
obvious similarities, inspection being concerned with caretaking
rather than with the creative shaping of the garden to one's will.
Both are likely to be labours of love more pleasureable than irksome,
in that triumphs are happily a good deal more common than
disasters. Regular inspection should, however, be considered as much
a responsibility as a well deserved reward. So, when appraising our
personal Edens from day to day, we must keep a sharp eye open for
signs of the serpent at work, so that trouble in whatever form may be
arrested before real damage is done.

Part Four

Preface to the Working-Calendar

And now for my main objective—the provision of a ready-reference guide to the seasonal jobs in the shrub garden, to keep us up to date with what we should be doing, and when. No matter how widely experienced as gardeners, few busy amateurs will be constantly aware that the right fleeting moment is at hand for this job or that in the shrub borders. This is not to suggest that the right moment is always uncompromisingly fleeting—indeed I hope to stress later that it is not—but most of us have outside interests and occupations, and time whisks by at a spanking pace when one's back is turned on the garden. Season after season I unintentionally neglect to prune and tie in certain clematis until the tangle is past unravelling, or find, too late, that the opportunity to fend off initial attacks from assorted pests and diseases has eluded me for yet another season. The calendar of perfection is too much to carry in one's head.

No doubt we know just where to turn up the pertinent information: but that is not the point. What *I* need, and so I hope may you, is a fairly elastic programme of operations in the form of a seasonal reminder to keep us up to the mark, so that we may see at a glance what we have left undone of those things which we ought to have done. Oversights will thus be reduced to a minimum and, even if we have been a little neglectful, with any luck we may find that there is still time to catch up.

My work roster has largely been put together from the jottings in my garden notebook, in which pertinent facts about my own assortment of trees and shrubs have been recorded from voracious reading and personal observation over the past 20 years or so. By now I can no longer distinguish the one source from the other, but obviously much of it will have been said before. However, if there is little originality either in content or in format, as far as I can discover the two have not hitherto been so combined as to do for the shrub gardener what any number of the calendar type of guides have done for other aspects of gardening. It is perhaps significant that one of the most reputable of the 'Complete' horticultural omnibuses (of almost 800 pages) devotes a scant six lines to trees and shrubs, and

in one month only out of twelve–and of these, four lines are taken up
with propagation and a fifth with hedges!

Such samples of the usual form of gardening calendar as I was
able to examine were mostly based on a rigid *weekly* timetable, making
them much less flexible than what I had in mind for our purposes.
They were, of course, primarily or wholly concerned with the care
of the 'flower garden' (oddly enough a shrub garden is rarely
thought of as a 'flower garden'), the rock garden, annuals and other
bedding plants, bulbs, fruit and vegetables and plants grown under
glass. The syllabus starts in January and its disciples are kept hard
at it from earliest spring to late autumn in their kind of garden, being
then excused all but a few outdoor duties in winter, which is looked
upon as the time for browsing through seed and bulb catalogues by
the fireside, snug and smug in the knowledge that their naked soil
has been dug over in time for the frosts to do their work. If green
fingers itch for a little more active gardening in the close season,
there are always flower-pots, it seems, to be washed, or cosy chores
to be performed in the greenhouse.

Whereas the weekly programmer is obliged to pinpoint suitable
dates for each job because he is the slave of his format, professional
advisers on shrub gardening are able to allow us a lot more latitude.
Take for instance their 'prune after flowering', which is so frequently
applied to spring- and early summer-flowering shrubs in particular.
What could be more elastic as a date for one's diary? My own
experience is that minor liberties may be taken with most counsels of
perfection and that where essential pruning, for instance, has been
neglected it may, at a pinch, be done at quite the wrong time of year
without disastrous consequences, the loss of a season's bloom being
the worst that need usually be feared from untimely attentions of
this kind. It is not as widely realized as it should be, though I have
done my best to remedy this in the Pruning Section of Part Three,
that most trees and a number of shrubs need no pruning at all.

And how are we to interpret 'after flowering' to fit an inflexible
weekly programme? Who is to say whether, in this fickle climate, my
Cytisus x *praecox* will have finished flowering by mid-May, or earlier,
or later? At one time I tried to keep an annual record of flowering
periods for all my trees and shrubs, and although, like most New
Year resolutions, it usually petered out after a month or two, along
with the last of the spring display, at least it served to show the wide
fluctuation in flowering times at this season, when a shrub normally
due to bloom in the third week of April, for example, sometimes did

so as much as four weeks earlier or almost four weeks later, in abnormal weather conditions.

So I shall not be urging you to plant, trim, prune or get to work with sprays and dusts within precisely specified dates. The framework within which my horticultural tasks are fitted is in fact altogether too elastic to be described as a calendar in the strictest sense, though I do so for the sake of convenience—for it rarely covers less than two months as an operational 'Period', nor does it neatly start on New Year's Day.

The physical work may begin sometime—any time—in autumn, when a casual stroll round the garden suddenly reminds us that summer is done, and that any day now we can make a start on the initial work or on the improvements we have been planning off and on for months. Now, at last, we can move that rhododendron which has been parched in its present position to a moister, shadier spot, nor need we longer delay the re-siting of those foliage cultivars of heath and heather into full exposure, in order to do justice to the splendid leaf colour, which has become dimmed by the gradual encroachment of semi-shade from maturing trees and shrubs nearby.

The bulk of such work does not start in earnest until leaf-fall, when deciduous trees and shrubs enter their dormant period, usually during November, and planting and transplanting may continue, whenever soil and weather conditions permit, until the end of March or into April, for these, and into May for evergreens and a number of other oddments, mostly of tender constitution.

As you see, the shrub gardener's year does not shut down with the coming of the frosts, and for us winter is often a busy season. We find our reward in summertime, however, when others are enslaved by their seed-sowing, thinning out, pricking out, bedding out, weeding, disbudding, staking and propping up with twiggery, and all the rest of it. For us it should usually be possible to fit in the odd bit of pruning, training or deadheading when clouds or cool breezes drive us out of our garden chairs—and we are constantly assured that our roses should not be sprayed in full sunlight for fear of scorching the foliage. And so, with conscience clear, and with British weather and other commitments permitting, we may take our ease in the sunshine and give ourselves up to the enjoyment of our gardens at a season of the year when this is most likely to be practicable.

Topsy-turvy though it may be by general standards, my Working-calendar starts in September, and is loosely based on six seasonal periods only. Because only some of the instructions will apply to any one garden it is bound to look a lot more onerous than it actually is. For instance, the natural fertility of your soil or the mildness of your garden climate may eliminate the need for feeding or for anti-frost measures. And, as I have already said, the programme must necessarily include individual pruning instructions for an assortment of trees and shrubs far wider than any one average garden is likely to contain. Then again, the pests and diseases which plague some districts and certain kinds of plant may give little or no trouble elsewhere. I also felt that I owed it to the perfectionist to deal with some of the less common or less important problems rather more fully than perhaps most of us require, although well aware that few may find time for any but the most inescapable chores. For this reason I have included a summary of the more important jobs at the end of each Working-period, basing my selection mainly on those about which I try to be most conscientious in my own garden, whatever else may have to be left undone. But even these, however strongly recommended, are not invariably so essential that occasional neglect will bring inevitable disaster in its wake.

In my view, the provision of space for personal notes adds so much to the usefulness of any book intended for practical reference that in this one a blank page has been included at the end of each Working-period in the calendar for the reader's convenience.

Working-Calendar

PERIOD ONE: AUTUMN

Mid- or Late September to Mid- or Late November,
according to season

Certain jobs at the start of this Period are summer hang-overs rather than autumn pipe-openers, e.g. continued protective measures against pests and diseases and the removal of spent blooms from late summer-flowering subjects. But with the beginning of the planting season we come to the true start of the shrub gardener's calendar.

Planting

Evergreens Late September to mid-October, or spring (late March onwards) are the best times for the planting or transplanting of evergreens, but the least hardy should be left until spring in cold districts (see pp. 44–7).

Deciduous Subjects Most trees and shrubs which shed their leaves in autumn, except the least hardy, may be moved at any time from November to the end of March in suitable weather (i.e. when the soil is neither frost-bound, snow-covered nor waterlogged), as soon as they become dormant. Within one's own garden they may, with care, be transplanted without waiting for dormancy if absolutely necessary. Here again, the less hardy deciduous subjects are better left until spring.

Evergreen or Deciduous Winter-flowering Subjects A start may be made on the planting of winter-flowering trees and shrubs at the end of this Period, any time from November to the end of March being suitable.

Hardy pot-grown subjects of all kinds may of course be planted at any season, but the possibility of heat and drought in summertime makes it preferable to delay planting until autumn, even for the all-seasons output of the Garden Centre, unless one is prepared to pay constant attention to watering.

Pruning

Finish any essential pruning outstanding from Period Six by the end of September, and remove dead or diseased wood at any time. Generally speaking, the pruning of late summer-flowering subjects, if any pruning is necessary, waits until spring.

Abelia, evergreen forms   Only occasional pruning is needed, in autumn, to shorten over-long shoots, cut out weak stems and remove some of the old, unproductive wood at ground level.

Hebe (Shrubby Veronica), **flowering varieties**   Deadhead and thin out crowded growth only when necessary in autumn. If more drastic pruning is needed, wait until April (see Period Four p. 209).

Humulus lupulus 'Aureus' and other decorative Hops   Cut to the ground when the hops are finished, annually.

Lapageria rosea   Weak shoots may be cut away when it has finished flowering, and wall plants reduced as necessary. Pruning is not otherwise desirable.

Polygonum baldschuanicum (Russian Vine)   Cut back in autumn or early winter, removing some of the old wood if necessary.

Potentilla (Shrubby Cinquefoil)   Either cut some of the unproductive old wood back to ground level in autumn occasionally (after flowering), or March (see Period Three p. 195). Brown wood beneath the bark does not mean that it is dead, because potentilla wood is one of the few that is never green.

Rose
>   Bush types Shorten the shoots before winter to prevent wind-rocking.
>   Ramblers (mainly *wichuraiana*, e.g. 'Dorothy Perkins', 'Hiawatha', 'Crimson Shower', 'Sanders' White' and others which throw up new canes from the base each season). Cut all the old canes to the ground in September if there are plenty of new ones to take their place; if not, keep some of the previous year's growth, shortening the side-shoots on these to 2 or 3 buds. Do not prune newly planted ramblers (for climbers see Period Three, p. 196).

Spartium junceum (Spanish Broom)   Cut back annually to within 2 buds of the older wood after flowering. This is essential in order to keep the plant from becoming leggy. Do not allow seed pods to form.

Vitis vinifera 'Purpurea' (Claret Vine) **and other ornamental grape vines**   Once the plant has filled its allotted space spur back side-shoots made during the summer to 2 or 3 eyes at the end of this Period or early in the next. The sooner this annual pruning is done after leaf-fall the better, but it can still be done up to the end of December.

Deadheading

Ballota   Remove flowered stems in late September.

Buddleias   For as long as you can keep pace with spent flower panicles. At least try to remove the terminal ones to encourage stronger flowering on the side-shoots.

Convolvulus cneorum   If it has produced a second crop of flowers.

Roses   Continue to deadhead for as long as they remain in bloom.

Mulching

Place your order for leaves with the local Council as soon as they begin to fall, and apply the leaf-mulch to the borders as soon after delivery as possible. They may hardly have arrived by the end of this Period, but by giving the job priority I hope to ensure that it will receive the attention it deserves. Mulch the low-growing front row plants with moist peat, bracken or hop manure rather than with fallen leaves, which are liable to suffocate the dwarfs.

Pests

A number of summer insect pests will still be about in the early part of Period One, especially if summery weather persists into autumn.

Earwigs Large-petalled blooms such as roses, clematis and romneya (Tree Poppy) are chiefly affected. Dust the plants and the
ground beneath with gamma-BHC, Sevin or other modern anti-
earwig chemicals, or spray with a liquid formulation of g-BHC.

Rose Pests Most of these will be controlled by one last application
of a systemic insecticide spray. Earwig damage may be checked by
dusting the ground and the blooms with BHC or treating with one of
the new substitutes for DDT.

Weevils, Clay-coloured and Vine Although chiefly harmful to
rhododendrons, they also attack roses, clematis and other shrubs.
Spray or dust the undersides of the leaves at intervals during
September with malathion, Sevin or other substitutes for DDT to
defeat adult weevils, and the ground beneath the plants should also
be sprayed or dusted periodically with BHC, Sevin or other DDT substitutes during Periods One, Two and There, in order to kill their
larvae overwintering in the soil.

Animals

Birds Spray such ornamental fruits and berries as are normally
palatable to birds with the harmless but effective repellent,
Curb.
    Towards the end of Period One it will be time to take precautions
against bird damage to spring-flowering subjects, which are often
attacked well in advance of hard weather. Again, use Curb.

**Rabbits, Squirrels, Deer, Rats, Mice, Dogs, Cats and other
four-footed Nuisances** Keep these out, as far as possible, by
spraying Curb on means of access, and use it to spray plants or paint
bark to deter the gnawers. Local friends have kept deer at bay at
least for one season by surrounding vulnerable plants such as roses
with rags soaked in creosote, but they say that it ceases to work once
the deer get used to it.

Slugs Protect vulnerable plants once a fortnight until the end of
October, after which once a month is enough. Winter baiting of
hedge-bottoms, dry walling and other hideouts may also prove
rewarding. Slug Gard (PBI), or Draza (Baywood Chemicals Ltd. and

Boots product), all containing methiocarb, are the most effective
of modern baits, in mini-pellet form.

Diseases

Leaf-curl   Trees or shrubs which have been infected by leaf-curl
should be sprayed with Bordeaux Mixture or lime-sulphur just as the
leaves start to fall, and again immediately leaf-fall is completed (see
also Period Three, p. 199, Period Five, p. 230 and Period Six, p. 240).

Rose Diseases   Continue spraying until the end of October with
a rose fungicide against black spot and mildew if necessary.

Tree Peonies   In the interests of hygiene, collect and burn dead
leaves which tend to cling to the plant, encouraging grey mould
(botrytis) and other fungal infections.

General   Keep watch for signs of disease at all times and treat as
recommended in the general section on Disease Control (pp. 117–29).

Watering

Newly planted evergreens, in particular, may need watering, or
spraying of the foliage, in a dry autumn.

Stakes, Ties and Labels

Stakes and ties will need looking over before winter gales put them
to the test, so check also that ties are not strangling expanding
trunks and limbs and that labels are present and correct.

Miscellaneous

Falling Leaves   Clear these off dwarf and carpeting plants with a
rubber-toothed rake periodically and use them as a mulch among the
taller subjects, together with leaves swept up from lawns and paths.
Do not waste this valuable mulching material on the bonfire, except

in the case of disease-prone foliage, e.g. that of roses, hydrangeas and tree peonies.

Weeds Remove the odd weed seedlings which may occur along the verges of the shrub plantings before the peat mulch is applied to them. Elsewhere weeds are almost non-existent in a well mulched shrub garden.

Variegated Foliage Plants Keep a look-out for plain green shoots and cut them out at once at their junction with the parent limb.

Training Combine the training and tying in with any pruning of climbers done in this Period.

Layering Now is a good time to layer woody shrubs such as cotinus, eucryphias, magnolias, pieris, rhododendrons, viburnums, etc.

Hydrangea Colour Treatment at Planting Time The hydrangea specialist, Mr M. Haworth-Booth, suggests the following blueing treatment as an alternative to the more expensive proprietary colourants, though he considers young plants to grow on better without colour treatment of any kind in their earliest years. To obtain blue flowers when planting in limy, neutral or only slightly acid soil, mix in aluminium sulphate at the rate of 2 lb. to each barrow-load of soil (probably 2 barrow-loads will be needed), but do not let it come into contact with the roots. Even on acid soils transplanting often results in pink flowers for a time. This can be corrected by mixing in aluminium sulphate at the rate of about 1 lb. per barrow-load of soil if slightly acid, and about ½ lb. if the soil is slightly more acid. Keep the soil thoroughly moist after treatment until next season's leaf-fall. Established specimens need further liquid treatment in autumn as described in Period Three, p. 201.

For pink or red flowers, if the soil is not naturally limy, these colours may be achieved by thoroughly mixing 2 lb. of ground limestone to each barrow-load of soil at planting time, or by watering with ½ oz. ground lime dissolved in 2 gallons of water in spring (see Period Four, p. 216–17).

No amount of treatment will alter white flower colour. When white varieties become tinged with pink as the flowers fade, this is due to the action of sunlight and not to soil conditions.

Summary of the More Important Jobs in Period One

Planting	Reasonably hardy evergreens, especially in mild districts	Late September onwards
	Reasonably hardy deciduous subjects	November onwards
Pruning (Annual)	Rambler roses	September
	Roses, bush types—shorten to prevent wind-rocking	Late autumn
	Humulus lupulus 'Aureus'	Late autumn
	Ornamental grape vines	Late November to December at latest
	Spartium junceum	September
Mulching		The sooner the better
Pests	Bird damage to spring-flowerers	Late October
	Clay-coloured and vine weevils (adult and larvae)	September onwards
	Rose pests, various	September–October
	Slugs	Fortnightly to end October, then monthly
Diseases	Rose black spot and mildew, if still present	To end October
	Leaf-curl	To end October, or even later
Watering	Newly planted evergreens, if necessary	i.e. in a warm, dry autumn

NOTES: PERIOD ONE

PERIOD TWO: LATE AUTUMN AND EARLY WINTER

Mid- or Late November to Mid- or Late December,
according to season

Planting

This is one of the most favourable periods for planting or transplanting the large majority of deciduous trees and shrubs, including the winter-flowerers, and it is also suitable for the *hardier* evergreens. In particular it is advisable for new roses to have been planted by the end of November or early December if possible.

Pruning

Catch up with any essential pruning left over from Period One, if possible, at the start of this Period—that is, before the tail end of autumn. And keep cutting out dead and diseased wood whenever it is detected.

Trees *If*, and only if, necessary, most deciduous trees, except cherries and certain other members of the *Prunus* genus, may be pruned any time in winter, from the time they shed their leaves until the first signs of awakening growth in spring. Cutting out live wood will only be required if a tree has outgrown its position, is robbing shrubs beneath it of the light necessary to their well-being, or is badly lacking in symmetry. The wounds resulting from the removal of either live or dead wood, if over ¾ in. in diameter, should be painted with Arbrex.

Hedges, deciduous If not clipped in August, these may be dealt with in winter (see Period Six, p. 238).

Campsis (Trumpet Vine) Keeping a few of the strongest new shoots and training these into position, spur-prune the rest to within 2 or 3 buds of the old wood once the plant has covered its allotted space. Prune annually any time from December to March. A certain amount of die-back at the tips of the shoots is a fairly regular occurrence and need cause no alarm.

Clethra Occasional thinning of overcrowded bushes consists of removing weak, twiggy shoots and a few of the oldest stems in winter.

Jasminum officinale (Common White Jasmine) Either cut back or remove some of the old wood altogether, each year in winter. Or prune after flowering (see Period Six, p. 237).

Lonicera (Honeysuckle), **climbing types** Annual treatment as for *Jasminum officinale*.

Rosa species and their hybrids and cultivars No pruning, as it applies to bedding roses, is required, but the occasional removal of some of the toughest old stems at ground level and the thinning of weak, unproductive twigs cluttering the plants, particularly in the centre, is beneficial in winter (see also Period Three, p. 196).

'Old' Roses Shorten the long shoots in winter annually, but do not prune hard.

Solanum crispum and S. jasminoides Leaving a few of the strongest shoots unpruned, spur back the rest annually to within 2 or 3 buds of the old wood in winter or early spring.

Stephanandra Keep up the supply of strong new shoots by getting rid of old growth at ground level annually in winter.

Syringa (Lilac) *Neglected* bushes may be rejuvenated by cutting the top-hamper down to about 2 ft. from the ground in winter. Next winter discard all but 3 or 4 of the most vigorous shoots sprouting from each stump, cutting the others right out, and retaining those unpruned until they have flowered. Normal pruning in summer, after flowering, should then be resumed (see Period Five, p. 226).

Viburnum, deciduous types Thin bushes only when overcrowded, by removing some of the oldest stems in winter.

Vitis vinifera 'Purpurea' (Claret Vine) **and other ornamental grape vines** If pruning as described in Period One is not done by the end of December it is better left undone, because of the risk of damage from loss of sap, known as 'bleeding' (see also Pinching Out, Period Five, pp. 226–27).

Mulching

This task is now becoming more urgent and should if possible be completed while there is still some remaining warmth in the soil. Mulches should not be applied when the soil is frozen.

Pests

Clay-coloured and Vine Weevils Spray or dust the ground beneath rhododendrons and other affected plants with BHC or Sevin periodically to kill the larvae in the soil.

Birds If early spring-flowering subjects have not yet been sprayed with Curb do so by the end of November or early December to last until mid- or late January (see directions for mixing to obtain long-lasting effects).

Four-legged Animal Pests As in Period One, p. 178. If the Curb spray was mixed to last eight weeks and was applied in the previous Period it should last throughout this one, but repeat application earlier, if in doubt.

Slugs Apply bait once a month in winter, treating hedge-bottoms, dry walls etc., as well as vulnerable foliage.

Diseases

Bud Blast Look over rhododendrons for browned or hairy blackish buds, which should be removed together with about 2 in. of stem and burned.

General Collect and burn any diseased foliage e.g. from roses, tree peonies etc.

Watch for signs of disease at all times and treat as recommended in the general section on the subject (pp. 117–29).

Winter Protection

Frost and Wind For such shrubs as need shelter from winter gales and severe icy spells take your pick from among the protective devices described on pp. 143–51 and get them into position by mid-December. See also special instructions for the protection of plants in containers.

Very young trees and shrubs may need protecting only for the first winter or two (e.g. young eucalypts need screening at the base of the trunk in their earliest years), whereas others considered barely hardy enough for the area concerned may need regular winter cosseting; a number of the less hardy silver-leaved shrubs such as *Artemisia arborescens* and *Convolvulus cneorum* will be likely to come into this category. Though not commonly listed as tender, hydrangeas may need protection in exposed situations in cold districts. Leaving the old flowers on the mophead kinds helps in this respect. Romneyas (Tree Poppy), phygelius (Cape Figwort) and other shrubby subjects which die to the ground in winter may be covered with bracken or similar litter, but for fuchsias use weathered ashes, unless they grow through some kind of evergreen carpeting plant which provides a living blanket.

Snow Only knock off snow if it threatens to break or overbalance the plant, as in the case of certain top-heavy evergreens and tap-rooted subjects, e.g. eucalypts, conifers, brooms, genistas, ceanothus and tree heaths.

Bind or tie in pyramidal conifers and tree heaths if necessary and truss up phormiums (New Zealand Flax) in districts of heavy snowfall as described on pp. 150–51).

Repairs As soon as the ground thaws after a spell of hard frost, re-firm recently planted specimens if lifted or loosened by frost.

Fill in hollow collars caused by wind-rocking, and stake if necessary.

Bandage splits as described on p. 151–2; trim irreparable breakages smoothly, and paint wounds of more than $\frac{3}{4}$ in. diameter with Arbrex.

Stakes and Ties

Check without delay for strength and durability, if not already attended to in Period One.

Miscellaneous

Falling leaves, weeds, variegated foliage plants, hydrangea colour treatment, training of climbers   As in Miscellaneous, Period One, pp. 179–80.

Water Butts and Similar Containers   Drain frost-vulnerable kinds to avoid distortion or bursting in icy weather and lag standpipes in the open.

Inspection   Keep an eye open for winter damage in particular.

Summary of the More Important Jobs in Period Two

Planting	Almost all trees and shrubs except the least hardy	Throughout this Period
Pruning (Annual)	Campsis	December onwards (to March)
	Jasminum officinale	,,
	Lonicera, climbing	,,
	Solanum crispum and	
	S. jasminoides	,,
	Stephanandra	,,
	Ornamental grape vines	Before end of December if not yet done
Mulching		Finish by Christmas, or sooner, if possible
Pests	Prevention of bird damage to spring-flowerers	Late November, if not yet attended to
	Clay-coloured and vine weevil larvae	Throughout this Period
	Slugs	Monthly in winter
Diseases	Bud blast on rhododendrons	Throughout this Period
Winter Protection	As necessary	Before Christmas
	Re-firm new plants lifted by frost	When necessary

	Repair snow and other breakages	When necessary
	Check on wind-rocking	Periodically
Stakes and Ties	Check for soundness	By first half of December
Miscellaneous	Drain damageable water butts and lag stand-pipes	Early to mid-December

NOTES: PERIOD TWO

PERIOD THREE: WINTER

Mid– or Late December to Early or Mid–March, according to season

Planting

Deciduous Trees and Shrubs and Hardy Evergreens As in Period Two. For the general run of deciduous subjects planting should be completed by the end of this Period, or at least by the end of March. Roses should, if possible, go in before Christmas, though planting is possible throughout this Period whenever the soil is neither frozen nor waterlogged. The hardy evergreens are the least urgent and may be left, with advantage, until Period Four.

Pruning (Late winter to earliest spring)

Check the list in Period Two and do any necessary pruning advised for winter or early spring which has not yet been done, but avoid pruning in frosty weather. An early spring may put a stop to winter pruning from any time after the end of February.

Deciduous Hedges If not clipped in August, or during the previous Period, they should be attended to during this one (see also Period Six, p. 238).

Early spring pruning (i.e. late February or March according to district and season) is recommended for the following, if necessary:

Abelia, deciduous types Long, straggling shoots may be cut back, weak twiggery removed, and some old wood taken out at the ground line occasionally.

Berberis, deciduous types Regular pruning is only necessary to obtain colourful young foliage on the purple-leaved varieties such as *B. thunbergii atropurpurea* (but not its dwarf form) and the pink and white variegated 'Rose Glow'. The main branches of these should be shortened back to strong new growth annually, and one or two of the oldest limbs occasionally removed. Other deciduous barberries may be similarly treated when pruning is necessary. The new, yellow-leaved *B. thunbergii* 'Aurea' seems similar in habit to

'Rose Glow' and the same regular treatment might therefore be expected to induce brighter foliage colour and bushier growth. I have slightly reduced the shoots on my tiny new plants, but am unable as yet to judge of the necessity for annual pruning.

Buddleia davidii and x weyerana varieties (Butterfly Bush) The long rods of the previous season should be ruthlessly cut back annually to within a few buds of their junction with the old wood, making the cut just above a strong live pair of buds. In backward areas, where these are not yet developed, leave the pruning until they are. In the case of gaunt old giants, cutting everything down to 1 ft. from the ground is risky, but may prove rejuvenating.

Callicarpa Overcrowded shoots may be reduced as necessary, retaining as much of the newer growth as possible.

Calluna (Heather) Clip over annually, preferably with secateurs, to remove last year's flowers, just before new growth starts. If shears have to be used on large drifts, alter the angle of the blades frequently to achieve a more natural effect.

Caryopteris As with roses, the weaker shoots are pruned harder than the strong ones, cutting the former to within a bud or two of their base and leaving 1 ft. of live growth on the strong shoots–if live it is, at the end of the winter. In cold districts I would advise leaving caryopteris alone until April.

Cassinia fulvida (Golden Heather, not a heather, but a daisy) Unless this is cut hard back for the house throughout the year, it will need an annual trimming now to prevent it from becoming gaunt and untidy (see also Period Six, p. 235).

Ceanothus, late summer-flowering types (e.g. 'Autumnal Blue', 'Gloire de Versailles') In the case of wall shrubs prune quite hard annually, leaving no more than 1 ft. on strong shoots and thinning out weak, muddled growth. In these positions they must not become crowded. Plants grown in the open borders do not need much pruning, except in cold districts to achieve a frost-defying density.

Ceratostigma Cut back to living wood annually, usually in very

early spring, depending on the weather. This may mean cutting
it to ground level.

Chaenomeles (Japonica)   Shorten long, wispy shoots devoid of
embryonic flower buds, but be careful to stop short of the coming
spring's flower buds in the process (see also Period Five, pp. 220–21).

Clematis   Breeders of modern clematis assure us that parentage
is now so mixed up that we need no longer bother with a mass of
pruning instructions governed by the Section (e.g. Lanuginosa,
Patens, Viticella, etc.) to which each one belongs. Instead, pruning
principles are based on three distinct flowering periods. Pruning
instructions included in this calendar are mainly condensed from a
lecture entitled *Sense about Clematis* delivered to the Royal Horticultural Society by the specialist grower, Mr W. E. Pennell, which
may be obtained in the form of a leaflet from his firm for a few pence
(see also R.H.S. Journal, Vol. CXI, Part one, Jan. 1966).

Group 1 covers early spring-flowering species and hybrids, which
are pruned after flowering, in May or June, and for which pruning
instructions are given in Period Five, p. 223.

Group 2 covers those which flower during May and June and
sometimes into July, with a repeat flowering in most cases in the
autumn. Pruning for these is not essential, *so long as they are regularly
trained and tied in*, but weak growth and dead parts should be cut
out in February or March, and strong shoots may be *slightly*
shortened at the same time. Any further reduction should wait
until after flowering (see Periods Five and Six, pp. 224, 235). Despite
reckless advice sometimes aired on the radio that all large-flowered
hybrids should be cut hard back at this season I have three times
proved this fatal for Group 2. All Groups and their treatment are
given in the specialists' catalogues and in the few cases in which
they differ regarding individual hybrids I find it safer to prune
cautiously (as for Group 2), rather than severely (as for Group 3).

Group 3 consists of those which flower *only* in late summer and
autumn, from July onwards. These will stand hard pruning. Cut
the growth of the previous season hard back almost to its point of
origin on the older wood in early spring, annually. One is advised
that if space is restricted they may even be cut to within 3 or 4 ft.

of the ground, though I personally distrust treatment as drastic as this. Group 3 also includes certain small-flowered species and their varieties which bloom in late summer.

New Plants   Young clematis of all kinds should be cut back to within about 1 ft. of the ground in February, making the cut just above a strong pair of buds. It takes as much strength of mind as the correct construction of a rock garden (in which costly rocks are buried in about the same proportions as an iceberg under water) to cut away so much top growth for which we have paid a high price. But this treatment may later be expected to repay us with sturdier growth in established plants. In selecting suitable buds at which to make the cut, 'a strong pair' should not be taken to mean the first to start into growth. The important point is to cut the top growth back as nearly as possible to 1 ft. above ground level if a healthy-looking pair of buds occurs thereabouts. 1 ft. above ground level is ideal, but as little as 6 in. is permissible if this is where the best growth buds between these two limits are placed. (It should perhaps be explained that the distinction between growth buds and flower buds made in Fig. 14A will not be detectable in young buds of clematis, since the embryonic flower buds are ensconced within the tightly furled leaf wrapping at this stage.) Most specialists recommend that this first pruning should be left until the plant's second season, which may be the best thing for the plant but increases the risk of one's overlooking the job altogether. Certain nurseries which send out their clematis in spring will already have pruned them before despatch.

Colutea (Bladder Senna)   In the case of wall plants, cut back the young growth fairly close to the parent limbs and clear out thin twiggery annually. Less regular pruning on the same lines suits open-ground specimens.

Cytisus nigricans   Unlike earlier-flowering brooms, *C. nigricans* flowers on the current year's growth and therefore needs differently timed treatment, trimming fairly hard back annually in February, but without cutting into old, hard wood.

Daboecia (St Dabeoc's Heath)   Shorten the flowered shoots of the previous season fairly hard just before growth starts each year, to prevent its tendency to straggle.

Erica (Heath), **summer-flowering types**   Clip over annually to remove last year's flowered shoots before the new growth appears, varying the angle of the cut if shears are used on large drifts.

Fuchsia   In cold gardens hardy or semi-hardy fuchsias will have died back to ground level and need no attention as yet. But in mild districts where top growth may survive, the side-shoots should be cut back fairly close to the main branches now, and dead wood removed.

Garrya elliptica (Tassel Bush)   Cut back, if necessary, immediately after flowering and before new growth begins, removing worn out wood and shortening some woody growth if the plant has become too dense to encourage the development of vigorous new shoots. Plants against walls are likely to need more frequent pruning than open-ground specimens. Never prune garrya in summer.

Hippophae rhamnoides (Sea Buckthorn)   Remove weak growth as necessary or, in the case of gaunt old plants, cut the whole down to about 3 ft. in early spring.

Hydrangea paniculata varieties   Remove the flowered tips annually in March or April, cutting back to a strong pair of buds. Light pruning results in more numerous but smaller flower panicles which, in the shrub borders, seem to me more appropriate than the fewer large heads produced by harder pruning.

Hydrangea villosa   Remove the flowered tips, shortening the shoots only slightly to the first good pair of growth buds.

Hypericum, Shrubby (St John's Wort)   Fairly drastic annual pruning makes for better bloom, reducing strong growth in the taller varieties such as 'Hidcote' by about three-quarters of its length and removing thin, muddled twigs altogether. Alternatively, the whole plant may be cut to the ground and then left to its own devices for a few years before repeating the treatment. The dwarf *H.* x *moseranum* (note unfamiliar but correct spelling!) usually dies to ground level in cold winters, so wait until signs of new growth appear before cutting out dead wood.

Indigofera   Where the top growth survives the winter, last year's shoots should be reduced annually at the end of this Period to about half their length or less, and weak growth eliminated. Any wood which has been killed back should be cut away.

Jasminum nudiflorum (Winter Jasmine) The flowered shoots should be pruned hard back annually after flowering.

Leycesteria formosa Shorten the flowered shoots fairly hard towards the end of this Period, and remove some of the old wands at the ground line each year to prevent overcrowding.

Lupinus arboreus (Tree Lupin) Regular pruning is important from the start, to prevent extreme top-heaviness in this fast-growing, rather short-lived subject. Remove old wood and weaker growths and shorten last year's more vigorous shoots pretty severely towards the end of this Period. (See also Pinching Out, Period Five, p. 227.)

Passiflora caerulea (Passion Flower) Cut most, but not all, of the strong new shoots hard back to within an inch or two of the parent branches in February or March annually. (If the top growth is killed in winter it usually springs again from the base.)

Potentilla (Shrubby Cinquefoil) There is a choice of treatment for the taller varieties (of which 'Katherine Dykes' and 'Purdomii' are typical) which may either be reduced to ground level in early spring each year to produce small, bushy specimens or, less drastically, relieved of some of the old growth only, in autumn (see Period One, p. 176). The latter form of pruning suits the dwarfer kinds.

Rhododendron, Hardy hybrids only Overgrown or gaunt old specimens may be cut down to about 2 ft. if necessary in March or early April, but many modern hybrids of lower hardiness ratings (especially the smooth-barked types) are loath to make new growth after any kind of hard cutting.

Rose, General Comments Opinions differ as to the best time for pruning roses, but the most reasonable course would seem to be to prune soon after the first signs of new growth appear, usually in late February or early March, but often later in cold districts. One should be prepared to go over the bushes a second time if hard frosts occur after pruning, to ensure that all dead, damaged or diseased wood is removed. Newly planted roses of the bedding types should be cut hard back at this time to within about 6 in. of the ground, though on poor soils it is advisable to postpone this operation until the second year. The hard pruning of established plants practised to obtain exhibition blooms does not make for maximum garden display.

Hybrid Teas   Healthy growth may be reduced by about half its length, the weaker shoots being pruned harder than the strong ones, cutting back to just above an outward-pointing bud. The cut should be a clean one and should be slanted so that the tapered end comes slightly above the bud. Where two buds or more are growing side by side, keep only the stronger one and rub out the other(s). Very vigorous sorts such as 'Peace' tend to be shy-flowering if hard pruned. If blind shoots are produced, cut them back to the second leaf joint.

Floribundas and Polyanthas   Either prune lightly all over, bearing in mind the principles mentioned above, or follow the currently popular staggered technique, i.e. lightly prune one-year-old wood, cut two-year-old wood back moderately hard and hard prune three-year-old wood, in order to achieve continuity of blooms.

Climbers   No pruning other than deadheading is advised for the first year. Subsequent pruning depends on the amount of growth made during the previous season, shortening the side-shoots where old wood needs to be retained, and cutting the old wood back to strong new growth where the latter exists. The majority of climbers do not need much pruning except to guide them in the way they should go. *Rosa banksiae*, climbing 'Peace' and 'Mermaid' in particular resent pruning.

Ramblers   see Period One, p. 176.

Shrub Roses   This heading covers a wide assortment such as 'Constance Spry', 'Nevada', 'Aloha' and the Hybrid Musk varieties. These require little pruning except in their first year, when strong shoots should be shortened and weak growth cut hard back. Species such as *Rosa moyesii*, *R.* x *cantabrigiensis*, etc., benefit from the removal of one or two of the oldest stems at ground level occasionally in winter.

Sambucus (Elder) Yellow-leaved forms produce finer foliage if the newer growths are cut back almost to the old wood annually.

Spiraea, late summer-flowering types Cut last season's growth back fairly severely each year and occasionally remove some worn-out wood at the ground line.

Symphoricarpos (Snowberry and Coral berry) Remove some of the oldest stems and weak growth annually.

Tamarix pentandra (autumn-flowering Tamarisk) Cut the previous year's shoots hard back almost to the older growth annually for maximum flowering. (Do not confuse this with the May-flowering *T. tetrandra*, for which see Period Five, p. 226.)

Vaccinium, deciduous types Occasional removal of old wood to ground level, or cutting back of the main branches to vigorous young growth in January or February, prevents the bushes from becoming overcrowded.

Wisteria Cut all side-shoots back to no more than 2 buds annually in late winter, when grown as wall shrubs. Little pruning is necessary for wisteria grown through trees, except where it threatens to strangle its host (see also Period Six, p. 237).

Deadheading

Some of the first rhododendrons of the year will be ready for some deadheading during this Period (see Fig. 25). Some camellias such as the x *williamsii* types are self-cleaning. The rest may be dead-headed for appearances' sake, but since they are not much inclined to set seed in most parts of the country their vigour is unlikely to be impaired if deadheading is neglected.

Mulching and Feeding

If available, apply a thin layer of well rotted farmyard manure in winter to the soil around clematis, roses, syringa, deciduous viburnums, and foliage plants such as fatsia, phormium, leucothoe and variegated weigela. On very light, hungry soils rhododendrons may also be included. Where farmyard manure is unobtainable some form of organic fertilizer may be substituted.

Calluna and summer-flowering Erica (Heather and Heath) These appreciate a topdressing of peat or weed-free compost (which must also be lime-free in both cases) just before growth starts in spring.

Rose Give the first application of special rose fertilizer in early spring, being careful that it does not come in contact with the stems.

Syringa (Lilac) Lightly fork in a handful or two of hoof and horn in February or March.

Trees if necessary apply a general fertilizer in March.

Pests

Clay-coloured and Vine Weevils Dust the foliage of rhododendrons and other affected plants periodically with BHC, Sevin, or other promised new substitutes for DDT dust from March onwards to combat any newly emerging adults (probably clay-coloured only as yet), and the ground beneath the bushes to defeat the last of the larvae of both kinds of weevil. When dusting rhododendron foliage with coloured indumentum on the undersides of the leaves, apply the dust as lightly as possible so as not to spoil the appearance of this velvety or woolly covering, on which the powder tends to cling, showing up conspicuously if applied in heavy-handed fashion.

Animals

Birds If Curb (mixed according to the longer-lasting formula) was applied in late November to early spring-flowering shrubs, another application will be due towards the middle or end of January.

Four-footed Animals As in Periods One and Two, pp. 178 and 185.

Slugs Protection will now be required for new green basal shoots on hydrangea plants and other young growth. Continue to bait hedge-bottoms, dry walls and similar places. Monthly applications are adequate throughout this Period.

Diseases

Bud Blast Look over rhododendrons for buds bristling with a hairy black growth. Cut these away with about 2 in. of the shoot and burn.

Chlorosis If due to the presence of lime in the soil, apply Murphy Sequestrene to discoloured plants in late winter or early spring. It is usually necessary to repeat the dose annually.

Leaf-Curl (Prunus subjects) Spray with Bordeaux Mixture or lime-sulphur when the buds are swelling, just before they are due to burst (see also Periods One, Five and Six, pp. 179, 230 and 240).

Rose Black Spot and Rust Collect fallen leaves before watering the soil with Jeyes' Fluid or Bordeaux Mixture during dormancy. Spray with a rose fungicide, such as captan for black spot, or zineb for rust, after pruning, if the leaves have started to unfold.

General Keep a watch for signs of disease at all times and treat as recommended on pp. 117–29.

Winter Protection

Any winter protective measures required by trees and shrubs of questionable hardiness should be urgently dealt with at the beginning of this Period, as recommended in Period Two, if still undone.

Snow As in Period Two, p. 186.

Repairs As in Period Two, p. 186.

Stakes and Ties

Check stakes and ties after gales or heavy snowfall and repair if necessary without delay.

Watering

The searing north and east winds of early spring may do more damage in the shrub garden than frost and snow, especially to immature plants. Give newly planted subjects a good soaking if necessary, and if evergreens lose an excessive amount of moisture through their leaves spray with cold water during windy periods, or with the plastic spray, S-600 (which should be stored in a warm temperature).

Miscellaneous

Falling Leaves   The last of these will need to be raked off verge plants, lawns and paths and deposited within the shrub borders during December, with the exception of diseased foliage, which should be burned.

Variegated Foliage Plants   Remove plain green shoots, cutting them right back to their point of origin, whenever they appear.

Training Climbers and Wall Plants   Much of this may be combined with pruning in this Period, tying the existing growth into place before the new season's shoots complicate matters further. Rampant climbers, such as clematis and honeysuckle, will need repeated training from now on throughout the growing season.

Disbudding   It pays to remove most of the flower buds on new young camellias and rhododendrons in early spring, and if established rhododendrons produce large clusters of flower buds at the end of a shoot, finer flowers will be obtained if all except one bud are removed.

Heeling In or Storing   Plants arriving during hard frost or other unsuitable weather should be dealt with as described on pp. 47–8.

Water Butts Keep these drained during severe weather if liable to damage.

Weeding The earliest of the annual weeds, if any, should be removed before they have a chance to multiply.

Blueing of Established Hydrangeas (macrophylla varieties) For blue or violet flowers instead of red or pink, treatment should start in earliest spring, that is, at the end of this Period or early in the next, according to season. Mix $\frac{1}{4}$ oz. aluminium sulphate and $\frac{1}{4}$ oz. iron sulphate in 1 gallon of rain-water (or about 1 heaped dessert-spoon of each to 2 gallons of water) and leave it to stand for at least half a day. Water over the entire root area at the rate of about 2 gallons weekly until midsummer, or until the flowers are fully open, and again in autumn, saturating the soil in contact with the roots. It is unwise to treat young plants because it tends to check their growth.

A more extravagant and more risky alternative is to scatter aluminium sulphate on the soil over the root area, mixing it thoroughly into the topsoil in spring and again in November, and watering it in with $\frac{1}{4}$ oz. iron sulphate dissolved in 1 gallon of rain-water. Repeat the watering at regular intervals unless equally regular natural rainfall does the job for you. A large bush may need as much as 10 lb. of colourant.

Inspection Keep watch for trouble of any kind, as usual.

Summary of the More Important Jobs in Period Three

Planting	Almost all trees and shrubs except the least hardy	Finish deciduous plantings if possible by the end of this Period
Pruning (Annual)	Berberis, deciduous, purple-leaved and others grown for foliage colour	Early spring
	Buddleia davidii and x *weyerana* varieties	Early spring
	Calluna	Early spring
	Caryopteris	Late March (or April)

	Cassinia	Early spring
	Ceanothus, late summer-flowering, on walls	Early spring
	Ceratostigma	Early spring
	Clematis, Group 3 (also Group 2 if needed)	Early spring
	Clematis, 2nd-year plants of all kinds	February
	Colutea	Early spring
	Cytisus nigricans	Early spring
	Daboecia	Early spring
	Erica	Early spring
	Fuchsia	Late March (or April)
	Hydrangea paniculata varieties and *H. villosa*	March
	Hypericum	Early spring
	Indigofera	Early spring
	Jasminum nudiflorum	Early spring
	Leycesteria formosa	Early spring
	Lupinus arboreus	March
	Passiflora caerulea	Early spring
	Potentilla	Early spring
	Rose	Early spring
	Spiraea, late summer-flowering	Early spring
	Symphoricarpos	Early spring
	Tamarix pentandra	Early spring
	Wisteria	Late winter

Dead-heading Early rhododendrons   As flowers fade

Feeding

Clematis	⎫	Winter
Foliage plants	⎪	Winter
Roses	⎬ Farmyard	Winter
Syringa	⎪ manure	Winter
Viburnums, deciduous	⎭	Winter
Roses	Rose fertilizer, first application	Early spring
Syringa	Hoof and horn	Early spring

Pests	Birds: second treatment for spring-flowerers	Mid- to late January
	Clay-coloured and vine weevils: foliage of rhododendrons and other likely victims, and surrounding soil	March onwards
	Slugs: Apply bait monthly	Throughout this Period
Diseases	Black spot and rust:	
	soil treatment	Winter
	plant treatment	Early spring
	Chlorosis: sequestrene application	Late winter or early spring
	Rhododendron bud blast	Winter to spring
	Other diseases	As necessary
Winter Protection	As necessary	Urgent at the start of this Period
	Repair damage	As necessary
	Re-firm plants lifted by frost	As necessary
	Check on wind-rocking	Periodically
Stakes and Ties	Check for soundness	After gales or heavy snow
Watering	Newly planted subjects, especially evergreens	During periods of wind or drought
Miscellaneous	Keep water butts drained if liable to damage	During severe weather
	Start training climbers and wall plants	Early spring

NOTES: PERIOD THREE

PERIOD FOUR: SPRING

Mid-March to Late April or Early May
according to Season

Much of what comes under the first two headings in this Period might have been done at any time during the winter, but if the weather has landed us with a backlog of planting and pruning to be completed during dormancy these jobs now become urgent.

Planting

The majority of deciduous trees and shrubs should have been planted by the end of March in the average season. Some exceptions which should wait until May are listed in Period Five. So long as the garden is neither waterlogged, exceptionally dry, nor still in the grip of winter, late March and April are favourable times for planting most of the more difficult evergreens, spring planting being preferable to autumn in all but the mildest districts. This also applies to the hardier silver-leaved subjects such as *Atriplex halimus* (Tree Purslane), ballota, *Euryops acraeus*, most helichrysums (but not *H. petiolatum*), santolina (Lavender Cotton), *Senecio greyi*, and a number of plants also usually specified by nurserymen for spring planting. Others such as evergreen magnolias, bamboos, clematis and the least hardy outdoor silver-leaved shrubs may wait until May.

Pruning

In average circumstances there should still be time in March for any winter pruning recommended in Period Three.

It is perhaps hardly necessary to mention that from spring onwards any subject which needs annual pruning after flowering may just as well be cut in flower for indoor decoration, cutting as far as possible as though pruning—not butchering.

Look out for wood killed by winter weather and cut it out as soon as it is distinguishable from live (i.e. newly budded) growth.

Suckers should also be removed as soon as they appear.

Late March and Early April Pruning

Buddleia alternifolia, to form a weeping standard Leave
unpruned for the first two years, then cut away all but one vigorous
basal shoot. Keep this disbudded until it reaches a height of about
6 ft. and stake very firmly. When the single stem is tall enough for
the intended trunk, pinch out the tip to induce branching growth
and continue to disbud the trunk itself. Once the weeping standard
framework has been achieved annual pruning takes place in late
summer, after flowering (see Period Six, p. 235). *Buddleia davidii*
and x *weyerana* cultivars: as in Period Three, if not yet done.

Cornus (Dogwood), **types grown for bark colour** Either
coppice-prune all last year's shoots to within two or three buds of
their base annually or, preferably, remove only half the total
number each year (see Fig. 17).

Danae racemosa (Alexandrian Laurel) If the clumps become
crowded thin out some of the oldest wands in spring. This is however such splendid cutting material that little other pruning is
likely to be necessary in a flower arranger's garden.

Escallonia Free-standing bushes may be cut back occasionally
either in spring or after flowering (wall plants are pruned after
flowering, Period Six, p. 237).

Eucalyptus, hardy species A very young tree makes a better,
bushier specimen if the top is cut out just before growth starts in
the spring following planting. If after a year or two a plant fails to
make good growth it is said by the experts to respond to being cut
back to ground level in March. (I have not had the courage to
test this maxim.)

Other forms of spring pruning depend upon the type of growth
required, i.e. coppiced or pollarded forms, shrub, tree or hedge.
Immensely detailed advice on pruning for each of these forms is
contained in Part II of an article entitled *An Introduction to Some
Garden Eucalypts* by Mr R. C. Barnard, published in the Journal of
the Royal Horticultural Society, Vol. XCI, Part 6 (June, 1966).
These instructions cannot usefully be condensed but would, I am
sure, be available for study in the Society's library if required.

Some browning of the foliage in a hard winter is a fairly common
occurrence, and will usually have righted itself by early summer.

Hedera (Ivy)   Do any clipping or more drastic pruning that may be necessary in April, for preference.

Hydrangea macrophylla varieties   As soon as hard frost is no longer likely, remove the desiccated flower heads left on the mop-heads for winter protection of the growth buds beneath, cutting back to a plump pair of buds. In cold gardens leave them till April if necessary, but try to finish any pruning before the new growth buds are really plumped up, because they are then so easily knocked off when reaching into the plant to remove the dead heads or a gnarled old stem or two and to cut out wood killed by frost. The new green shoots pushing up from ground level will need thinning pretty drastically, leaving room for only a few of them to grow on strongly without crowding, provided the slugs do not get them.

Itea ilicifolia   Long, straggling shoots may be reduced in April.

Ligustrum ovalifolium 'Aureum' (Golden Privet)   If open-ground specimens need to be reduced, shorten the shoots in spring or late summer with secateurs, not shears.

Lithospermum diffusum varieties   Cut away all winter-killed growth as hard as necessary (see also after flowering, Period Five, p. 224).

Mahonia japonica   This is best left alone as long as the entire plant looks well furnished, but very occasionally the lower portion of a woody limb becomes so bare and leggy that it is worth while removing its top whorl of foliage, with some length of the woody stem, just after flowering, in order to induce it to break into fresh growth lower down, which it usually does.

Phygelius capensis (Cape Figwort)   In cold areas it will probably be necessary to cut last year's wood back to ground level, if killed by frost. Otherwise merely cut back to new growth when it appears in spring.

Salix (Willow), **types grown for bark colour**   As for cornus.

Sorbaria   Prune all growth either to the ground, or nearly so, annually, cutting back in the latter case to a good, strong bud.

208   PERIOD FOUR

Late April Pruning

Late April or early May is regarded as the best time to prune the majority of evergreen shrubs *if necessary*, unless they happen to be in bloom, in which case it may be deferred until they have finished flowering.

If overgrown evergreens, including evergreen hedges, need really severe treatment involving cutting into the old wood this, too, is best done in April.

Arundinaria and other bamboos   The oldest canes should be cut right out periodically, to thin crowded clumps. (Trim and dry the old canes for use as stakes.)

Atriplex halimus (Tree Purslane)   If not cut sufficiently hard for flower arrangement, odd shoots may occasionally need shortening to keep it shapely or to contain it in a limited space.

Ballota   Prune back to about 6 in. in late April or early May, at least every other year.

Berberis, evergreen species   Only occasional thinning of the oldest stems to ground level, or shortening them to strong new shoots, is necessary. Wait until after flowering if April-flowering species require pruning.

Buddleia globosa (Chilean Orange Ball Tree)   Gaunt, overgrown bushes may be cut hard back to the old wood, instead of the normal pruning after flowering, for which see Period Five, p. 223.

Bupleurum fruticosum   Thin occasionally any time in April, or cut fairly hard annually, if limitations of space require it.

Camellia   Old specimens which have grown out of hand may be reduced by one half, or more if necessary, in April. Otherwise do no pruning.

Caryopteris   In cold districts leave the annual pruning until April, following the instructions given in Period Three (p. 191) for warmer gardens.

Chimonanthus (Winter Sweet) In the case of wall shrubs cut all the side-shoots back almost to their parent branches each year after flowering.

Cytisus battandieri Spring pruning is not essential, but some trimming of straggling shoots improves its appearance and may, in particular, be necessary in wall positions where this delightful and unusual broom is commonly grown.

Euonymus fortunei varieties Bush or carpeting specimens may be trimmed as necessary. Wall specimens need little or no pruning.

Euphorbia characias and E. veneta (*wulfenii*) (Giant Spurge) Remove dead stems and any with frosted tips which will be unable to flower. (Promise of flower is indicated by a crook-head as distinct from an upright tip as early as mid-winter.)

Fuchsia In backward districts new growth should now be appearing, making it possible to cut back the old wood to live buds if any, or to remove dead wood to the ground line annually.

Genista aetnensis (Mt. Etna Broom) For a semi-weeping standard, pinch out all the side-growths on the new plant and continue to do so in spring for several years until the trunk is tall enough, keeping it very firmly staked meanwhile.

Hebe (Shrubby Veronica) Reduce overgrown bushes by cutting hard back, as necessary, every few years.

Helichrysum Cut back the hardier kinds such as *serotinum* (*angustifolium*) and *plicatum* close to the old wood each year in April.

Lavandula (Lavender) Cut fairly hard back to the new growth near the base annually, to prevent legginess which causes early demise.

Magnolia, evergreen types If wall plants need restraining, prune as required, or thin the growth.

Magnolia x soulangiana varieties When grown against a wall cut back, if you must, after flowering, but deciduous magnolias are inclined to resent pruning.

Olearia x haastii (Daisy Bush)   Scraggy old plants will make an enormous amount of new growth from the old wood if cut back drastically in late April.

Osmanthus (syn. Siphonosmanthus) **delavayi**   Lanky old specimens will 'break' readily from the old wood if cut down to about half their height.

Perovskia atriplicifolia (Afghan Sage)   Prune annually to the base of last year's growth, or even harder.

Phormium tenax (New Zealand Flax)   Cut dead or damaged leaf blades out at ground level when the protective winter trussing is removed each year.

Prunus 'Cistena'   Unlike some of its relations this prunus will stand hard pruning after flowering if desired.

Pyracantha (Firethorn)   Hard pruning of neglected wall shrubs may be done in April, sacrificing the flowering growth. Other wall shrubs may have shoots shortened where necessary, but this should be limited to a minimum until after flowering (see Period Five, p. 225).

Raphiolepis   The shortening of long shoots may occasionally be necessary for the sake of symmetry.

Ribes (Flowering Currant)   Cut back to strong young growth after flowering every few years.

Romneya (Tree Poppy)   This is usually cut to the ground in a hard winter, but whether the top growth is live or dead it may all be reduced to the ground line in spring, to be replaced by strong new growth from the base.

Rosmarinus (Rosemary)   Overgrown bushes should be cut hard back now, but other pruning should wait until after flowering (see Period Five, p. 225).

Ruta graveolens varieties (Rue)   Cut very hard back each April for the best foliage effect.

Santolina (Lavender Cotton)   Cut back to the fuzz of new growth at the base of the shoots, if only pruned once a year. If the plants are kept trimmed periodically during the summer less drastic reduction will be necessary now.

Senecio greyi   Cut back in April annually–hard if necessary. Well grown plants in the fullest exposure will probably need only light trimming, but where weak, bare growth and dead wood are cluttering up the bushes these should be removed. For drastic treatment of scrawny old plants see Period Five, p. 222. (See also pinching out and de-flowering in Period Five, pp. 226, 227.)

Spartium junceum (Spanish Broom)   It is important to rid the plant of winter-killed growth annually, as well as to trim hard after flowering (see Period One, p. 177).

Stachyurus   Flowering branches make delightful cutting material. Any other shortening of overlong shoots or thinning which may be necessary should be done after flowering.

Stranvaesia   Shorten some of the longer shoots and thin crowded branches if necessary.

Styrax japonica (Snowbell)   If wanted on a single stem, the basal growth may be cut away in April to leave a clean trunk, painting all but the smallest scars with Arbrex. Otherwise no pruning is necessary.

Ulex europaeus 'Plenus' (Double Gorse)   Legginess in old plants may be remedied by cutting all the gnarled old wood down to 1 ft., at the cost of the season's bloom.

Vaccinium, evergreen species   Any shaping of evergreen vacciniums should be done in April, as needed.

Yucca   Cut the dead leaves out to the base yearly.

Deadheading

Early flowering rhododendrons, pieris, tree peonies and so on.

Feeding

Clematis   Apply 2 oz. of a general fertilizer, or water with a good liquid feed, in spring (and again in July–see Period Six, p. 239, and also see Period Three, p. 197).

Eucalyptus   Feeding is not generally recommended for these exceptionally fast growers, but I have read (I cannot recall where) that in the case of plants on infertile soil or of those which are hard pruned annually, a handful of sulphate of ammonia per sq. yd. applied to the soil in spring provides necessary nitrogen. As mentioned under Specialized Planting Hints (pp. 61–2), even at planting time fertile soils need no enrichment for eucalypts; but both Mr Barnard and his successor, Mr Bayles, approve the addition of bonemeal to *poor* soils and of moist peat to *dry, sandy ones*, during the planting process.

Eucryphia   On hungry soils an early spring mulch of well rotted farmyard manure mixed with acid peat or compost will be appreciated, especially if not kept adequately mulched with fallen leaves.

Hydrangea   On poor, hungry soils spray with a foliar feed soon after they come into leaf.

Lithospermum diffusum varieties   Unless topdressed regularly in spring with weed-free, acid compost or peat, the size of the flowers is likely to dwindle and the growth to deteriorate.

Magnolia   Mulch with well-rotted farmyard manure, hop manure or leafmould in spring, being careful not to disturb the easily damaged surface roots. Such feeding is especially beneficial during the first few years.

Pests

Aphids   These may begin to appear quite early in the spring, depending on the weather. For the type of isolated huddle likely to occur early in the season in particular, I find it convenient to keep one of my several Acme Blowers charged with malathion dust or to give them a squirt from my Metasystox Aphid Gun. Look out for early infestation not only on roses but on various tender young foliage shoots, e.g. greenfly on camellias, evergreen magnolias, clematis, honeysuckle, hydrangeas and so on, and blackfly on some cherries and viburnums and on *Euonymus europaeus* (Spindle).

Caterpillars, various If too numerous to pick off, dust or spray with malathion or derris, or use a systemic insecticide.

Clay-coloured and Vine Weevils Spray or dust the leaves with BHC, Sevin (dust only), or other substitutes for DDT, paying special attention to the undersides, starting in late March and repeating periodically until September. In the case of rhododendron foliage with coloured undersides, dust lightly and evenly, to preserve their beauty, repeating periodically until September. (This treatment will also, incidentally, take care of rhododendron bug and rhododendron whitefly.)

Rabbits These will now be turning their attention from bark-gnawing to the nibbling of lush young greenery. Spraying with Curb is said to be effective (as against other four-footed pests), but fortunately I have had no opportunity to test its effect on rabbits, though it has undoubtedly discouraged dogs from invading the garden.

Rose Leaf-rolling Sawflies and Tortrix Caterpillars Spray or dust with BHC or Sevin, or apply liquid substitutes for DDT in April or early May as a deterrent, and hand-pick affected leaves at an early stage. Once these pests are established the innermost parts of the rolled or cocooned leaflets are most likely to be reached with a special rose systemic such as Toprose (PBI) or Murphy's Systemic Insecticide.

Slugs Increase applications of slug bait from monthly to fortnightly throughout the growing season. Pay special attention to *Danae racemosa* (Alexandrian Laurel), fuchsias, hydrangeas, romneyas (Tree Poppy) and ground-covering foliage plants.

Diseases

Azalea Gall Affects dwarf evergreen azaleas. Spray with a copper or zineb fungicide such as Dithane (PBI) just before the new foliage unfurls. If the swellings appear on the new leaf-shoots or flowers pick these off and burn them. Neglect of the disease will undoubtedly increase the severity of the attack, in which case repeated spraying throughout spring and summer will be necessary.

Clematis Wilt   Cut out wilted shoots immediately or, if all growth is affected, raze the entire plant to ground level, and thereafter water regularly and copiously throughout the growing season, even though there may appear to be nothing left to water. Watch for new shoots at ground level and protect them from slugs, mice, rabbits, greenfly and other foliage-eating pests.

Fire Blight   Watch for early symptoms and remove affected parts to prevent spread of infection.

Hydrangea Botrytis   Start the application of a foliar feed as a prophylactic, especially in areas of previous infection.

Peony Wilt   As soon as the leaves appear spray fortnightly until flowering with captan, Dithane (PBI) or other fungicide, in gardens where the disease is prevalent. If necessary, continue the treatment after flowering to prevent damage to the leaves. Cut away diseased portions immediately and burn. The tool used should then be sterilized.

Powdery Mildew   This may affect all manner of shrubs, usually rather later in the season, but prevention of mildew is easier than cure, so likely victims should be dusted or sprayed with dinocap (Karathane) at an early stage, and then periodically during the growing season, unless a more all-purpose fungicide is being used, as for example those which control both black spot and mildew on roses.

Rose Fungus Diseases, various   Fungicide dusts and sprays currently available for the control of black spot, mildew, rust and others need to be applied about once a fortnight from spring to late autumn, depending upon the weather; but when the systemic fungicides which are now being developed become obtainable they should be considerably more long-lasting, because they are not washed off by rain. Young shoots seen to be infected by the powdery yellow (spring) stage of rose rust should be cut out and burned.

General Keep a look-out for symptoms of disease likely to strike at any time and treat as recommended on pp. 117–29.

Winter Protection

In some seasons it may still be necessary to re-firm plants lifted by hard frost during March.

Various temporary shelters and other protective devices may be removed as soon as the danger of prolonged frost and snow and arctic gales is at an end.

Snow If snow occurs from late March onwards it is unlikely to be heavy or long-lasting, and there is nothing one can do but grin and bear it.

Sudden Overnight Frost A sharp, overnight frost is possible even at midsummer in the worst frost hollows, and is a very real danger to burgeoning shoots and flowers in all but the mildest districts in April and May. If air frost is forecast give what makeshift protection there is time for to favourite items in the spring display, covering these with almost anything available–even newspaper. A stock of $\frac{1}{4}$ in. mesh plastic netting such as Rokolene Windbreak, is one of the easiest and quickest forms of protection. Further details of emergency measures are given on pp. 152–4. (See also Watering, below.)

Watering

Versus Late Spring Frost A shrub border on which water can be sprayed throughout a frosty night should be safe from damage. Where no overnight covering or spraying has been possible, water the frost off the plants (with *cold* water) in the early morning before the sun reaches them. It is however rarely possible to salvage anything in fully open flower, as distinct from opening bud.

Versus Drought Drought is a common feature of this Period, due to drying spring winds. If watering becomes necessary, despite the moisture-conserving properties of the leaf-mulch, an occasional soaking is much more beneficial than frequent dribbling.

Plants growing against house walls are likely to be particularly short of water. Special attention should be paid to any clematis which have previously shown signs of wilt disease.

If very dry weather follows spring planting of evergreens, it may be advisable to spray the foliage each evening with cold water during periods of wind or drought. Alternatively the plastic spray, S-600, which envelops the leaf surfaces in a fine film, may be preferred as being more long-lasting in its effects.

Miscellaneous

Training of Wall Shrubs and Climbers These will need regular attention from now on, especially climbers of the clematis type, which turn into an untidy and debilitating tangle if neglected.

Unwanted Buds on Tree Trunks If trees grown on a clean stem produce growth buds on the trunk, rub these out by hand before they have time to develop.

Variegated Foliage Plants Remove plain green shoots, as always, whenever they appear.

Weeds Newly planted ground-cover should be kept free of weeds until it has, in fact, become ground-covering. Such annual weeds as may appear in the shrub garden should be exterminated before they multiply.

Non-vegetable Mulches If applied for winter protection over fuchsias and so on they should be removed before the tool used for the job risks damage to newly emergent shoots.

Colour Treatment for Established Hydrangeas As described on p. 201. To obtain blue hydrangeas, start watering suitable sorts, as soon as growth begins, with the solution of aluminium and iron sulphates. It is not a bit of good attempting to influence flower colour by delaying treatment until the plants are about to bloom. One additional dose should be given in the autumn (see Period Three, p. 201).

Red or pink flowers may be obtained by mixing $\frac{1}{2}$ oz. ground

lime with 2 gallons of water and applying over the root area. One
annual treatment in spring should be enough in this case.

Layering   As in Period One, p. 180.

Inspection   Routine tours of inspection should be made daily if
possible, combining duty with pleasure, now that the spectacle is
under way.

Summary of the More Important Jobs in Period Four

Planting	The more difficult ever-greens, some of the hardier silver-leaved subjects and a few oddments customarily sent out in spring	Late March or April
Pruning	Ballota	Late April or early May
(Annual)	Caryopteris, cold districts	April
	Chimonanthus, wall plants	April
	Cornus, for bark colour	Late March
	Eucalyptus, one year after planting	March
	Fuchsia	April
	Helichrysum, hardier sorts	April
	Hydrangea macrophylla	March or April
	Lavandula	April
	Lithospermum diffusum varieties	March or April
	Perovskia atriplicifolia	April
	Phormium	April
	Phygelius	March or April
	Romneya	April
	Ruta	April
	Salix, for bark colour	Late March
	Santolina	April
	Senecio greyi	April
	Sorbaria	March or early April
	Spartium	April
	Yucca	April

Dead-heading	Pieris, early-flowering rhododendrons, tree peonies, etc.	As flowers fade
Feeding	Clematis: general fertilizer or liquid feed	Spring
	Eucryphia: farmyard manure, etc.	Spring
	Lithospermum diffusum varieties: acid compost or peat	Spring
	Magnolias: farmyard manure or similar	Spring
	For many subjects in need of a boost: foliar feeding	Spring and early summer
Pests	Aphids, caterpillars (including tortrix), clay-coloured and vine weevils, and leaf-rolling sawflies	From spring onwards
	Rabbits attacking new green growth	From spring onwards
	Slugs–bait fortnightly	Throughout growing season
Diseases	Look out in particular for azalea gall, clematis wilt, fire blight, peony wilt, powdery mildew and rose fungus diseases	Throughout growing season
Watering		As necessary
Miscellaneous	Training of climbers and wall plants	Frequently from now on
	Inspection	Daily, now, if possible
	Remove non-vegetable winter mulches	Just before new shoots are due to emerge

NOTES: PERIOD FOUR

May to Early or Mid-July, according to season

Planting

Although one may take liberties with transplantation at almost any time within one's own garden, only certain subjects recommended for late spring despatch are customarily sent out from the nurseries in May or early June. These include:
  Ceratostigma
  Cistus (Rock Rose)
  Eucalyptus, hardy species
  Fuchsia
  x Halimiocistus
  Halimium
  Helianthemum (Sun Rose)
  Romneya (Tree Poppy)
  Tropaeolum speciosum (Flame Flower)
  Some less hardy silver-leaved subjects such as *Artemisia arborescens, Convolvulus cneorum, Senecio cineraria, S. leucostachys* and *Teucrium fruticans* (Shrubby Germander).

Properly pot-grown subjects may be planted throughout this Period, provided they are put into moist soil and are never allowed to dry out.

Pruning

Catch up on any essential pruning left undone in April at the beginning of this Period, if suitable weather allows.
  Continue to remove suckers whenever they are spotted.
  Generally speaking, pruning during this Period will be chiefly concerned with spring-flowering shrubs when their display is finished.

May Pruning

Chaenomeles (Japonica) On wall plants the side-shoots should be spurred back close to the main branches after flowering, and I find it necessary to do the same for open-ground plants, though less drastic treatment is usually advised for these. If old specimens are very sparsely flowered, having first made sure that the buds have not merely been stripped by birds, cut them hard down and give them a handful of hoof and horn to help them to make a fresh start. (See also Period Three, p. 192 and Pinching Out in this Period, and the next, p. 236.)

Cistus (Rock Rose)   Wait until May to examine these for frost damage, by which time the live growth should be identifiable. Cut out all dead wood and peg down suitable shoots. (See also Pinching Out in this Period and the next, p. 236.)

Corylopsis   Cut out muddled, spindly twigs and exhausted old wood occasionally.

Erica arborea 'Alpina', E. australis and other Tree Heaths Reducing the flowered shoots by about 1½–2 ft. annually, though not perhaps *de rigueur*, is the surest way to obtain really bushy specimens with vivid young green foliage plumes well feathered to the ground. Unpruned bushes tend to become bare-legged and wispy.

Erica carnea varieties and other winter-flowering Heaths Clipping every two or three years after flowering is probably enough for these.

Forsythia x intermedia varieties   Cut back all vigorous flowered shoots annually.

Forsythia suspensa   This is the rather more floppy, paler yellow species (usually grown against a wall or other support), which needs harder pruning, cutting all side-shoots back almost to the old wood.

Kerria   Quite severe annual pruning, especially for the double variety and for the variegated one, is advisable after flowering, getting rid of some of the older wood altogether and shortening other branching wands back to vigorous young shoots.

x Osmarea 'Burkwoodii'   Give this a light trim annually, or less frequently, after flowering.

Prunus (Ornamental Cherry, also almonds, peaches, apricots) Most are better left unpruned, but if it becomes necessary to amputate a live branch or to remove side-growths, do this in late May or early summer (not later than 15th July), when there is least risk of silver leaf infection. Paint the cut surfaces with Arbrex.

Prunus tenella (Dwarf Russian Almond)   This is an exception which benefits from being cut fairly hard back after flowering—or, of course, when in bloom.

Rosmarinus (Rosemary)   Light cutting back of the tips of the shoots and the trimming of hedges may be done after flowering, as necessary.

Rubus (Ornamental Bramble)   Those with decorative stems, e.g. *R. cockburnianus*, need to be thinned to ground level in early May to make way for new growth. Those with ornamental flowers, e.g. *R.* 'Tridel', also need to be relieved of some of the old wood at the ground line to stimulate new growth.

Senecio greyi   Scrawny old specimens will usually respond to severe cutting back into the old wood in early summer, though in cold districts this may be a little risky.

Spiraea thunbergii   Cutting back yearly, after flowering, to strong new shoots springing from fairly far back on the old wood keeps the bush well furnished, and more graceful flowering sprays result from the removal of muddled little twigs.

May Pinching Out (see Fig. 22)

Silver-leaved Subjects, Newly Planted   Pinch out the extreme tips of the shoots frequently during their first season, from May to the end of July, to encourage bushiness.

Vitis vinifera 'Purpurea' (Claret Vine) **and other ornamental grape vines**   Pinch out the tips of the new growth occasionally

from now on (or as soon as there is anything to pinch out) until
about the end of July.

May Deadheading
Continue to attend to tree peonies, pieris, rhododendrons, deciduous
azaleas (the latter as for rhododendrons, Fig. 25).

Summer Pruning

Hedges   For those that are to be trimmed several times during the
growing season clipping should start in June. (For less precisely
clipped hedges see Period Six, p. 238.)

Buddleia globosa (Chilean Orange Ball Tree)   If not cut back to
the bone in April for rejuvenation, a little shortening of the flowered
shoots, but not hard pruning, in July is advisable but not essential.
In cold districts hard cutting should be undertaken with care, as
considerable injury may result.

Ceanothus, spring-flowering types   When grown against walls,
etc. the side-shoots should be regularly spurred hard back to within
an inch or two of the main branches after flowering. For plants in
the open some shortening of the flowered growth is adequate, but
the compactness induced by rather harder pruning makes them
better able to withstand winter weather in cold districts.

Cercis siliquastrum   (Judas Tree) Spur-prune on walls after
flowering for greater floriferousness.

Clematis, Group 1, Winter and Spring-flowering (January to
May)   This Group covers many of the small-flowered species and
their hybrids, including all varieties of *alpina, armandii, chrysocoma,
cirrhosa, balearica* (syn. *balearica*), *macropetala* and *montana*. The less
vigorous of these *may* need no pruning at all, but such as is necessary
for any of the above should be done immediately after flowering. A
strong grower such as *montana* may be *sheared* after flowering, to
within a few inches of the basic framework of branches which should
have been formed in the plant's first few years. *Armandii* may grow
vigorously if well suited, but will not stand shearing or hard pruning.
Only thin and shorten growth in this case.

Clematis, Group 2, May and June-flowering Where space is limited some *old* wood may be shortened after flowering, but be careful not to cut away new growth (see also Period Three, p. 192).

Cytisus scoparius and similar types (Broom) These should receive their first trimming after flowering, never cutting into any wood thicker than a No. 9 knitting needle. Cut very circumspectly in the case of the dwarfs, such as the semi-prostrate *C.* x *kewensis*, so as not to destroy its natural habit.

Deutzia Cut the flowered shoots back annually to a strong new wand and remove an old, unproductive stem occasionally at the ground line.

Dipelta If not cut hard for the house, cut back the flowered shoots annually and eliminate one or two of the oldest growths in a strongly growing specimen in most years.

Genista hispanica (Spanish Gorse) I find clipping over after flowering necessary to keep this dwarf bushy, though it is said not to need pruning. Unlike some of the species, gangling old unpruned specimens will stand hard cutting back into the old wood.

Helianthemum (Sun Rose) The earliest of these will now be ready for a light trim immediately after flowering (but see warning in Period Six, p. 236).

Kolkwitzia amabilis (Beauty Bush) The flowered wands should be cut back (if not cut for the house), and growth renewed by eliminating one or two of the oldest stems annually at ground level.

Leucothoe Thin out some of the oldest wood occasionally after flowering.

Lithospermum diffusum varieties Cutting back fairly hard is necessary each year after flowering in order to maintain a dense evergreen flowering carpet rather than a tangle of old bootlaces.

Neillia Thin out some of the old wood after flowering if the bushes are overcrowded.

Paeonia suffruticosa varieties and other Tree Peonies
Occasionally remove some of the oldest wood, if dense (see also
Deadheading).

Philadelphus (Mock Orange)   Hard cutting after, or during,
flowering, keeps up a plentiful supply of vigorous young wood. Cut
back to strong new shoots, or to the ground in the case of wood
bare of such growth, and clear out spindly twiggery at the same
time.

Phlomis fruticosa (Jerusalem Sage)   Cut back the flowered
stems annually not later than July.

Physocarpus opulifolius 'Luteus'   It does not seem to matter
when this is pruned, so I include it here on the 'after flowering'
principle, though I cut any number of enormous wands of foliage
throughout the growing season. Some hard pruning seems necessary
to get the finest foliage, cutting back to strong new wands and
removing some of the oldest wood at the ground line each year to
avoid overcrowding.

Prunus laurocerasus and P. lusitanica (Laurel)   July is the
best time for pruning these, if necessary, when grown as open-ground
specimens, cutting as hard as you please.

Pyracantha (Firethorn)   Free-standing bushes benefit from some
cutting back after flowering, to give the berries every opportunity
to ripen. Wall plants will need more drastic restraint, while bearing
in mind that removal of spent flowers will prevent berrying (see
also Period Six, p. 237). For neglected wall specimens see Period
Four, p. 210.

Rosmarinus (Rosemary)   Prune after flowering for the sake of
density and shapeliness, without cutting into the old wood.

Ruta graveolens varieties (Blue Rue)   The glaucous foliage
colour is more effective without the intrusion of the insignificant
little yellow flowers, so it is advisable to remove these in bud,
unless the rather neat seed heads are wanted for drying.

Santolina (Lavender Cotton)   Plants may be lightly trimmed at intervals throughout the summer as an alternative to the more drastic pruning described in Period Four (p. 211), but do not trim if flowers are wanted. If they are not, remove the flower buds as they appear.

Senecio greyi   If the bushes are allowed to flower, cut all the spent flower shoots hard back immediately afterwards, to give the plants time to refurbish themselves before the winter.

Senecio, other species and hybrids   Here again the flower buds should be removed before they open if they are not wanted. In any case do not allow them to set seed.

Spiraea x arguta and **S. x vanhouttei**   Prune after flowering as described for the rather earlier *S. thunbergii* (May Pruning, p. 222).

Syringa (Lilac)   When cutting away spent flower trusses annually, by-pass the first few growth shoots and cut back to one lower down, in order to produce finer flowers. Cut out some of the young shoots at the same time, to let in light and air, and remove suckers whenever they appear. For treatment of neglected bushes see Period Two, p. 184.

Tamarix tetrandra (Spring-flowering Tamarisk)   Spent flower shoots may be shortened in June if necessary. This tamarisk is not to be confused with *T. pentandra* (summer-flowering), for which see Period Three, p. 197.

Summer Pinching Out

As soon as new growth makes this feasible, start the periodical pinching out of the extreme tips of soft growth (see Fig. 22) on the following:

> Ceanothus, spring-flowering types
> Chaenomeles (Japonica)
> Cistus (Rock Rose)
> Cytisus (Broom), young plants
> Embothrium (Chilean Fire Bush), in youth
> Eucalyptus, first growing season

Fuchsia
Genista, young plants of the taller types
x Halimiocistus
Halimium
Lupinus arboreus (Tree Lupin) in youth
Phlomis fruticosa (Jerusalem Sage)
Prunus (Cherry)
Salvia officinalis varieties (Ornamental Sage)
Santolina (Lavender Cotton), or trim
Senecio species and varieties—both young and mature plants
Spartium (Spanish Broom)
Vitis vinifera 'Purpurea' (Claret Vine) and other ornamental
grape vines.

Summer Deadheading

It is not possible to deadhead the incredibly floriferous dwarf evergreen azaleas or the small-flowered alpine rhododendrons except
in their earliest infancy, but the appearance of the former may be
improved by clawing through the plants with the fingers, to remove
most of the browned corollas. Deciduous azaleas, various late spring-
flowering rhododendrons as well as some of the hardy hybrids of
early summer, kalmias, pieris, *Convolvulus cneorum* and *Euryops
acraeus* will need deadheading in this Period. The spent flower
stems of *Euphorbia characias* and *E. veneta* (*wulfenii*) (Giant Spurge)
should also be cut back to the base, and *Lupinus arboreus* (Tree Lupin)
should not be allowed to form seedpods. The spent blooms of tree
peonies should be cut back to the first healthy growth bud before they
begin to exhaust themselves in seed production. When deadheading
roses in the earlier part of the season, remove only a short length
of stem at a good growth bud. Removal of immature laburnum
seedpods is advisable if within reach of young children, because
the seeds are very poisonous. This is not, however, necessary for the
good of the plant.

Mulching

Cut young green bracken, if available, before the fronds are fully
unfurled, for first-class mulching material for front row plants and

for others in need of a tonic. It should, preferably, be roughly chopped before applying.

Feeding

Camellia Apply farmyard manure or a liquid feed annually in July to boost the production of flower buds. As an occasional tonic for a plant in poor health, saturate the soil with a liquid fertilizer twice at fortnightly intervals in early summer. Tub-grown specimens in particular benefit from regular foliar or liquid feeding.

Chaenomeles (Japonica) Old specimens which have been cut hard back for rejuvenation will benefit from a handful of hoof and horn.

Erica carnea varieties and other winter-flowering Heaths These appreciate an occasional topdressing of peat or weedfree compost when cut back after flowering.

Hydrangea For red flower colour there must be some trace of lime in the soil, but the addition of dried blood to the soil in early summer at the rate of $\frac{1}{2}$ oz. per sq. yd. helps the quality of the colour. In poor soils all benefit from a dose of general fertilizer such as Growmore. For general use the recommended rate of application is 1–2 oz. per sq. yd., but on a fast-draining, sandy soil such as mine, the hungry and thirsty hydrangeas can do with 3 oz. They also greatly benefit from periodical foliar feeding in the earlier part of the season, especially if they have suffered past neglect in the matter of feeding and watering, when growing in poor soil.

Rose Give a second application of rose fertilizer in early summer and a third (the last) at the end of this Period (i.e. early or mid-July). Foliar feeds are also particularly suitable in the earlier part of the season, from spring to late June.

Tree Peonies These 'gross feeders' require regular annual applications of some kind of fertilizer after flowering. Liquid or foliar feeds are probably the most effective, or, where bracken is available locally, you may care to try mulching with dried bracken rhizomes.

General Most shrubs, except those requiring the most spartan diet, much appreciate two or three applications of a good foliar feed during the growing season, starting in late spring or early summer. This is a particularly convenient way of providing nourishment for plants in tubs and containers generally.

Pests

Aphids, caterpillars (including tortrix) and rhododendron pests As in Period Four, pp. 212–13.

Rose pests A systemic insecticide will take care of the majority, and of the sucking varieties in particular, if applied about once in three weeks, and contact sprays are probably effective for about ten days, depending on the weather. But even the makers are unable to be very precise on these points, so repeat the treatment whenever the pests begin to reappear. For the individual treatment of various rose pests see the Pests and Diseases section in Part Three, pp. 127–28.

Four-footed Pests Deter with Curb repellent spray.

Slugs apply slug bait fortnightly.

Diseases

Azalea Gall Pick off and burn infected shoots as far as is feasible and spray periodically with a copper or zineb fungicide throughout this Period. Dithane (PBI) seems especially effective (see also Period Four, pp. 213–14).

Bud Blast Spray or dust rhododendrons liable to bud blast with BHC or malathion to protect them against leafhoppers, which are thought to be the indirect cause of this disease.

Clematis Wilt As in Period Four, p. 214.

Fire Blight Watch for the symptoms described on p. 121 and cut out diseased parts, or remove the plant altogether if necessary.

Hydrangea Botrytis If early-flowering varieties develop brown blotches on the 'flowers' or leaves, remove affected parts before the trouble spreads and start regular spraying with captan, thiram or zineb.

Leaf-curl Mostly affecting ornamental cherries, almonds, peaches. Early detection is important. Pick off diseased leaves as early as possible and certainly before the diseased parts produce a 'bloom', and burn them. Infected wood should also be promptly cut out and burned.

Peony Wilt In mild, damp seasons, or in gardens where the disease is troublesome, spraying of the foliage with captan or Dithane should be continued after flowering, and diseased wood cut right out.

Powdery Mildew As in Period Four, p. 214.

Rose Diseases As in Period Four, p. 214.

Silver Leaf Likely victims are eucalyptus, laburnum, poplar, rhododendron, various *Prunus* species including Portugal Laurel and some other members of the rose family. Cut out dead or diseased wood before mid-July and burn, painting the cuts with Arbrex. Neglect by private gardeners is likely to have serious consequences in the neighbourhood of commercial plum, and to a lesser extent, apple orchards.

General Keep a look-out for disease at all times and treat as recommended on pp. 117–29.

Watering

Versus Frost In case of need, see Period Four, p. 215.

Versus Drought As in Period Four, pp. 215–16. Some plants which resent dry root conditions are listed under Watering on p. 135.

Stocktaking and Inspection

The one is concerned with the long view and the other with

immediate action. As regards inspection, regular tours become increasingly useful from now on, chiefly in order to spot trouble and to put it right if possible without delay. Stocktaking, on the other hand, is contemplative and can only be done when the shrub garden is in full leaf. Go round with a note book whenever time permits during the growing season recording mistakes and planning alterations for implementation at the proper season.

Miscellaneous

As in Period Four, pp. 216–17.

Also twig-stake the young growth of romneya (Tree Poppy) if it tends to flop.

Summary of the More Important Jobs in Period Five

Planting   A few pot-grown oddments only   May to early June

Pruning (Annual)		
Ceanothus, spring-flowering	After flowering
Chaenomeles	After flowering
Clematis, Group 1	Early summer, after flowering
Cytisus, most	After flowering
Deutzia	After flowering
Dipelta	After flowering
Erica carnea and spring-flowering tree heaths	After flowering
Forsythia	After flowering
Genista hispanica	After flowering
Helianthemum	After flowering
Kerria	After flowering
Kolkwitzia	After flowering
Lithospermum diffusum varieties	After flowering
Paeonia suffruticosa varieties and other tree peonies	After flowering

Philadelphus	After flowering
Phlomis fruticosa	After flowering
Physocarpus	Any time
Prunus tenella	After flowering
Rosmarinus	After flowering
Rubus, for ornamental stems or flowers	May
Senecio greyi (if allowed to flower)	After flowering
Spiraea, spring-flowering types	After flowering
Syringa	After flowering
Hedges, if close-clipped	Start trimming in June

Pinching Out	See lists, pp. 222–23 and 226–27	Periodically, during summer
Dead-heading	See lists, pp. 223, 227	Throughout this Period
Feeding	Camellia: farmyard manure	July
	Erica, winter-flowering: peat or compost	After flowering
	Hydrangea: Growmore and/ or foliar feeds on poor soils	Growmore, one application (1–2 oz. per sq. yd.) 3 oz. in exceptional cases. Foliar feeds periodically
	Rose: two applications of rose fertilizer. See also foliar feeding under General	One at the beginning and one at the end of this Period
	Tree Peonies: see choice of feeds	After flowering
	General: foliar feeding benefits the majority of shrubs	Several times during spring and the early part of the summer
Pests	The worst are aphids, caterpillars (including tortrix), clay-coloured and	Throughout this Period

	vine weevils and various rose pests	
	Slugs—bait fortnightly	Throughout growing season
Diseases	Look out in particular for azalea gall, clematis wilt, hydrangea botrytis, leaf-curl, powdery mildew, rose fungus diseases and silver leaf	Throughout this Period
Watering		As necessary
Stock-taking and Inspection		Frequently
Miscel-laneous	Training of climbers and wall plants	Frequently during this Period

NOTES: PERIOD FIVE

PERIOD SIX: LATE SUMMER

Early or Mid-July to Mid-September, according to season

Pruning

Any necessary pruning outstanding from Period Five should be completed as soon as possible, and suckers promptly removed.

Pruning for Period Six consists almost entirely of cutting back mid-summer-flowering shrubs when they have faded, whereas those which flower in late summer and autumn are mostly left unpruned until the spring. There is no hard and fast dividing line between July and August pruning, but the following will mostly have finished flowering before those in the later list.

July Pruning

Buddleia alternifolia   Remove flowered shoots annually.

Buddleia globosa (Chilean Orange Ball Tree)   If necessary cut back straggling shoots to keep the bush neat. More drastic reduction may be done in April (see Period Four, p. 208).

Cassinia fulvida (Golden Heather)   A second trimming to remove spent flower heads improves the appearance (see also Period Three, p. 191).

Clematis, Group 2 (as in Period Five, p. 224)   The latest of these may continue flowering into July. Some of the *old* wood may be cut back after flowering if space is limited. (See also Period Three, p. 192.)

Cytisus scoparius and similar types (Broom). Clip over *lightly* several times during the growing season, without cutting into old wood.

Deutzia   Remove all the old flowered growth annually, cutting back to a strong new shoot, and eliminate one or two of the oldest stems at the ground line from time to time.

Genista, taller species   As for *Cytisus scoparius*.

Genista lydia   This spectacular dwarf makes a lot of dead wood, which must be cut out, but further pruning should be sparing, shortening individual flowered shoots a little with scissors, for preference, without destroying their arching habit.

Helianthemum (Sun Rose)   When the main flush of the June-flowering varieties is over they may be lightly clipped over to increase density and, possibly, induce a second flowering. If not cut back they quickly become stringy, but in cold areas trimming of these not over-hardy carpeters has sometimes proved a little risky. The important point is to cut them back *immediately* after flowering, if at all, so as to give the new growth time to ripen before the winter.

Ruta graveolens varieties (Rue)   Continue the removal of flower buds according to taste.

Santolina (Lavender Cotton)   If lightly clipped throughout the summer rather than hard pruned in spring, a trim in July will be the last for the season. If not clipped, remove the flower buds, unless the yellow button daisies are wanted.

Senecio greyi   If these have been allowed to flower, cutting the flowered shoots hard back before they set seed should not be delayed after July.

Weigela ssp. and hybrids   Shorten the flowered shoots and cut out a few unproductive old stems at the base annually.

July Pinching Out

Continue to nip out the soft tips of new growth periodically on the plants listed in Period Five until the end of July. Pinching out should then be discontinued, since any new growth made at this season will not have time to harden before the winter.

August and Early September Pruning

Carpenteria californica   Shorten flowered shoots and cut out any weak growth annually.

Cytisus scoparius and similar types (Broom)   Give one last light clipping in August.

Escallonia   An occasional cutting back of free-standing bushes either after flowering or in spring is beneficial. For wall plants, etc. cut back regularly after flowering as much as their position requires.

Feijoa sellowiana   If grown against a wall, cut back as space dictates after flowering.

Genista, taller types   Give one last light clipping in August.

Jasminum officinale (Common White Jasmine)   Thin fairly drastically either after flowering or in winter (see Period Two, p. 184).

Ligustrum ovalifolium 'Aureum' (Golden Privet)   If it becomes necessary to control the free growth of open-ground shrubs, shoots should be shortened (not sheared) in late summer or in spring (see Period Four, p. 207). Bushes look their best when grown naturally, without formal pruning, except where hedges require it.

Pyracantha (Firethorn)   Careful shortening of foliage growth where necessary to expose incipient berries helps these to ripen and to display themselves better when they do so.

Ruta graveolens varieties (Rue)   Continue to remove the flower buds if not wanted.

Santolina (Cotton Lavender)   The same applies, unless regular clipping has prevented flower formation.

Staphylea (Bladder Nut)   Cut out unproductive old wood, and shorten long straggling shoots if necessary, after flowering.

Teucrium fruticans (Shrubby Germander)   Cut back the flowered shoots before they set seed.

Wisteria   The young shoots should be reduced to about 6 in. each year in mid-August—that is, leaving three or four buds only on each spur (see Figs. 14A and 14B).

Zenobia   I differ from the experts in that I find it necessary to prune back to good strong shoots after flowering annually in order to improve the naturally rather sprawling, untidy habit (which is more than redeemed by the beauty of the flowers).

Hedges, close-clipped   Another trimming will be due in August.

Hedges, evergreen   Assuming no more than one annual trim will be given, this is best done in August.

Hedges, deciduous   August is also the best time for an annual clipping of beech, hornbeam and other deciduous hedges, but these may wait until winter if necessary (see Periods Two and Three, pp. 183 and 190).

Deadheading

Buddleia davidii varieties (Butterfly Bush) **and other late flowering types**   It pays to remove at least the terminal flower panicles as they fade, to direct more vigour into the rest of the flower crop, but one can rarely keep pace with deadheading beyond this stage. White varieties look worse than purple ones if neglected in this respect.

Cistus (Rock Rose)   Prevent seeding by cutting out dead flower clusters as soon as flowering is finished.

Convolvulus cneorum   If a second flower crop is produced it should not be allowed to set seed.

Lavandula (Lavender)   Remove dead flower stems only—this can be done roughly by the fistful, but avoid cutting beyond the bare flower stems, leaving pruning proper until spring (see Period Four, p. 209).

Phormium (New Zealand Flax)   Cut out flowered stems (if any) to their base.

Rhododendrons   Late-flowering varieties.

Roses Cut spent blooms away with a fair length of stalk in late summer, as a kind of pruning. Sizeable new shoots lower on the flower stem will often dictate where to make the cut (see Fig. 26).

Yucca Cut out the flowered stems to their base.

Feeding

Camellia Treat at the start of this Period as in Period Five, p. 228, if not yet done.

Clematis Apply 2 oz. of general fertilizer, or water with a good liquid feed in July. (See also Periods Three and Four, pp. 197 and 212.)

Rose Do not apply quick-acting stimulants such as dried blood or fish manure after July.

General Foliar feeds will still be welcome periodically during the early part of this Period, not forgetting plants grown in tubs and other containers.

Pests

Sucking insects will have thinned out by late summer, when the juicy young shoots which form their diet have toughened up, but a number of them will still be about. The majority of these, and also caterpillars, may be controlled by systemic insecticides, and the biters mainly by BHC, malathion or Sevin dust. In general, treatment is as in Period Four, pp. 212–13. Earwigs are most active in this Period and may be combated with BHC or Sevin dusts.

Four-footed Pests deter with Curb repellent spray.

Slugs Apply bait fortnightly to the end of this Period.

Diseases

Azalea Gall If bad attacks persist into late summer, treat as in Period Five, p. 229.

Bud Blast   Spray or dust rhododendrons again in the early part of this Period with BHC or malathion, as in Period Five, p. 229.

Clematis Wilt   Continue regular watering and protect new shoots, if any, as in Period Four, p. 214.

Fire Blight   Cut out and burn diseased parts, or grub out the plant if necesssary.

Hydrangea Botrytis   The late-flowering types should be treated if necessary as described in Period Five, p. 230.

Leaf-curl   Spray or dust likely victims with captan just before leaf-fall (see also Periods One, Three and Five, pp. 179, 199 and 230).

Powdery Mildew   As in Period Four, p. 214.

Rose Fungus Diseases   If black spot and other ailments persist, continue spraying with a rose fungicide until late October.

General   Keep a look-out for symptoms of diseases likely to occur at any season.

Watering

Assuming that the need for watering against overnight frost is past by the beginning of July, we are unlikely to be bothered as yet by early autumn frosts, so drought will be our only concern in this Period.

Nowadays St. Swithun's Day, whether wet or fine, is commonly followed by a good many more than the legendary 40 days of rain. But if periods of drought occur in late summer pay particular attention to new plants, house beds and other wall plantings, moisture-loving subjects and evergreens. For plants which resent dry root conditions see the list under Watering in Part Three, p. 135.

Stocktaking and Inspection

There is not much time left 'to stand and stare' before leaf-fall, so *make* time if necessary for a final assessment of shortcomings and successes in the shrub garden, noting proposed alterations before you forget what was decided.

Continue frequent routine inspections in order to remedy trouble promptly.

Miscellaneous

Plant Orders   Lose no time in completing orders for the nurseries, if any, once plans for improvements or for new plantings have been finalized, and keep a record of the orders, with dates.

Training of Climbers   Continue this until the end of the growing season.

Weeds   Weed as necessary, especially among newly planted ground-cover.

Variegated Plants   Cut green shoots right out, if any.

Blueing of Established Hydrangeas   Continue the weekly liquid treatment, as described in Period Four, p. 216, in the early part of this Period, for late-flowering varieties, until the flowers are fully open.

Summary of the More Important Jobs in Period Six

Pruning	*Buddleia alternifolia*	After flowering
(Annual)	*Carpenteria californica*	After flowering
	Cytisus scoparius varieties and similar	Periodical clipping
	Deutzia	After flowering
	Escallonia, wall plants	After flowering
	Genista	Periodical clipping
	Helianthemum	After flowering
	Jasminum officinale	After flowering (or in winter)
	Teucrium fruticans	After flowering
	Weigela	After flowering

242

	Wisteria	Mid-August
	Zenobia	After flowering
	Hedges	August
Pinching Out	As listed in Period Five	Until end of July
Dead-heading	As necessary	Throughout this Period
Feeding	Clematis: general fertilizer or liquid feed	July
	General: foliar feeds as necessary	Early part of this Period
Pests	Suckers: mostly controlled by systemic insecticides	As necessary
	Biters: mostly controlled by BHC, malathion or Sevin dust	As necessary
	Slugs: bait fortnightly	To the end of this Period
Diseases	Look out in particular for clematis wilt, fire blight, leaf-curl, powdery mildew, rose fungus diseases	Throughout this Period
Watering		As necessary
Stock-taking and Inspection		Frequently
Miscellaneous	Despatch of plant orders	As early as possible
	Training of climbers	To the end of the growing season

NOTES: PERIOD SIX

APPENDIX ONE

Recommended Reading

Camellias for Everyone	Claude Chidamian	Faber	£1.50
Climbing Plants for Walls and Gardens	C. E. Lucas-Phillips	Heinemann	1.25
Climbing Roses Old and New	G. S. Thomas	Dent	2.75
Design of Small Gardens	C. E. Lucas-Phillips	Heinemann	1.80
Dictionary of Gardening (4 vols.) Supplement (1 vol.)	Royal Hortic. Soc.	O.U.P.	23.50
Diseases and Pests of Ornamental Plants	Pirone, Dodge and Rickett	Constable	4.20
Dwarf Conifers	H. J. Welch	Faber	4.50
Effective Flowering Shrubs	M. Haworth-Booth	Collins	2.50
Evergreens for your Garden	D. Bartrum	Gifford	1.25
*Fertility without Fertilisers	Lawrence D. Hills	HDRA	17½p
Garden Design	K. Midgley	Penguin	63p
Gardening by the Sea	J. R. B. Evison	Pan Piper	30p
Gardening Chemicals		R.H.S.	37½p
Gardening on Chalk and Lime	C. Lloyd	Pan Piper	30p
Gardening on Clay and Lime	M. Fish	David & Charles	1.75
Hedges for Farm and Garden	J. Beddall	Faber	2.10
The Hydrangea	M. Haworth-Booth	Constable	1.50
Making a Shrub Garden (acid soil)	H. E. and J. Bawden	Faber	2.50
The Old Shrub Roses	G. S. Thomas	Dent	2.00
*Pest Control without Poisons	Lawrence D. Hills	HDRA	17½p
Pesticides and Pollution	K. Mellanby	Collins	1.50
Plants for Ground-cover	G. S. Thomas	Dent	3.00
Pruning Hardy Shrubs	A. Osborn	R.H.S.	15p
The Pruning of Trees, Shrubs and Conifers	G. E. Brown	Faber	9.00
Rhododendrons and Azaleas	J. Berrisford	Faber	2.10
Seaside Gardening	Christine Kelway	David & Charles	1.75
The Small Garden	C. E. Lucas-Phillips	Pan Piper	37½p
Topiary and Ornamental Hedges	M. Hadfield	Black	3.00
Trees and Shrubs Hardy in the British Isles (4 vols.)	W. J. Bean	Murray	8.00 (per vol.)
The Well-tempered Garden	C. Lloyd	Collins	2.10

* available from The Henry Doubleday Research Association, Bocking, Braintree, Essex

APPENDIX TWO

Some Tree and Shrub Nurserymen, with Addresses

Because of the ever-increasing cost of carriage and packing on goods sent by road or rail, delivery of plants is on the decrease as more and more gardeners prefer to fetch their plant orders, not too far from home, to suit their convenience. This also reduces the damaging length of time spent by plants in transit and the rough handling they so often meet with on the way.

I have therefore purposely made the list a long one, including both small and large nurseries, in an attempt to spread the network as fairly as possible throughout the country, despite which it may seem that an undue proportion of the large shrub nurseries have been picked from the southern counties. The fact is, however, that these have mostly been attracted southwards because of the greater suitability of the soil and climate. Naturally it is not possible for me to answer for the reliability of many of the nurseries known to me only through their latest catalogues at the time of writing, and even among the best of those with which I have had personal dealings standards tend to see-saw, owing to shortage of labour, or cash, or other problems of these difficult times.

I have by-passed all specialist rose growers—defeated by sheer weight of numbers—despite the importance of shrub roses and many others (with the exception of most Hybrid Teas) for their colour contribution to the shrub borders. With so many rose nurseries proliferating throughout the British Isles, their omission here should not much inconvenience the reader, who will find large numbers of suitable roses included in many of the general tree and shrub catalogues issued by the nurserymen on my list.

I have in a number of cases been asked to mention that it has become necessary to make a charge for catalogues, in order to offset the high cost of their present-day production.

Plant Finding

One last hope for Fellows of the Society unable to track down a

scarce plant is to send all necessary particulars to the Secretary of the
Royal Horticultural Society's monthly journal, for inclusion under the
heading: *Fellows wishing to obtain plants rare in cultivation.* The Fellows
must then sort things out between themselves, supplying wants on a
buy or barter basis, or for nothing, with what proportion of successful
appeals I cannot say. I only tried it once–and it worked, for me.

Tree and Shrub Nurserymen

Aldenham Heather Nursery, Round Bush, Aldenham, Watford,
   Herts (heath and heather specialists).

Barnham Nurseries Ltd., Barnham, Nr. Bognor Regis, Sussex.

A. J. T. Bayles, Grey Timbers, Chapple Road, Bovey Tracey,
   Devon (ex R. C. Barnard, leading hardy eucalyptus specialist,
   now retired).

S. Bide and Sons Ltd., Alma Nurseries, Farnham, Surrey.

J. and W. Blackburn Ltd., Pennine Nurseries, Shelley, Huddersfield,
   Yorks.

Bodnant Garden Nursery, Tal-y-Cafyn, Colwyn Bay, N. Wales
   (short but interesting lists issued spring and autumn).

J. Cheal and Sons Ltd., Park Farm, Stopham Road, Pulborough,
   Sussex (also Garden Centre, Horsham Rd., Crawley, Sussex).

J. Coles and Sons, The Nurseries, Thurnby, Leicester LE7 9QB.

Colourful Gardens Ltd., Llwyn Hudol, Criccieth, N. Wales (heath
   and heather specialists, and general).

P. G. Davis, Timber Tops, Marley Common, Haslemere, Surrey
   (heath and heather specialist–strictly for personal shoppers).

Dolley's Hill Nurseries, Normandy, Guildford, Surrey (heath and
   heather specialists).

W. Drummond and Sons Ltd., Blairingone by Dollar, Stirling.

Everton Nurseries Ltd., Everton, Nr. Lymington, Hants.

Exbury Gardens Ltd., Exbury, Nr. Southampton SO4 1AZ (rhododendron, azalea and camellia specialists, and some general,
   including large-size standard trees).

Margery Fish Nursery, East Lambrook Manor, S. Petherton,
   Somerset (more shrubs than hitherto, in a short but interesting
   list, including wide choice of ivies, euphorbias and hebes).

Fisk's Clematis Nursery, Westleton, Nr. Saxmundham, Suffolk
   (clematis only).

Four Winds Nursery (K. R. Potts), Holt Pound, Wrecclesham,
   Farnham, Surrey (short list of considerable interest).

Glendoick Gardens Ltd., Glendoick, Perth (E. H. M. and P. A. Cox,
well-known hybridists specializing in rhododendrons and azaleas.
All plants sold on their own roots).

Goatcher's Nurseries, Washington, Sussex.

Great Dixter Nurseries (Christopher Lloyd), Northiam, Sussex
(clematis specialist and interesting general list—advises personal
shopping, but will send if required).

Haskins Nurseries Ltd., Trickett's Cross, Ferndown, Dorset (camellia
specialists and general).

M. Haworth-Booth, Farall Nurseries, Roundhurst, Nr. Haslemere,
Surrey (expertly selected short list for seasonal displays).

Headley Nurseries, Headley, Bordon, Hants. (telephone before
visiting).

Heath End Nurseries, (D. W. Hatch), Heath End, Farnham, Surrey
(dwarf conifer specialist, also a few other shrubs).

Hillier & Sons, Winchester, Hants. (largest selection in the country).

Hydon Nurseries Ltd., Hydon Heath, Nr. Godalming, Surrey
(rhododendron, azalea, camellia and heather specialists, and
small general list).

W. E. Th. Ingwersen Ltd., Birch Farm Nursery, Gravetye, E.
Grinstead, Sussex (mixed list, mainly alpines, but including a
number of shrubs).

Jackmans Nurseries Ltd., Egley Road, Woking, Surrey (clematis
specialists and general).

Knap Hill Nursery Ltd., Barrs Lane, Knap Hill, Woking, Surrey
(rhododendron and azalea specialists, and general).

Knights' Nurseries Ltd., Hailsham, Sussex.

Peter Lloyd Nurseries, Hale, Fordingbridge, Hants. (short but good
list of evergreen azaleas, heaths, conifers and other shrubs).

C. J. Marchant, Keepers Hill Nursery, Stapehill, Wimborne, Dorset.

Maxwell and Beale, Corfe Mullen, Wimborne, Dorset (chiefly
heaths and heathers, with small additional general list).

Notcutt's Nurseries Ltd., Woodbridge, Suffolk.

Oliver and Hunter, Moniaive by Thornhill, Dumfriesshire (heath
and heather specialists).

Pennell and Sons Ltd., Princess Street, Lincoln (clematis specialists
and general).

Proudley's Heather Nursery, Two Bridges, Blakeney, Glos. GL15
4AF (heath and heather specialists, listing only a selection from
larger stock).

G. B. Rawinsky, Primrose Hill Nursery, Bunch Lane, Haslemere,

Surrey (includes a number of rare items—personal shoppers
preferred, at week-ends only, otherwise by appointment).

G. Reuthe Ltd., office: Fox Hill Nurseries, Keston, Kent; branch
nursery at Crown Point, Nr. Ightham, Kent (rhododendron and
azalea specialists, and general).

Robinson's Gardens Ltd., Knockholt, Kent.

R. V. Roger Ltd., The Nurseries, Pickering, Yorks.

Roseacre Garden Centre, Kidderminster Road South, West Hagley,
Worcs. (retail part of the Blakedown Nurseries Group).

L. R. Russell Ltd., Richmond Nurseries, Windlesham, Surrey.

John Scott and Co., The Royal Nurseries, Merriott, Somerset
(price of catalogue 15p. quoted at their special request).

J. O. Sherrard and Son, Shaw Nursery, Newbury, Berks. (much of
special interest to gardeners on limy soils).

Slieve Donard Nursery Co. Ltd., Newcastle, Co. Down, N. Ireland.

Walter C. Slocock Ltd., Goldsworth Nursery, Woking, Surrey
(two catalogues, one specializing in rhododendrons, and the
other, general).

James Smith and Sons, Darley Dale Nurseries, Nr. Matlock,
Derbyshire (mainly heath and heather specialists, remainder
rather pedestrian, but cheap).

Sunningdale Nurseries Ltd., London Road, Windlesham, Surrey
(shrub rose specialists and general).

F. Toynbee Ltd., Barnham, Nr. Bognor Regis, Sussex.

Treasures of Tenbury Ltd., Tenbury Wells, Worcs. (clematis
specialists and general).

James Trehane and Sons Ltd., Ham Lane, Longham, Nr. Wimborne, Dorset BH22 9DR (camellia, evergreen azalea and blueberry specialists).

Treseders' Nurseries Truro Ltd., Truro, Cornwall (many rare
plants, especially those for mild climates).

Mrs. D. Underwood, Colchester, Essex (specialist in silver-leaved
plants).

G. Underwood and Son, Hookstone Green Nurseries, West End,
Nr. Woking, Surrey (specialists in brooms, heaths and heathers).

Washfield Nurseries, Hawkhurst, Kent (ex Davenport Jones. Short
but interesting mixed list, including a proportion of shrubs).

George G. Whitelegg Ltd., Knockholt, Sevenoaks, Kent.

Wyevale Nurseries, Kings Acre, Hereford.

APPENDIX THREE

Some Manufacturers of Chemical Products Approved by the Ministry of Agriculture, Fisheries and Food for Use in the Cultivation of Hardy Ornamental Trees and Shrubs

Note: Although the A, topped by a crown, granted by the Ministry of Agriculture, Fisheries and Food, is generally accepted as the hall-mark of safety, combined with efficiency for its purpose, in a gardening chemical, this is not to say that the rest are necessarily dangerous or unreliable. In view of the considerable cost of submitting a chemical for an official test, a number of manufacturers find it necessary to forgo the possible distinction of the A sign by marketing their products without their having been tested by the Ministry.

The list below consists mainly of manufacturers of approved products, with certain exceptions which may in some cases be too new at the time of writing to have been sufficiently tested for official approval.

Armillatox, Old Smugglers, Henley, Fernhurst, Haslemere, Surrey.

Baywood Chemicals Ltd., Eastern Way, Bury St. Edmunds, Suffolk (representing the German firm of Bayer); includes Draza Slugkiller.

Boots Pure Drug Co. Ltd., Station St., Nottingham; also includes their own Draza Slugkiller

Bugges Insecticides Ltd., London Road, Sittingbourne, Kent.

J. D. Campbell and Sons Ltd., Liverpool Road, Warrington, Lancs.

Cory & Co. Ltd., Evesham, Worcester; includes Topvil Mole Fuses.

Fison's Ltd., Agrochemical Division, Harston, Cambridge.

ICI/Plant Protection Ltd., Fernhurst, Haslemere, Surrey.

May & Baker Ltd., Dagenham, Essex.

The Murphy Chemical Co. Ltd., Wheathampstead, St. Albans, Herts.

Pains-Wessex Ltd., Fumite Division, High Post, Salisbury, Wilts.; includes Fumite Mole Smokes.

Pan Britannica Industries Ltd., (=PBI), Britannica House, Waltham Cross, Herts.; includes Slug Gard slug killer.

Sphere Laboratories (London) Ltd., 1 and 2 Onslow Mews East, London SW7 3AA; for Curb bird and animal repellent.

Synchemicals Ltd., Grange Walk, London SE1; includes SBK Brushwood Killer and S-600 anti-transpiration spray.

Zoan-Midox Ltd., Smarden, Kent (Casoron G).

Index

* Since the text of this book went to press the manufacturers have changed the name of this product from Sequestrene to Sequestered Iron.

* Since the text of this book went to press the manufacturers have changed the name of this product from Sequestrene to Sequestered Iron.

Printed in Great Britain by Western Printing Services Limited, Bristol